Is Life Like This?

Is Life Like This?

*A Guide to Writing Your First
Novel in Six Months*

JOHN DUFRESNE

W. W. NORTON & COMPANY

New York | London

For information about permission to reproduce selections from this book,
write to Permissions, W. W. Norton & Company, Inc.,
500 Fifth Avenue, New York, NY 10110

For information about special discounts for bulk purchases, please contact
W. W. Norton Special Sales at specialsales@wwnorton.com or 800-233-4830

Manufacturing by Courier Westford
Book design by JAMdesign
Production manager: Julia Druskin

Library of Congress Cataloging-in-Publication Data

Dufresne, John.
Is life like this? : a guide to writing your first novel in six
months / John Dufresne.—1st ed.
p. cm.
ISBN 978-0-393-06541-1 (hardcover)
1. Fiction—Authorship. 2. Creative writing. I. Title.
PN3365.D84 2010
808.3—dc22

2009039296

W. W. Norton & Company, Inc.
500 Fifth Avenue, New York, N.Y. 10110
www.wwnorton.com

W. W. Norton & Company Ltd.
Castle House, 75/76 Wells Street, London W1T 3QT

1 2 3 4 5 6 7 8 9 0

For Chris Kelley,

Andres Moxey,

and Ricky Smith

We are such stuff

As dreams are made on; and our little life

Is rounded with a sleep . . .

—WILLIAM SHAKESPEARE,

The Tempest

Contents

Is Life Like This?

Introduction

A novelist must preserve a child-like belief in the
importance of things which common sense
considers of no great consequence.
—W. Somerset Maugham

YOU'VE ALWAYS WANTED to write a novel, but you haven't
been able to. Not yet, you haven't. Perhaps you've been too
intimidated to even begin. (Who do I think I am?) Or you've started
writing several novels over the years, each with abundant hope and
enthusiasm, but you soon became discouraged when the characters
in your head did not breathe on the page. Or maybe you keep pulling the same novel out of the desk drawer whenever you have some
downtime, and you work on it again for a week or a month—you
feel a feverish sense of urgency—and the novel keeps growing, year
after year, but seems unwilling to resolve itself, and then, alas, the
so-called real world summons you, or you lose confidence in your
creative or organizational abilities, and you shove the manuscript
back into the drawer and push your chair away from the annoying
desk. Well, you should know that you're not alone. We've all done
the same thing. Writing is hard, and it's harder for the writer than
it is for anyone else. *Is Life Like This?* is aimed at getting you past
the inevitable obstacles and the inescapable dejection, and helping

you get a competent and compelling draft of your novel done— that means beginning, middle, and (the hardest part) end—in six months.

You begin writing your novel at the same place everyone else begins. That is, you begin the journey not knowing where you'll end up. You may have a destination in mind, and you may well set off in that direction, but what you'll encounter along the way will likely alter your course. In other words, you begin writing your novel in doubt and uncertainty. This uncertainty, though daunting, is crucial to the writing process. Cherish it. Uncertainty allows for, even encourages, revelation and surprise, while it prevents the manipulation of character or plot to suit your preconceived, and usually ill-conceived, notion of what the novel must be. In writing the first draft, you begin to work through all the uncertainty and advance toward meaning.

The premise of this book is that if you come to understand how the writing process works—by fits and starts, with equal parts elation and frustration—you won't give in to despair when you feel stuck, as you inevitably will. If you understand that the novel-writing process is messy, chaotic, and perversely irrational at times, if you know that you *will* lose your way (because if you don't get lost, then you're not exploring; you're following a worn path, one we've been down before) and that you will excise words, delete sentences, and remove whole chapters because that's just the way it goes—for you and for everyone else—then maybe you won't raise your arms in surrender when you feel besieged; instead you'll do what you need to do—you'll write your way through the difficulties.

Writing a novel is a commitment of energy, passion, and intelligence, all of which you've plenty of. And it's a commitment of time, which is, unfortunately, in short supply for most of us. You've got a job and familial obligations. You've got a social life. You've got important matters to attend to—those pesky kids, the lawn maintenance, the unrelenting e-mails. How can you justify sitting around and making things up? Know this: Everything in your life is incompatible with writing and always will be. You are going to have to be fierce in defense of your writing time in these coming months if you are serious. The daily task of writing your novel may cause some tension around the house and within your close circle of friends. So be it. You've got characters to nourish and cities to build. You have matters of consequence calling for your undivided attention.

You bring patience and tenacity to the writing desk. You set loose your imagination, and this book provides the method to help you shape your requisite madness, as it were, into a coherent narrative. You've got enough to deal with in creating your brave new world. You shouldn't have to worry about what comes next. You've found your central character, and you think, "What do I do now?" What you do now is follow the weekly writing plan; you do the writing exercises, and now you have a setting, a narrator, a plot, and so it goes. Trust in the process. That's what this book is for: to point the way and to organize the thousand steps in the novel-writing process. Your writing schedule for the next twenty-six weeks is laid out. You'll start with a blank slate. You'll begin by exploring your own life for fictional and thematic material and then drive on deep into the imaginative world of the novel. You'll start by thinking of characters and then places, plot, theme, scene, point of view, and so on all the way to revision. While you're writing serenely, while you're focused on the week's subject, you'll be encouraged, reassured, and interrupted on occasion for a chat about what a novel might be, and about the forms and structures of novels.

Novels are written, not wished into existence. You have to sit your ass in the chair or nothing gets done. Remember that you always find time to do what you love. You only have to want to write as much as you want to watch TV or listen to music. You can do this! So get to the writing desk. Check your impatience at the door, but bring your enthusiasm and passion. You're going to live a dozen lives; you're going to learn about your own life, about the world around you, and about the human condition. The world you'll create is going to be more vivid and provocative than the one outside your door. This is going to be fun. This is the year your novel gets written.

A Modest Proposal

LET'S DO THE impossible. Let's decide we're going to write the first draft of our novel in six months, three hours a day. Our total writing-time goal is twenty-one hours a week. Three hours a day. Twenty-one hours for twenty-six weeks. If you can manage only twelve hours during a particular work week, you can easily write for three *extra* hours on the weekend. Don't skip a day. If you have only five minutes on some horrific day when the car breaks down and the lines at Fresh Market are out the door, use those five minutes to write. In fact, write while you're waiting for the car in the dingy repair shop reception area or write in the supermarket checkout line. Characters will be all around you. If you slip into bed one night only to realize that between the Hendry account, the impromptu staff meeting, the birthday party for the twins in the steno pool, and the Little League doubleheader, you didn't get a minute to write, then grab the pen and the memo pad on your bedside table and write. In a letter to Maria Kiselyova, who wanted to know how to become a writer, Anton Chekhov offered this bit of unvarnished advice: "Write as much as you can!! Write, write, write until your fingers break!"*

*Chekhov also wrote this to Maria: "But the writer is not a pastry chef, he is not a cosmetician and not an entertainer. He is a man bound by contract to his sense of duty and to his conscience. Once he undertakes this task, it is too late for excuses, and no matter how horrified, he must do battle with his squeamishness and sully his imagination with the grime of life."

Let's talk about where you'll be doing all this note-taking and writing. In your writer's notebook. Keep a notebook for several reasons. It's a reminder that you're a writer and that what you're currently doing while you're out of the house, away from the desk, is taking notes for your novel. You know that you think differently when you have a pen in your hand. You think differently, and you observe differently. You see what's really there, not what's supposed to be there. You keep a notebook to teach yourself to pay attention. You keep a notebook to encourage yourself to create. You keep a notebook to serve notice to the world: Writer at Work! When you're writing a novel, the novel becomes a magnet for everything that happens in your life, and the notebook is where you store what has been attracted.

Writing regularly in your notebook keeps the creative juices churning; it preserves thoughts, images, overheard lines, dreams, whatever it is that catches your imagination. A notebook affords you the opportunity to write when you may only have five minutes to do so. And writing engenders more writing. The image you capture now might show up in the novel you write in ten years. The notebook is the repository and source of writing material. It's also a refuge. Open it up when you need to think. Read what you've written; write about what you've just read. Note-taking can be a creative act. It may not be your purpose to write a novel based on the image you just discovered—birds nesting in a human skull—but once you get started, you may just keep writing.

> "It's never too late to be what you might have been."
> —GEORGE ELIOT

The notebook is not so much about what happened, as about what *could* happen. It's for your eyes only, not for publication. It doesn't need to be neat, ordered, or logical. You don't need a system; only collect! Write down remarks that you hear or read on the craft of writing, conversations that you overhear in restaurants;

tape in newspaper articles, photographs that you might use in a story sometime; write down phrases or words that might become titles or chapter headings or dialogue; list story ideas, titles, names, words, images. Keep your senses alert and gather your data in the notebook.

The constant use of the notebook keeps you working, writing, and provides a mine of material to be used today and down the road. Keep all of the writing exercises from this book in your notebook. Keep anything pertinent to your development as a writer: character sketches, found poems, observations, all of the preliminary stuff that is the first stage of the writing process. What you write down now goes toward all the writing you will ever do. The

"We work in the dark—we do what we can—we give what we have. Our doubt is our passion, and our passion is our task. The rest is the madness of art."
—HENRY JAMES

sentence you overheard—"It's good to be back, but where am I?"—might not be appropriate for the novel you're working on, but might be the seed of the novel you're going to write next. And you don't need to know how that'll come about. Trust in the material. A notebook is a warehouse, not a museum. You're taking it down so it's there when you need it. And you don't need a system—write it all as fast as you can. The notebook is not an end, but a means.

Chekhov kept a notebook. He titled one of his notebooks "Themes, Thoughts, Notes, and Fragments." Here's an entry:

At twenty she loved Z., at twenty-four she married N. not because she loved him, but because she thought him a good, wise, ideal man. The couple lived happily; everyone envies them, and indeed their life passes smoothly and placidly; she is satisfied, and, when people discuss love, she says that for family life not love nor passion is wanted but affection. But once the music played suddenly, and, inside her heart, everything broke up like ice in spring;

she remembered Z. and her love for him, and she thought with despair that her life was ruined, spoilt for ever, and that she was unhappy. Then it happened to her with the New Year greetings; when people wished her "New Happiness," she indeed longed for new happiness.

Here are some more provocations from the master, all from his notebooks:

A pregnant woman with short arms and a long neck, like a kangaroo.

A serious phlegmatic doctor fell in love with a girl who danced very well, and, to please her, he started to learn a mazurka.

He flatters the authorities like a priest.

The ice cream is made of milk in which, as it were, the patients bathed.

One of the most fascinating artist's notebooks is not a writer's but Leonardo da Vinci's. The notebooks were "mirror written," backward from right to left. In the notebooks are notes on anatomy, music, painting, sculpture, remarks about light, ideas for future projects, reminders about neighbors in possession of certain rare books, drawings, natural observations ("The shadows of plants are never black, for where the atmosphere penetrates there can never be utter darkness"), exercises ("Describe the tongue of the woodpecker and the jaw of the crocodile"), and sententiae, like this:

We are deceived by promises and time disappoints us.

He who thinks little, errs much.

The greatest deception men suffer is from their own opinion.

When I was looking for the name of a beauty parlor while writing *Deep in the Shade of Paradise*, I read through my notebooks and found the one I used, Pug Wolfe's Curl Up & Dye. Pug Wolfe is a real beautician in Cleveland, Mississippi. My friend the poet Carolyn Elkins got her hair done at Pug's New Generation beauty shop. I stole Pug's name. What I learned when the book came out was that Pug first wanted to call her shop Curl Up & Dye, but her family vetoed the idea. Maybe now she'll change.

You can write down quotes on writing or on thinking in your notebook. ("Diane Arbus: 'I really believe there are things nobody would see if I didn't photograph them.'") Keep lists of words that you want to use in your next novel. Record interesting facts ("All Europeans descend from five females") or curious behaviors ("Chambermaid at the Hotel Gunther drinks water right out of the pitcher"). Write them down because something about them intrigues you. You don't have to know how you'll exploit them yet. Your job is to jot. Glue in newspaper articles that suggest intriguing narratives. Write down your dreams. Glue in cartoons, postcards (like the one from the Moses Motel in Monroe, Louisiana—who knows what

> "Writing is a process of dealing with not knowing, a forcing of what and how."
> —DONALD BARTHELME

character might check in), photographs you've taken of possible settings for scenes. If you hear a line that you like, write it down. "I stayed up all night with this chicken, and you're not going to eat it?" Or a situation: "A fundamentalist preacher is harassed by a guy with a remote-control car."

Now that you've got the notebook, take it with you. Try writing in different places. Write in a bar. (And at some point someone will ask you what you're doing, and you'll say you're a writer, and he'll tell you his story.) Try writing in other places where people gather—cafés, malls, bus stops. If your characters drive expensive cars, then you might bring that notebook out to the country club and settle into the nineteenth hole. Write in a church, an old church if you can, a Catholic church if possible. Can you smell the incense? What is the effect of the light flooding through the stained glass? Write in a cemetery or in a rowboat drifting on a pond. Write in an art museum. Write in a library. Write about the people you see. And the books they are reading. Why is it that some people's voices carry across the room?

"When you write about what you don't know, this means that you begin to think about the world at large. You enter dream and imagination. So write about what you don't know, so that you can bring imagination into play, so you can create and explore. If you write something and don't learn anything new, you've failed. A fiction writer wants to create a world as real as, but other than, the world that is."
—CYNTHIA OZICK

You may be tempted to get the novel draft done even more quickly than our proposed six months. I've planned for us to spend two weeks finding our characters, and you figure three days is plenty. You're wrong. You have hardly begun to know your characters. Spend the hours every day for the two weeks learning as much as you can about these people who have only just been born, but who have been born with dreams and sorrows and childhood traumas and secrets and fears and talent and what all else. Take your time here. You ought to be learning things about the characters that surprise and maybe even shock you, things that the characters don't want you to know, things they don't even want to know about themselves. The better you get to know your characters, the better you will like them, and the better you like them, the more you will care about them.

You may already have notes for a novel in your drawer. You may even have a hundred pages of an abandoned novel. You may have nothing but a dream. And that's what I'll assume—we're starting with a blank slate. When the first draft is done, then the real writing begins. In one sense the first draft is always a failure. It's not the story you set out to write. It's not supposed to be, however. It's simply the first step. In another sense, the first draft is always a resounding success because now you have something to revise. The draft did what it was intended to do—got you a brave new world and many goodly creatures in it and trouble and scenes and themes and tone and voice and so on.

Here's what I'm suggesting we do to get a draft in six months:

Weeks 1 & 2: *This Is Your Life.* We'll spend the time exploring your own life as a source of fictional material. We'll look for characters and events and examine your emotional history. What's important to you? What keeps you up at night? What do you know? What don't you know? What don't you want to know? How did you get into all that trouble? Why were people saying all those nasty things about you?

Weeks 3 & 4: *Character.* Character is the heart of fiction. We read novels for the people who live in them because we read to learn about ourselves. We're not alone, after all! We read to explore the human condition. Who are these people in the novel, and why do they do what they do?

The first month is finished already, and you haven't written one word of the novel. Perfect! Writing a novel does not proceed in a linear fashion even if the novel itself eventually does. Writing a novel is messy; it's labyrinthine at times; it's recursive and indirect; it sputters and lurches and frustrates and generates. The way is tortuous. Your novel may not meander, but your writing of it surely will. Writing fiction enables you to think—in fact, it insists that you think—in ways you've never thought before, and so it is by definition irrational, but not without reason, and illogical. It both uses and makes uncommon sense. Think of your day's writing task as bricolage. You take what you have at hand, and you use it. You do that knowing that soon you'll have lots more at hand to work with because what you assemble today, what you discover today, will lead to insight and to the generation of more material. And you cannot know what that material is ahead of time.

Week 5: *Place.* Those people in your novel have to live someplace, and that someplace has defined them to a degree. Nothing can take place nowhere. So let us build us a city or a town or a neighborhood or a tenement building or a trailer park. And let's look around and see who's there and who's lurking in the shadows.

Week 6: *Theme.* What are you writing about? What about what it's about? What is the central character's problem? What is it like to be a human being, and how does that feel?

Week 7: *Point of View.* Who's telling the story to whom and at what distance from the characters and from the reader? What's that voice I hear?

Weeks 8–11: *Plot.* What happens in this world and to whom and why. What is the architecture of action and how can you use it to build your novel? Yes, a novel is a story. In fact, it's many stories.

Week 12: *Review.* You're halfway home. What have you wrought? Take stock of the novel. Read it and take notes. Assess the product and the process. Look ahead.

Week 13: *The Opening Scene.* What comes first may not happen first. What exactly is a scene anyway? What is the opening image of the novel? In the opening scene you have the chance to teach the reader how to read your story. Write the opening scene. Revise it. Edit it. Polish it. It's all rehearsal for what you'll be doing for the rest of the novel.

Weeks 14 & 15: *The Obligatory Scenes.* What's your contract with the reader? How does your central character struggle to get what he wants? Illustrate the struggle. Describe the necessary action.

Week 16: *Miscellanea:* Here we'll talk about all those things we've forgotten to even mention yet, like titles, chapters, tense, atmosphere, details, and so on.

Weeks 17 & 18: *Character.* More on the heart of fiction. How can you turn your characters into people?

Weeks 19 & 20: *Plot and Subplots.* Text and subtext. Let's consider the architecture of action, the shape of your story, the arc of the character development, the beginning, the middle, the end, the climax, and the resolution.

Weeks 21–24: *Writing the First Draft.* Connect the dots, the scenes. Get black on white. Fly through the story; read and write.

Weeks 25 & 26: *Revision.* Read what you've written with a pen in your hand. Tear it apart and build it up again. Cut, note, question, prepare. Have a drink, toast your great success. You did it!

———

AND BY NOW your notebooks are full, and you've got scribbled papers in folders all over the place, and your desk is a mess, and so is your life, come to think of it. Isn't it great? You might want to call some of those people you've been ignoring. (You might get material.) You have a beginning, a middle, and an end that you're not completely pleased with, but still you admire it, as you should. You've brought something new into the world, some people and places that did not exist before, people who are as real as the people in your workplace. (And much more interesting.) You've already done the hardest part, and you've done it quietly, determinedly, serenely, and secretly. You've done what so many people talk about doing, dream about doing, but never do. Be happy, but understand that this is only the start. You've shown courage and tenacity, and now you'll need more of the same. We'll be talking about the forms and the theory of the novel in the pages ahead, and we'll be writing. Weeks one and two start with our next chapter.

YOU ARE WHAT YOU READ . . . Here's an exercise I got from my friend John Bond, who claims to have read five novels a week for most of his life. His house is a library—the stacks to the ceiling, the ladder, the whole nine yards. There are two ways to learn how to write a novel. By writing them and by reading them. If you are not reading them, the obvious question I'd ask is, why would you want to write something you wouldn't want to read? Are you one of those folks who really wants to make movies and figures writing a novel is easier than writing a screenplay? (It's not.) Or you think the novel will be your entrée into Hollywood? (It very well could be.) If you confess to the above, then you might be disappointed in these particular exercises. If you want to be a novelist, you have to read novels. You're kidding yourself if you think otherwise. Your daily view of the world is affected by what you've been reading, and what you write will also be affected.

> *"Wisdom begins in wonder."*
> —SOCRATES

You should always be reading a novel or a collection of stories.

When you find a novel you like, read everything by that writer, or read him until you've had enough. You're reading to learn. How does this writer do what she does, and how can I do it? I've heard writers say they can't read fiction while they are writing it. Are they afraid of being influenced? If you're reading good stuff, what would be the fear? Some critic says you write like Fitzgerald! Well, praise God and send the critic a thank-you note. If you're reading trash, then you're going to write trash. If you can't read fiction, what's the point of going on? You think the author's style will undermine your own. Then read someone whose style (whatever that is) is so outré or so Victorian that it couldn't possibly interfere with your own. But read!

> "You can't want to be a writer, you have to be one."
> —PAUL THEROUX

So then, what are the *last five novels* you read? Go to the bookcase. Remember. Make a list. You might check off the ones you liked of the five. You might consider why you liked those, not the others. Now what are *your five favorite novels* (as opposed to those you think are the best)?

For each of these ten novels, ask the following questions:

- What is the point of view?

- What is the "timescape" of the novel—when does it begin and when does it end? Does it go into its own past through flashback? What other time elements are there? Why does it begin when it begins?

- What does the main character want? Why does she want it? When do you know? Is there a false want/need? If so, when do you discover that it's false and find out what the true want is?

- What is the first obstacle the hero encounters? How far into the book—in terms of pages and in terms of the book's time? The second obstacle?

- What is the protagonist's single most interesting characteristic?

- What are the dominant themes of the book?

- Does the book explore a particular world or subculture (i.e., *One Flew Over the Cuckoo's Nest*, Ken Kesey—mental hospitals; *Strip Tease*, Carl Hiaasen—strip clubs; *The Monkey Wrench Gang*, Edward Abbey—environmental activism)?

- Is there a clearly defined antagonist? How does the antagonist reflect the protagonist's character flaws (if the antagonist does)?

- What do you like best about the book?

- What is the book's most apparent weakness?

THE WRITER'S LIFE. Flaubert called it a dog's life, but the only life worth living. Today you're a writer, and from today on. So look at the week ahead and plan your writing time. Writing is your priority now. Pencil in your writing hours Monday through Sunday (start with tomorrow, of course) in that new DayMinder you just bought when you picked up the pens and the paper and the DO NOT DISTURB: WRITER AT WORK sign. Because it's your first week at work, you might want to give yourself assignments other than what we have in the exercises. Just to get the pump primed, and so you won't waste even a minute staring at a blank page or screen. Like this: Monday: *Write about my favorite meal*; Tuesday: *Where I want to go before I die*; Wednesday: *Things I'd like to do over*; Thursday: *Things I'd like to forget*; Friday: *Describe my hands*; Saturday: *Saturdays when I was young*; Sunday: *What it feels like to have written every day for a week*.

THEY DID AND THEY DIDN'T. I've just read a book called *101 Plots Used and Abused* by James N. Young, published in 1945 when it sold in hardcover for $1.25. Mr. Young, then the associate editor of *Collier's* magazine, which many of you will not remember, outlines 107 (not 101) plots that he calls "tired and tiresome." Maybe you can prove him wrong. Here's number 51. "Two old people — a man and a woman who had once, years before, been in love with each other—correspond, with a view to looking each other over and possibly marrying. The man is a widower; the woman is a widow. They make arrangements to meet somewhere—usually the lobby of some great hotel; and they describe each other. Each is to wear a distinguishing mark of some sort—a flower perhaps. But they never actually meet. Each manages to steal a peek at the other; and both sneak away—and, later, report that they had been unavoidably detained by something or other." Write about these two; give them names and addresses in separate cities. Write about their youthful love affair and the eventual breakup. Summarize their years of marital bliss or suffering, whatever it was. Describe their separate lives until now. Maybe sample their recent correspondence. How did they hook up again anyway? Now give us the scene in the hotel lobby—describe the lobby using all of your senses. Let's suppose that they do, in fact, avoid each other as Young suggests. Let's follow them back to their homes and to their lives. Do they wonder what they may have just let slip through their hands? What now for each? Now let's suppose that they do meet, and hit it off, and get married and start a new life. Write about that new life. Is it happy? Maybe you play both scenarios out in the same novel—if you want to write this as your novel. You begin at that moment when she was going to walk away but turns once more to look at him . . . and thinks? And feels? And . . . And what else do you imagine here? Then write two plots that you braid together, one in which they meet, one in which they do not, and follow their lives.

In the Beginning Were the Words

Beginning a book is unpleasant. I'm entirely uncertain about the character and the predicament, and a character in his predicament is what I have to begin with. Worse than not knowing your subject is not knowing how to treat it, because that's finally everything. I type out beginnings and they're awful, more of an unconscious parody of my previous book than the breakaway from it that I want. I need something driving down the center of a book, a magnet to draw everything to it—that's what I look for during the first months of writing something new.
—*Philip Roth*

WHERE DO YOU begin writing a novel? At the desk, of course. And how do you begin? Let me count the ways. You can begin by asking yourself what it is you want to know. Make a list: (1) What is it like to realize that you're dying? (2) How can you be in love and then out of it again? (3) What would make me happy? (4) What makes people behave in ways that they detest? (5) What if I won the lottery? (6) Why is there something and not nothing? (7) How could a person abuse a child?

The idea for a novel might come from the events of your life. Examine your past. Write about what hurts, what broke your heart. Write about what you don't understand. Write about what you can't forget. Write about your regrets and your outrage. A novel might come from the events of someone else's life. A novel might be inspired by what you've read, in fiction or in a newspaper. It might begin as an anecdote overheard or a snatch of dialogue from the folks at the next table in the restaurant. Novelists are inspired by whatever attracts their attention, by what pops up in their note books. A novel might begin with a strong emotion, a character or a situation, a place, an overheard line, a provocative image. In short, a novel can begin anywhere, with anything, so long as it fascinates you, worries you, or makes you wonder.

My novel *Louisiana Power & Light* began as an attempt to write about a place, a small city in northeast Louisiana, to try to understand what drew people to the place, what kept them there, what influence the topography and the commerce had on their speech, folkways, and relationships. The novel began with my taking copious notes about the cotton fields, the foodways, the idioms of speech, the markets, the flora and fauna in the brakes, bayous, and riversides, and the history, meaning the War Between the States, especially. It began with reading old newspapers and looking at countless historical photographs. I wasn't writing history or reportage, so I needed people. Characters. So I got my Billy Wayne Fontana, whose surname came from a road on the south side of town. I didn't know squat about Billy Wayne. Only his name. But then I realized that his family had a long and disastrous history in the town. The trouble didn't start with Billy Wayne. The Fontanas would be my Snopeses. Trouble would haunt them. That's all I knew. I wondered what was Billy Wayne's trouble now, in the time of the story. I needed a precipitating event,* an action that would

---

*Back in my first so-called career as a social worker/counselor, I worked at a crisis intervention hotline. We took calls from people in trouble and tried to help them clarify what was going on and what they might do about it. The fact that someone in dire emotional straits would call a stranger suggests that her normal

set the wheels of the novel into motion. One evening I was watching the news and saw a story of a man, a divorced father, who had kidnapped his child from a local elementary school. These were the days when missing children's photographs wound up on milk cartons. I wondered what would drive a man to perform so desperate an act. I knew that a man doesn't just kidnap his child. He has to plan, at least a little bit. He has to get a vehicle, has to drive to the school, has to find the right classroom, has to provide an excuse, has to drive off to some considered destination or to god knows where. I worked at the story awhile, and I seemed to be going nowhere plotwise (no surprise there), when I had my narrator say something about Billy Wayne that I didn't already know. (And this may be the moment, there at the kitchen table, that I became an honest-to-god writer, or felt like I had anyway.) What came to me nearly whole cloth, with some minor tinkering, was what would be the opening sentence of the story "The Fontana Gene," and subsequently of the novel:

"When Billy Wayne Fontana's second wife, Tami Lynne, left him for the first time, he walked into Booker T. Washington Elementary School, interrupted the fourth grade in the middle of a hygiene lesson, it being a Thursday morning and all, apologized to Miss Azzie Lee Oglesbee, the substitute teacher, fetched his older boy, Duane, and vanished for a year and a half from Monroe." I say it came whole cloth, but that was after I'd been taking notes for a month or

coping mechanisms had broken down. Usually, you'll talk to family, to friends, to a priest, perhaps. A call might, and often did, involve spousal abuse. One thing you knew was that this reported abuse was not the first episode of violence. No one calls the first time. There is a history here. So what has happened that makes the most recent episode different from all the others? Why didn't she call last month, last night? Why today, right now? What was the precipitating event—that which happened today, right now, which provoked (enabled?) the victim to call? What event in your novel gets the central character to act on her desires, to go after what she needs?

more. I pushed the chair back from the table and looked at what I'd wrought: two wives and two children, submerged trouble and palpable trouble, an adventure for a year and a half, and a return, a second split. I began to ask questions. Why not take the two boys? Who was that first wife? Why would this Tami Lynne take Billy Wayne back after what he'd done? Why would she leave him again? And who was that voice telling the story? (And that Azzie Lee, she'll need to come back to the story somehow, won't she?) I started answering the questions and in several months had a long, expository story that I liked. But I realized I had only just begun writing about the Fontanas.

Leo Tolstoy's neighbor Bibikov, the snipe hunter, lived with his mistress, Anna Pirogova—a juicy bit of gossip in the neighborhood. But then Bibikov shifted his affections to his children's German governess, decided, in fact, to marry the Fräulein. Anna's jealousy turned to rage. She ran away, wandering the countryside, crazed with grief. Then she threw herself under a freight train at the Yasenki station. The following day, Tolstoy went to the station, attracted by the scandal of the woman who had given all for love, who had died this trite, if tragic, death. He learned of a letter she had written to Bibikov: "You are my murderer. Be happy, if an assassin can be happy. If you like, you can see my corpse on the rails at Yasenki." This is just the sort of story that might show up in the morning papers.* Tolstoy, they say, settled down to write the novel

---

*As I begin this chapter, police have unearthed the remains of two thirteen-year-old girls buried beneath a concrete slab in Ward Weaver's Oregon City backyard. Weaver's in jail on the unrelated charges of strangling and raping his son's nineteen-year-old girlfriend, the mother of his grandchild. The son called 911 and told the operator his father had admitted to killing the two girls. Weaver's father, also named Ward, a trucker, is serving a death sentence for the murder of a man whose car had broken down and for the rape and murder of the driver's girlfriend. He buried her body in his backyard after having his ten-year-old son unwittingly dig the grave. The body remained there for seventeen months until

the day he read a piece by Pushkin that began, "The guests arrived at the country house," and realized that he could begin by plunging into the middle of the action. Tolstoy turned the shocking incident into one of the world's great nov-

> "Do not even listen, simply wait, be quite still and solitary. The world will freely offer itself to you to be unmasked, it has no choice, it will roll in ecstasy at your feet."
>
> —FRANZ KAFKA

els, *Anna Karenina*. He thought, no doubt, about what would have driven her to such desperation, and he began to imagine her life from the little he knew. (It's good to know just a little.) And he did not confine himself to Anna and her struggles, but brought to the novel the world of politics, poverty, scientific farming, and the military.

William Faulkner said, "With me, a story usually begins with a single idea or memory or mental picture. The writing of the story is simply a matter of working up to that moment, to explain why it happened or what caused it to follow." *The Sound and the Fury* began as the story of a funeral. And it all started with the image of, in Faulkner's words, "the muddy seat of a little girl's drawers in a pear tree, where she could see through a window where her grandmother's funeral was taking place and report what was happening

---

another of his sons led police to it. The senior Weaver's truck route matched up with twenty-six unsolved hitchhiker murders, but he was never charged. He also picked up a pair of runaways, had a friend shoot the eighteen-year-old boy while he raped the fifteen-year-old-girl. Ward, the son, knew the missing girls, treated Ashley Pond "like a daughter." He often drove her to school, took her on vacations —once they even stopped at San Quentin to visit the elder Ward Weaver. Ashley lived briefly with Weaver when her own father was jailed for abusing her. Despite the fact that at least two people, including a teacher, reported to state welfare workers that Ashley had accused Weaver of abusing her, and despite the fact that Weaver had flunked a lie-detector test, the Oregon City police did nothing until the call came from the son. And this is only the beginning of what might make a harrowing novel. But who's our central character? And do we want to live in this world for the time it'll take to write the book?

to her brothers down below." Surely, a girl worth paying attention to. When asked how he composed the novel, Faulkner said he followed Caddy around and wrote down what she did. And he hit on the notion of telling the same story four times, from four different points of view.

E. L. Doctorow said this about the genesis of *Ragtime*: "I was so desperate to write something, I was facing the wall of my study in my house in New Rochelle and so I started to write about the wall. That's the kind of day we sometimes have as writers. Then I wrote about the house that was attached to the wall. It was built in 1906, you see, so I thought about the era and what Broadview Avenue looked like then: trolley cars ran along the avenue down at the bottom of the hill; people wore white clothes in the summer to stay cool. Teddy Roosevelt was a resident. One thing led to another and that's the way that book began, through desperation to those few images."

Henry James talked about what he called the germs of stories—"the interesting truth about the stray suggestion, the wandering word, the vague echo, at touch of which the novelist's imagination winces as at the prick of some sharp point: its virtue is all in its needle-like quality, the power to penetrate as finely as possible. This fineness it is that communicates the virus of suggestion, anything more than a minimum of which spoils the operation."

> "All behavior consists of opposites . . . Learn to see things backwards, inside out, and upside down."
> —LAO-TZU

James remembered the genesis of an Englishwoman's novel about a French Protestant youth. She was asked how she learned so much about this recondite creature she'd created. She said that once, in Paris, she ascended a staircase, passed an open door where some young Protestants were seated at a table around a finished meal. The glimpse made a picture; it lasted only a moment, but the moment was experience. She had gotten her direct personal impression, let it incubate, and then got to work. As *Revelations* directs us: "What thou seest, write in a book. . . . Write the things which thou hast seen, and the things which are, and the things which shall be hereafter."

James described the beginning of his own *The Spoils of Poynton*. He was enjoying a holiday dinner when he heard a bit of gossip about a mother and son at odds over the ownership of a valuable piece of furniture. "There had been but ten words, yet I recognized in them, as in a flash, all

> "Chaos often breeds life, when order breeds habit."
> —HENRY ADAMS

the possibilities of the little drama of my 'Spoils,' which glimmered then and there into life." Joseph Conrad began *Nostromo* by recalling an anecdote he'd heard twenty-seven years earlier. Pay attention. Eavesdrop.

So let's say you've gotten that seed. You've got a character, maybe, or a place or a line. You're ready to begin. Here's a sketch I found in one of my notebooks. Let's see what we might do with it to get the novel going. I have the image of a man sitting in a car in a motel parking lot. He's waiting for someone and warming the car. It's cold, gray. A woman comes out of the motel room, taps her pocket, closes the door, smiles at him, and walks to the car. For a moment the man doesn't know who she is or why he's with her. I see the man looking at her through the windshield as she approaches. Something about this guy and this woman and this place intrigued me enough to make the note. The attraction might be that they're on the road. It might be the man's moment of dissociation that compels me. But something there is in that visual image that tells me there's a story lurking in that parking lot.

Where do we go from here? How does this moment, this singularity, expand into the universe of a novel? First, I wonder if I've ever experienced a moment like this myself. It occurs to me that I have. Now I understand that the man's feeling is not *Who is this woman?* but rather, *Who am I? Is this where I belong? Am I pretending to be someone I'm not?* I'm using the emotional material from my own past. Take the initial moment, the image, the line, and then connect it to the facts and, more importantly, to the emotions of your own life. You'll be able to go there again and again.

Let's remember what John Gardner said about the fiction writer's process. In his imagination, the writer sees made-up people doing things—sees them clearly—and in the act of wondering what they'll do next, he sees what they'll do next, and he writes that down in the best, most accurate words he can find, understanding that he may have to find better words later, and the change of a single word will sharpen the vision of the entire story. You look. You see. You see clearly, meaning you see the details, the nuances (the way the woman tapped her pocket before she closed the door). And you wait. You might take this one step further. When you're writing, don't ask what *happens* next, ask what *happened* next, and then see it and write down what did.

Writing a novel is talking to yourself and then talking to the world. You understand that meaning emerges from the flow of words and images. Meaning doesn't exist before the writing. And meaning is what you're after in writing a novel. But you're not sure you can do this. You've got two people in a parking lot—how on earth does that become a novel? You've got a sentence, maybe. You need three hundred pages.*

You know that the idea for a novel is not a novel. You're worried.

---

*You can give the motel a name, for starters—a few more words. The name's right up there on the sign by the road. *The Golden Motel/Beautyrest.* (I looked through a book of photographs, and found it.) Now you know the motel is not a chain, and that may tell you something about the man and the woman and/ or about the place.

Doubt and uncertainty, fear and intimidation are at the heart of
the novel-writing process. For everyone, not just you, and for every
novel you'll ever write, not just this one. Get used to it. Doubt and
uncertainty are not only a part of, but are fundamental to, the writing process. *Not knowing* is crucial to the making of a novel. It sets
wonder in motion. (Donald Barthelme: "A writer is a man who,
embarking upon a task, does not know what to do.") E. L. Doctorow explained the writing of a novel this way: "Writing a novel is
like driving a car at night. You can only see as far as your headlights,
but you can make the whole trip that way."*

All right, then, the woman is walking to the car. She's still smiling. She's got a blue backpack draped over one shoulder. Her hair
is brown. It's still a bit damp from the shower. The man watches
her. She opens the door and hops in. She kisses him. When their
lips touch in the dry, cold air, they are zapped with the sting and
click of electricity. She (they're going to need names soon) makes
a joke about his high-voltage smooch. I like that she does that. I
like her. His mind, however, is elsewhere. Why isn't he happy?
What's the trouble? Whenever I wonder why I'm writing the novel
I'm writing, I'll come back here, to the parking lot, and I'll remind
myself what first attracted me to these two—his bewilderment and
angst, his unsettled sense of self, and her wit, humor, and buoyant
sense of self.

I don't know what the trouble is yet because I don't know
enough about them. I need to consider what I have here. They
are about to drive somewhere. But where to? And where are they

---

*Not all writers agree that writing is a journey of discovery. John Barth: "I don't
see how anyone starts a novel without knowing how it's going to end." Katherine
Anne Porter: "If I didn't know the ending of a story, I wouldn't begin." Toni Morrison: "I always know the ending; that's where I start." But I would caution those
who do know the ending to be flexible and not wrest the plot to fit the end. You
may find a better ending as you write.

now? I know it's dry and cold. So I'm thinking out West, winter. California? The Sierras, say? California's the Golden State, the land of dreams and opportunity. I have a feeling that's not what I want here. The Great Basin seems more appropriate. The country's largest desert. Nevada. Okay, what else does Nevada afford? Gambling, of course. Space. Mining towns, ghost towns, empty highways. Area 51. Red rock canyons, salt flats. Cowboys and Basques. Quickie weddings, quickie divorces. Nevada is the most mountainous state in the country, the driest, the fastest-growing, surprisingly the most urban, and, perhaps, the most empty.

Our couple (well, that word *couple* articulates something that we had already guessed) need names. Names are important. Naming a character is like naming a child. You're going to be living with these people for a long time. Names signify, even if what they signify is ordinariness. (And you might want ordinary for some characters.) Names are never neutral. And remember that the names you use may suggest certain traits, perhaps, social and ethnic backgrounds, geography, and so on. Take care with your characters' names. If you are good, their names will be around longer than yours will. Don't use run-of-the-mill names, if you can help it. They are not memorable. If you give a character a name you dislike, it may prejudice you against that character. So let's call our couple Teddy Chauvin and Avery Bishop. I may decide to change them later, but for now they'll do. And note that Teddy has a French surname like my own, and that suggests that I know something more about his background and culture than I do about Avery's, which, by the way, might not work in Teddy's favor.

> "Whether it's something that happened twenty years ago or only yesterday, I must start out with an emotion—one that's close to me and that I can understand."
> —F. SCOTT FITZGERALD

Teddy and Avery are driving to—I open a map of Nevada and find a name I like—Battle Mountain—driving to Battle Mountain for breakfast, so I figure they're in Valmy, just up the highway. Teddy's a little preoccupied, we know, and Avery senses it. She trusts her intuition. She asks him what's wrong. He says nothing. She asks him if his back still aches and apologizes for the motel. She picked it out because of the motel sign—reminded her of a fairy tale. And now I know this about Avery: for years she has let signs guide her life. They do not appear by accident, she believes. If you need something, open your eyes and you will find it. It could be the sign outside a church announcing the Sunday sermon: LOVE IS WHAT IT IS. It could be an astrological sign. She's a Taurus; he's a Scorpio. (I'll have to read some astrology to find out what Avery will think that combination means for their relationship.)

I have a sense of Teddy's unease, irritability, discomfort. I'll make it even more uncomfortable for him. Their car is small. Too small for a proper road trip. Let's say it's a Mitsubishi Mirage—a name compatible with our desert imagery (and not only that, besides the illusion of water and inverted reflections of distant objects in the desert, *mirage* also means illusory or insubstantial—does this now become a theme in the nascent novel? Is it too good to be true? Or is it too heavy-handed?), and later when they may have to get the car repaired, the garage won't have the parts, and the mechanic will be a World War II vet who still holds a grudge against the Japanese. And, in fact, the car's developed a hesitation in the last few days. (My life has been a litany of bad cars and breakdowns. The last time I drove through Nevada, via Death Valley, the car quit eighteen miles from the closest town. I got a new fuel filter, bent to fit,

> "I start with a tingle, a kind of feeling of the story I will write. Then come the characters, and they take over, they make the story."
> —ISAK DINESEN

at the Death Valley Garage in Beatty. Every March in Beatty, they hold the Rhyolite Resurrection Festival—your guess is as good as mine. Book early!) So Teddy's worried about the car, especially out here in all this emptiness.

But I know that's not the real trouble. Wouldn't be enough for a short story, much less a novel. All right, then. The trip was Teddy's idea. (It occurs to me that the trip itself might be the structure I need for the novel [structure is always the key]. When the trip is done, so is the story.) He likes travel, likes the way it makes him pay attention to the world, likes the way everything is new. Likes the way you can reinvent yourself for the people you meet. But he hates the crummy motels, the freaking car that won't perform, hates the anxiety of that. He hates that he doesn't have his books with him, can't just kick back and spend the day reading. Hates so many of the bad restaurants. It was his idea to roam without destination—the opposite of what his life had been till then. (It's sounding more and more like this is Teddy's story, isn't it? I began with his point of view and have unconsciously looked at the material as his.)

So what was his world till then? What was Avery's world? Backstory. This may not all show up in the novel, but I need to know it. I'm looking for the trouble, remember. So Teddy was married for fifteen, twenty years, let's say. Not to Avery. (Teddy and Avery are in their forties, it sounds like.) Had a steady job—a teacher, let's say. (The books.) He got the idea, maybe from the books he was reading, that he was wasting his life, deferring his dreams, was midway in his life's journey and in dark woods, the right road lost. (I just stumbled onto Dante here [and Langston Hughes] and only at the end of the sentence do I understand its potential in my novel. Life as a journey may be our oldest metaphor. And Teddy and Avery are on a journey, are they not? Will they lose, or have they already lost, the right road? Will the wrong turn result in a descent into the nine circles of hell? We'll see.) Okay, Teddy left the wife and the job. (He had no kids. We might wonder why.) He met Avery, a free spirit, and the two of them hit it off, were up for an adventure. Avery's never been married, but she has a daughter and a grand-child. The daughter's married to a haberdasher (love that word, so why not?) and doesn't understand her mother at all. Avery has had long, monogamous relationships with a number of men. Losers, every one. (What attracts her to them?) Avery and Teddy have been traveling for a month. Teddy wants to keep driving, like he's trying to see everything he's missed all his life. Avery, on the other hand, likes to linger, to stay a few days at a place. Teddy admits that lin-gering is more pleasurable and sensible, but he can't help himself. He doesn't know why.

Avery, though, is just happy to be with Teddy. She's in love with him, admires him. It was Teddy's idea to travel, but she's actually better at it. She enjoys talking to the people she meets, likes learn-ing about the towns, the history, the foods, the cultures. Teddy sees it as them against the world sometimes. Everyone's out to take them. He's provincial, though he wouldn't ever admit to it. He can't understand how people could live like this, out in the middle of nowhere, not a theater in sight, not a bookstore for hundreds of miles.

They stop for breakfast. Teddy hates everything about the place, the brown Formica table with its cigarette burns, the plastic cruets of powdered nondairy creamer, the plastic squirt bottles of ketchup and mustard, the bamboo basket of saltine crackers, the sugar and sweetener bags stacked on their plastic caddy, the peel-back packets of jam piled in a cracked wooden salad bowl. When Avery doesn't order breakfast, but then snatches a slice of his bacon, Teddy flips. They argue and Avery tells him to go along. She won't take this kind of abuse. They make up, drive on into the novel. Specifically, they decide to drive to Austin across eighty miles of uninhabited road.

Teddy figures the car will be fine—hadn't acted up this morning. Must be the altitude.

I don't know what's going to happen, and I don't need to. I just need to keep intensifying the trouble and the struggle. I don't yet know what Teddy, my central character (for now—we're still in the audition stage) wants. And he may not know what he wants. When he does I'll have a better idea about where this is going. I may find out soon. I may not know for quite a while. Either way, I keep writing. I consider that I have a few contrasts already. (Novels often build on contrasts.) Illusion and reality. The past and the future. The rooted life and the nomadic one. The private self and the public self. Wariness and trust. Intuition and logic And I have themes: travel, the self, love, marriage, signs (and paying attention to them). (What *about* travel? The self? Love? Marriage?) And I just know that gambling and risk-taking will enter the picture. I know there will be plenty of images of physical, emotional, and spiritual aridity.

> "Writing is finally a series of permissions you give yourself to be expressive in certain ways. To invent. To leap. To fly. To fail."
> —SUSAN SONTAG

Here's one way the novel could go: The car breaks down on 376 near Alkali Flat. They're rescued by a truckload of guys who've been out hang-gliding. Teddy's so grateful that he wants to take the guys out for drinks in Carvers. Avery wants to leave. Something's not right. Teddy says she's being silly. They go to a bar. The first time Teddy senses danger is when one of the men asks him if he's a Jew. He says he isn't. We realize, as Teddy does, that there is no law in this town. A stranger could disappear, and no one would ever know it. The violence escalates. Avery is assaulted. Teddy escapes, but needs to get her back and execute his revenge. What he wants is now clear. And so are his obstacles—the bad guys, the desert (the inferno).

Or it could go another way, any number of other ways. Let's see. Teddy's doubt precipitated the action-so-far. Let's go there. He left a comfortable and predictable life. He set off on an adventure, and now he's not sure this was the right thing to do. He thinks he may not be finding the real Teddy—which was the pretense for the trip—but has learned instead that he's playacting at being the vagabond.

But I haven't answered my question—the question every novel needs to address: What does he want? He wants to know what he wants? Hmm. Whatever else the novel is about, it's about a relationship in trouble. It strikes me that it will be easier to write Avery's story. She's clear (at least I think she is—the truth about a good novel is that nothing is ever what it seems to be) that she loves Teddy and wants to be with him—on the road or settled down, makes no difference. (We love people who are in love.) She wants to make this love affair last. She wants to be with Teddy for the rest of her life. We know what she wants and why she wants it— she loves him. And we suspect there may be other motivations as well. She thinks this could be her last chance to make a relationship last. There's a hint of desperation. She's convinced that she's finally found a guy who is not organically flawed like all the exes. She doesn't have to settle for what she can get with Teddy, and she won't. If it doesn't work out with Teddy, she'll never make it work. Better to give up on love and sex entirely than to start all over with another guy. She wonders if it isn't she that's the problem. Maybe she doesn't want the partnerships to work. She doesn't believe that, but she doesn't disregard the possibility, either. She's trying to be honest.

> "I am always doing what I cannot do yet, in order to learn how to do it."
> —VINCENT VAN GOGH

So what are her obstacles? Well, right now, Teddy is one. He's beginning to act coldly toward her. This is the thing about men—when they meet you, they pretend (that theme again) to be someone other than who they are because they believe their real selves are unattractive and unlovable. And so you begin an affair with this compassionate, articulate man and soon enough you're dealing with a reticent and selfish lout. But every woman knows this, and so she steels herself against the revelation of oafishness. And here's what else women know—that the guy's real self is the presentation self, not the emergent self, this dolt-come-lately, this bore, this self-indulgent lummox. But the lummox never believes the truth.

Avery knows Teddy better than he knows himself. She understands his fears and won't let him run from them. She wants him to confront the fears, the doubts, the anxieties. She wants him to forget the past and live for now. If she can save Teddy from himself, she'll save their relationship. She'll get what she wants. She may become her own obstacle along the way. She might have to struggle against her own frustration and resignation, her own desire to flee this tepid romance. Other obstacles surface. The ex makes a phone call—why did

> "Nothing is harder than being a true novelist, unless that is all one wants to be, in which case though becoming a true novelist is hard, everything else is harder."
> —JOHN GARDNER

Teddy give her the cell phone number anyway? They run out of cash. We'll see what all else surfaces. But in the end, Avery gets Teddy to love her unconditionally and to understand the responsibilities of the lover and the beloved. They go to the Rhyolite Resurrection Festival that spring (rebirth and resurrection, how could I pass it up?—the festival's an arts and crafts exhibition, with funnel cake stands, Mexican food and hot dog concessions, games for the kiddies held in an old ghost town), and that's where Teddy rises from the inferno of doubt and misgiving and discovers the purity of his love for Avery. They drive to Vegas and get married by an Elvis impersonator (*pretend* again). Or they don't.

It occurs to me that the first plot—the revenge plot—would be easier to write because the requisite action is already well defined. But ease of execution is no reason to choose a plot. In the love plot, it's clear to me that I have much more energy with Avery as the central character than with Teddy. I should follow my intuition and go with her. The plot becomes the force that drives through the novel. But that's not all there is. Like Tolstoy we need to bring in the world. This is a novel, not a sonnet. One way to bring the world in is through subplots. Let's consider what some of these might be.

Think about what you're interested in. What political or social issues, for example, do you think are critical? Your characters might think the same. What's going on in Nevada these days? Trying to liberalize the marijuana laws. Burying all the nuclear waste on Yucca Mountain. Maybe Avery and Teddy get involved with the Yucca Mountain Resistance. Maybe they confront folks who have a vested interest in seeing the dump built. Teddy's ex-wife wants him back. She keeps calling. He thinks he owes it to her to listen. Avery's daughter is begging her to come home, to quit this foolishness and settle down. Her grandson misses her.

So you begin with a place or a line or an image, and you find yourself a character to live in the world suggested by that germ. And now you give that character trouble and find out what she wants to do about it. You wonder what she'll do, you see her do it, you write it down. You exploit the place where the character lives. Themes emerge, and you keep coming back to them as you write to see how they'll resonate. Every new thing you learn about your character expands the universe of the novel. You learn that your central character is a prosecuting attorney, and now you know something of his worldview, and you have some insight into his mind. He's very logical. Self-righteous. Relentless.

Your novel becomes a magnet for everything that happens in your life, for everything you read. Your dreams become your characters' dreams. The newspaper article you read this morning is also read by your character. You see a photograph in a fashion magazine and realize that's what your hero looks like, and that's the jacket he's wearing in the first scene. You keep your antennae up at all times.

YOU SHOULD KNOW that writing a novel may not be as easy as you think it's going to be before you finally sit down at the desk with your new writing tablet and your lovely fountain pen, stare at the blank page, drum your fingers, get up to freshen the coffee, tuck a pillow behind your aching back, make a list of what else you have to accomplish today, check your e-mail, switch to the computer where everything you type looks so polished and done with, make a list of possible titles, wonder if you should adopt a nom de plume, something exotic and unforgettable like *Sailor Modig* or *Jane Austen Jones*, get an idea for a better novel, smile to think how happy your mom will be when she sees the dedication page.

Monty Python has a sketch called "Novel Writing (Live from Wessex)" in which a crowd has gathered in a sports stadium to watch Thomas Hardy write *The Return of the Native*. Hardy walks out to thunderous applause and sits at his desk. The crowd goes quiet. Hardy thinks, picks up his pen, dips it in the inkwell, and begins—with a doodle. A meaningless scribble! And then he signs his name beneath it. The play-by-play commentator remarks, "Oh, dear, what a disappointing start." But then Hardy recovers and writes the definite article *The* to open the new novel. Five of his eleven novels, we're told, began with the same word. But then he crosses it out and gazes off into space. He signs his name again. He manages a phrase and the crowd goes wild, but he's misspelled *November*. Our commentator says, "It looks like *Tess of the d'Urbervilles* all over again." And so it goes. Writing a novel doesn't get any easier the second or the eleventh time you do it. And unfortunately, you won't have fans in your writing room to urge you on. There'll be no applause. Just month after month of putting it down and crossing it out and recasting the sentence once again. Everyone who has a life thinks he has a novel to write. And he or she may. But very few people understand that the life is not the novel, that chronology is not plot, that imagination is action, and action is eloquence. As I said, writing isn't easy. Simply because you have access to a pen, some paper, and a dictionary does not mean that you can write a novel any more than having access to a piano means that you can play the Goldberg Variations. Anyone can make noise. It's music we're after. Anyone can write on and on indefinitely. We're after the definite article.

If you want to be a novelist, write. Every day. Faithfully, serenely, and diligently. You have to want to write so badly that nothing, not jobs, not friends, not family, not TV or the movies, will stop you. You want it so badly you won't be deterred. You know that if you want to clutch a decent first draft of your novel in your tight little fists in six months or a year, one that you're justly proud of, but still dissatisfied with, then you have to sit down and start in on it today. Start by jotting notes. Your own procrastination is your first obstacle. Your lack of confidence may be the second. The confidence comes with the writing. *You* are the only person who can stop you from writing your novel.

Now let's write.

READING YOURSELF. Read over any stories you have written. What have you done well? What could you do better? Are there any themes you return to? Do you know why you do? Do you notice any stylistic tendencies that you have? What are they? Do these work for you or not? Who are your favorite characters and why? Are you stuck in one point of view, in one sort of world? Why is that, do you suppose? What about your settings? Write about your own writing. You might try to remember how you began the stories—what was the germ? Remember how you overcame the obstacles in writing.

READING OTHERS. William Faulkner said, "Read, read, read. Read everything—trash, classics, good and bad, and see how they do it." Make a list of your five favorite novels, whatever they are today. (Do more if you like.) No two by the same author. Look through your bookshelves to remind yourself. Pick out the contenders. Read the opening paragraphs. Look at the sections you've underlined or highlighted, read the marginalia—what do you mean, you don't write in your books? Select the five—rank them in order. Write a paragraph on each explaining the reason for your selection.

GERMS. Here are some germs for your writing. They come in different forms. You'll think of more. Get used to starting with something small and exact, not with anything as large and as vague as an idea.

- *A line.* I'll give you one. You can find them everywhere in what you read, in what you hear. Find them in poems, newspaper stories, on billboards, in the conversation of the people behind you at the supermarket checkout. Take the line as the opening of your story or novel. Write it out and keep going. Let it take you where it will. Write for ten minutes or until you want to stop. The line will likely be gone when you revise the piece, if you do. Maybe it becomes the epigraph for your story or novel. Here's the line: "Most things will never happen; this one will." Taken (with grammatical liberties) from Philip Larkin. Here's another: "Last night the moon seemed to say something." From Frank O'Hara. One thing I hope these lines do is pull you out of your world and plop you into an imagined one.

- *A list.* Your story or novel begins with a list. Who's making it? Why? What does it reveal about the list maker? The list is "Things That Make One's Heart Beat Faster." And another: "People Who Seem to Suffer." And read *The Pillow Book of Sei Shonagon* from which these potential lists were taken.

- *A title.* What does the title suggest to you? Certain themes, perhaps. Characters. A place? Titles are always important. They can be symbolic, can suggest tone, can characterize, and can push the reader along. The title is the essence of the story— which is why, despite our exercise, the title often comes last. Here are a few titles. Write about whatever they suggest, and then think about what you've written, and write some more. *The Heart Specialist; Murder Your Darlings; You Belong to Me, I Believe*; and *Stirred, Not Shaken.*

- *A character.* Many stories begin with a character. Here's one from the unfortunate news of the day. Your character is a parish priest who hears the confession of his colleague and fellow curate at St. Paul's Church, and learns that his trusted companion has molested a child. Here's another. A mother whose child has been abducted.

- *A situation.* The situation should be odd and perhaps a bit troubling. It should make you wonder. Here's an intriguing situation. Make it the opening of your story or perhaps the end of Chapter 1 of your novel. A landscape architect bathes in gasoline. And: A pizza delivery driver notices a body on his customer's floor.

- *An event.* A high school prom. A death in the family. The birth of triplets. A frightening diagnosis.

- *An image.* The smell of pencil shavings. The sight of salt-crusted work boots tucked under a radiator. The taste of Play-Doh. The sound of fingernails being scraped along a chalkboard. How it feels on your skin when a cloud passes before the sun.

- *A subject.* Happy Puppet Syndrome (a neurological disorder). A drought. Mountain climbing. Redemption. Foreclosure.

- *An oddity.* A neurology professor takes home human body parts and stores them in his freezer. Or: The poet Hart Crane committed suicide by leaping from an ocean liner into the sea. His father Clarence invented the Life Savers candy in Cleveland. Crane's Peppermint Life Savers. Since we're speaking of Cranes, Anton Chekhov had a pet crane in Yalta, a raggedy, one-legged creature that followed Chekhov around.

Weeks 1 & 2:

This Is No Memoir; This Really Happened

Biography and memoirs can never be wholly true, since they cannot include every conceivable circumstance of what happened. The novel can do that.
—*Anthony Powell*

SO HERE WE are setting out to write a novel, but I'm asking you to begin by writing about yourself. Let me explain my thinking. First of all, we want to begin writing easily and comfortably—we want to develop the habit of being writers. So starting out with material that we have easy access to makes sense. You've heard the advice before: Write about what you know. Just remember that what you know includes what you have researched and what you can imagine. What you know, in other words, is not confined to your biographical history. That given, you *do* know about your own life—or you will if you'll take the time to examine it. You were there for most of it. Some of us disparage our lives as not being exciting enough for the stuff of fiction. But we all have led interesting lives whether we know it or admit it or not. And we know the idea of using one's life for one's novel worked pretty well for Proust. Flannery O'Connor said, "Anyone who has survived his childhood has enough information about life to last him the rest of his days."

And let's consider memory itself a moment. Memory's primary job is to help us live in the present and prepare for the future, to keep us alive. You think, The last time I ate oysters I ended up violently ill, so I think I'll have the smoked mullet today. We don't need to remember what is not vital and salvific, so our memories are naturally fallible and malleable. We can remember that which did not happen, as false-memory studies have proven. It's called counterfactual thinking, and we all do it. We all create alternative versions of the past, phantom recollections, to cover up trauma, perhaps, or uncover trauma if you're writing a story, to avoid facing uncomfortable truths, or to explain the unexplainable. An inexact memory insists upon elaboration. Memories are remnants and impressions, and where there's a gap, we fill it in. When we remember, we remember the gist, not the unblemished caboodle; not the dialogue verbatim, but the essence of the conversation and its attendant emotions. Small talk evaporates. Details blur. Memory is the past revised—re-created and distilled.

As far as I can tell, I use the same mental system to envision tomorrow as to recollect yesterday. And it's the same system my unconscious brain uses to dream. In all three cases I'm forming a mental image of what is not actually present. I'm seeing and hearing what isn't here. Think of memory as reproductive imagination. So when we are remembering our past (memoir—that which didn't happen in quite this way) we are doing the same thing we'll do when we imagine a brave new world (fiction—that which happens).

What we're going to do for the next two weeks is take a somewhat systematic look at your life, at your experiences, at your emotions, your traumas, your values, and your aspirations. Some of these exercises will work better for you than others will. Some will suggest other areas you might want to explore. Go ahead and explore them. Don't limit yourself to these exercises. Follow the accident; go where the energy carries you.

Remember that you're not writing a memoir; you're writing a

novel. Your job is not to describe *one* life, but to create many lives, is not to report what happened then, but to dramatize what could happen now. You'll be delving ("to dig the ground, as with a spade") into your past, but recall what William Faulkner said about that: "The past isn't dead. It isn't even past." It's not the facts that you're after, but the important raw material of compelling narratives: the intriguing people, the evocative places, the haunting images, the dramatic moments, the resonant themes. In his magnificent memoir *Speak, Memory*, which he "self-plagiarized" for his novels, Vladimir Nabokov writes, "The following of such thematic designs through one's life should be, I think, the true purpose of autobiography."

Once you begin to examine your past, you'll see that your life opens up to you, provides you with an inexhaustible source of narrative material. And you don't even have to scrutinize the memories. You need only experience them and attend to your emotional responses. One memory connects to another, which fires another and another, and seldom in the neat and logical way you may have expected. Your memory has a mind of its own. Let it go to work. Pay attention.

Allow me to illustrate what can happen very quickly when you invite memory to join you at the writing desk. This morning as I was drinking my first cup of coffee, thinking about this chapter, and glancing at my hometown newspaper online, I saw that Omer Collette had died. Omer, whose name I had always heard as "Homer," was a paperboy who lived in my neighborhood. *Paperboy* sounds patronizing, since Homer was an adult when he sold papers, but *paperman* doesn't say it right (in the same way that *manfriend* doesn't replace *boyfriend*) and neither does *newspaper vendor*. For forty years Omer sold the *Evening Gazette* downtown, first at Harrington Corner, at Main and Front, outside Liggett's (and when I think of Liggett's, I think of drinking lime rickeys at the lunch counter and of my friends Kathy and Eileen McKiernan, the twins, who worked at the counter; they were both funny and interesting and smart, and Kathy died too young), and later in the entryway of the Slater Building a couple of blocks north on Main Street. This was in Worcester, Massachusetts. Omer stood by the sidewalk with a half dozen papers under his left arm and four or five stacks of papers on the sidewalk, mostly *Gazettes* and a few *Globes* and *Record Americans*. He'd take a paper out from under his arm and hand it to the buyer and take the payment in one efficient motion. My brother-in-law Conrad remembers Omer yelling, "Dyno-gee-gazette!" and not knowing what he meant. What Omer was yelling, I think, was "Final *Gazette!*" and pronouncing it, with its hard *g*, as "Vinyl Gee-ze-hette!"

> "Fiction is nothing less than the subtlest instrument for self-examination and self-display that mankind has invented yet."
> —JOHN UPDIKE

Omer was short. Five feet in his black leather boots. He rolled each cuff of his dungarees up six inches in a single fold. He wore a "Read the *Telegram & Gazette*" apron that had a couple of pockets at its waist. He wore a four-barreled steel coin changer attached to his belt and a billed cap except in the summer. His dark hair was cut short (and I suspect he, too, got his hair artlessly cut at Leon's Barber Shop on Orient Street like I did—twenty-five cents for a butch, thirty-five cents for a boy's regular). Omer's plastic-framed glasses were thick and slid down his nose. He had a toothy smile. His lower jaw never quite aligned with the upper. He seemed to always be in a hurry and walked with a forward lean. On the bus (the #18 Hamilton or the #5 Wheelock Ave.) Omer sat up front and on the edge of his seat, holding on to the chrome pole, so that he could talk with the driver. Omer was eighty-three when he died, slightly older than my parents. The obituary described him as "the special child" of Pierre and Rose Collette.

Omer was a fixture in our city. Our parents knew Omer; Omer

knew everyone. He was a mystery and a fascination to us kids. Rumors circulated that he was a millionaire, owned a block of triple-deckers on Plantation Street, saved every penny he'd ever earned. (I knew that part wasn't true, at least, because I'd seen him at the parish turkey raffle in the Monsignor Ducharme Center buying tickets for a chance at a wheelbarrow full of groceries from Iandoli's Market.) About once a month I went to the ten-fifteen French-language Mass at St. Joseph's with my grandparents. When I did, I'd see Omer there in a suit and tie, walking up the center aisle to Communion. I'd kneel in my pew and snap the hat clasp until my grandfather slapped my hand away, and when I wasn't losing myself in the series of biblical paintings below the clerestory windows (the apostles cowering in their fishing boat as Jesus stands at the bow and calms the stormy Sea of Galilee), I'd watch Omer, and I'd watch Pea Soup.

Pea Soup was our—mine and my siblings'—nickname ("pea soup" being our symbol of all things French-Canadian, which we were) for a gentleman who lived two streets away from us on Lamar Avenue. Lamar Avenue was where my paper route began, but Monsieur Potage de Pois did not subscribe to the paper, and I may have held that against him. Like Omer, then, I was a paperboy, but I went door to door with the morning *Worcester Telegram*, six days a week at five A.M. in the dark and the cold and the snow with dogs biting my legs and my fingers frozen stiff—but if I go down this road much farther, I'll never get back. Pea Soup had an enormous nose, a craggy, puckered bolus, a caricaturist's dream, and also a severe underbite. He was a vaguely menacing and unpleasant little fellow who never smiled and seldom spoke. I did see him once outside the church after Mass by the makeshift newsstand where my uncle Richard sold the Sunday

> "What is remembered is what becomes reality."
> —PATRICIA HAMPL

papers (another paperboy, another friend who died too young), and he seemed to be talking to a taller man. His lips were moving, but I was certain no words were being spoken. Pea Soup walked quickly, with mincing little steps and an erect posture. He always wore a fedora (straw in summer), even when he was standing on his porch in his T-shirt and suspendered gabardine trousers, keeping an eye on the neighborhood. A sign by his front door read NOTARY PUBLIC. I didn't know what that meant. I did note, however, that Smokey Stover in the Sunday funnies had a sign on his desk and sometimes in his two-wheeled Foomobile that said NOTARY SOJAC, and I assumed the two phrases were linguistically related.

> "Every thought tends to connect something with something else, to establish a relationship between things."
> —L. S. VYGOTSKY

In high school, my friends and I hung out downtown after school. We'd meet in front of City Hall or at Denholm's Department Store and walk a few block to Sibley's Jersey Bar. We'd walk by Omer and one or another of my friends would ask Omer what the number was. (The winning number in the local policy lottery, which was the pari-mutuel number at Suffolk Downs, the win, place, and show bets for the day. Or something like that.) Anyway, the question for some reason drove Omer crazy. He'd get furious, stamp his foot, yell something incomprehensible at us, and we'd pretend to run and would laugh. I never asked the infuriating question myself, but I also never told my friends to quit it. I imagined that Omer had put up with a lot of teasing his whole life from adolescent boys like us. He never seemed to remember my affront when I bought a paper from him and said hello. Over at the Jersey Bar, we'd get our tickets from the TakaCheck machine when we walked in, buy our coffees, and have the ticket punched with our total by a small red-haired lady who was shaped like a bell and mumbled to herself continually, usually about food or money. If I was flush, I'd buy a chocolate pudding which came with a cruet of cream. I'd crack the skin of the pudding and pour in the cream. Heavenly. Let me stop here.

In just a few minutes, prompted by the notice of a familiar stranger's death, I found not only Omer, but also Pea Soup and Uncle Richard and the McKiernan twins, Smokey Stover, and my grandparents and the vile neighborhood dogs (no leash laws then), and if I looked around the Jersey Bar I'd see old friends who've gone from my life. I revisited these sacred and haunted landscapes of my youth and found at least one dramatic moment—Omer's righteous wrath—and a dozen themes: death at an early age, intolerance, self-reliance, friendship, family, loneliness, religion, devotion, sacrifice, secrecy, "special children," and loss of innocence. All that in a few minutes.

I mentioned Nabokov earlier, and I'll mention him again. That memoir, *Speak, Memory* (which he wanted to call *Speak Mnemosyne,* and, when that was rejected by the publisher, suggested *The Anthemion,* and which was first published in the U.S. under the title *Conclusive Evidence,* and subtitled in its final edition *An Autobiography Revisited*), opens like this: "The cradle rocks above an abyss, and common sense tells us that our existence is but a brief crack of light between two eternities of darkness." Forty-five hundred heartbeats an hour into the abyss, into the darkness. We're writing against the clock, so let's get going. Let's keep writing. Here are two weeks' worth of writing exercises that will help you discover the resonant themes in your life, and will remind you of the significant people, some of them strangers, who have passed through your life, and will reacquaint you with evocative settings and provocative, and perhaps confounding, events. You're recalling your own past in order to imagine the future for your characters.

IN SEARCH OF LOST TIME. There's a popular name for involuntary memories provoked by the chemical senses (taste and smell). It's called the "Proust effect." And here's why. In *Swann's Way*, Proust wrote the following about the day his (Marcel's) mother offered him a cup of tea:

> She sent for one of those squat, plump little cakes called "petites madeleines," which look as though they had been molded in the fluted valve of a scallop shell. And soon, mechanically, dispirited after a dreary day with the prospect of a depressing morrow, I raised to my lips a spoonful of the tea in which I had soaked a morsel of the cake. No sooner had the warm liquid mixed with the crumbs touched my palate than a shudder ran through me and I stopped, intent upon the extraordinary thing that was happening to me. An exquisite pleasure had invaded my senses . . .
>
> And suddenly the memory revealed itself. The taste was that of the little piece of madeleine which on Sunday mornings at Combray . . . When I went to say good morning to her in her bedroom, my aunt Leonie used to give me, dipping it first in her own cup of tea or tisane. . . . and the whole of Combray and its surroundings, taking shape and solidity, sprang into being, town and garden alike, from my cup of tea.

(In an earlier version of the scene, according to Edmund Levin, Marcel is offered a bit of dry toast, which he dips in the tea, and the "bit of sopped up toast" triggers the familiar surge of memory. Proust knew, however, that the madeleines were more delicate and poetic, so the hell with what might have really happened—this is a novel, after all.) The millions of olfactory neurons (the only neurons outside the brain) are hardwired to the limbic system as well as to the cortex. The limbic system includes areas that control emotion, memory, and behavior. In evolutionary terms, smell is our most important sense. It's how we first recognized food and poisons, and we had to remember which was which to stay alive. A smell can trigger immediate and complete memories that come with emotions attached. Here's Diane Ackerman on the mute sense in her book, *A Natural History of the Senses*: "When the olfactory bulb detects something . . . it signals the cerebral cortex and sends a message straight to the limbic system, a mysterious, ancient, and intensely emotional section of our brain in which we feel, lust, and invent . . . Smell needs no interpreter. The effect is immediate and undiluted by language, thought or translation. A smell can be overwhelmingly nostalgic because it triggers powerful images and emotions before we have time to edit them." Take a whiff of a box of crayons or pencil shavings and, *bam!*, you're back there in first grade, and Sister Andrea's writing with yellow chalk on a green board, and what she's just written is your name, and you're to copy it in your tablet over and over until you can do it without looking up. You're glad you don't have a name like Kazimeras Rebikauskas. Poor Kaz is working his eraser overtime. He's torn another piece of paper.

> *"Art does not reproduce what we see; rather it makes us see."*
> —PAUL KLEE

So let's try to see what memories can be summoned by various smells. Gather your agents. Cologne or perfume, patchouli, the aforementioned box of crayons, a peppermint, a banana. Find some smells that you were familiar with in your past, in other words, and put them by the writing desk. Take one at a time, inhale, and write about what memory is triggered. And then try this. Try preparing a food that your grandmother or your mother made for you. Fill the kitchen with the aroma of frying garlic or bread. And then enjoy the meal and write about the meals just like it that you had as a kid. Who is at the table? What are they talking about? Bake some Toll House cookies, you lucky dog. Go to the market or to the florist and smell a flower and write about the memory that that provokes. While you're at the market, buy up every kind of product you had in your childhood bathroom. The aftershave your dad used, the toothpaste (do they still sell Ipana?), the mouthwash. When you get them home, dab some Vicks VapoRub under your nose, some Ben-Gay on your arm (but not at the same time). Wash your face with Ivory soap or Lifebuoy or whichever soap your mom bought when you were a kid. Sure, get the Cheracol cough syrup. Go to a toy store and buy some Play-Doh.

Buy some candy you used to love and devour. You don't have to eat it now, but you can smell it at least. Chew some Bazooka bubble gum. And then some Dubble Bubble. Juicy Fruit, Black Jack, Beemans, Clove. And then taste a breakfast cereal from your childhood. It's not enough to just remember that bowl of Wheaties, although even that will carry you back; you need to smell and taste it (sure, sprinkle on the three spoonfuls of sugar, why not?) to recall the emotion of the moment.

Was there a cleaner that your mom used around the house? Mr. Clean, maybe, or Lysol. Bab-O, Pine-Sol. (My great-grandmother used to tell me that she was the bonneted old lady with the broom-stick pictured on the can of Old Dutch Cleanser. And now I can see her kitchen so clearly over all these decades. I'm at her table eating two Oreos and drinking a glass of milk. The can of Old Dutch Cleanser is on the shelf over the porcelain sink in the sunny pantry, and on it the old lady is running in circles.) Something lemony or ammonia-y? There's a thought—find some unpleasant smells or tastes and see what they do for you. Boiled spinach, the diaper pail (thank god those days are gone), a wedge of Limburger, blood sausage, moth balls, rotten eggs. If it's not against your neighborhood association's bylaws, hang some laundry out to dry in the sun and smell it. What are you reminded of? I'll bet you're smiling.

ELEMENTARY, MY DEAR. Think about elementary school. Picture the building, or buildings if you changed schools. (And wasn't that traumatic?) The teachers, administrators. Your classmates. See their faces. Go through your class row by row and remember everyone that you can. For each class. Are there people from those days that are still in your life? That you would like to contact, if not? Have any of those old classmates died? Whom did you have a crush on? Who made you laugh? Who made you cry? Now go through each year beginning with kindergarten. Write about how it felt to be in each room. We were bused to our kindergarten (which was called pre-primary) at Sacred Heart Academy and went full days. We took a nap in early afternoon, and the first person to fall asleep won a prayer card. I tried to fake sleep, but kept peeking to see if Sister was looking at us. She was looking at me. I hated naps. Now think about an image that captures that particular school year for you. What is it? Or who is it? A map of South America on the wall? A favorite shirt that you wore? A boy you were crazy about? An incident that folks are still talking about? Go through each year and write about it. Remember all you can remember. Take your time, enjoy it. You're gathering material, remember.

LOST AND FOUND. Think about everything in your life that you have lost. (All those pairs of glasses, for starters, the keys, the money.) Write about what you have lost and how you miss what you've lost and how your life is different because of the loss. Write about looking for the lost item or person. Is anything lost right now? Where is the last place you saw it? If you were that object, where would you be? You realize that what you've lost might include friends and family and skills. And once you may have lost your way, or lost yourself, but now you are found. Some losses are to be wished for—weight and addiction, for two.

THE TOY STORE. You're walking in a strange town and pass a storefront window and a toy in the window catches your eye. You had one just like it when you were a kid. It's an old pressed steel biplane. You check the name of the store: Toys of Your Childhood. You decide to go inside. A couple of aisles piled high with toys. Describe the place. The smell of all this childhood memorabilia. Any noises? You're alone. The owner must be in the back room. Look at the toys. They all look familiar. You pick up the cap pistol and see that the white plastic on the grip is cracked right at the longhorn's nose, just like yours was. That's when you realize this is *your* toy store.

Somehow, someone has saved all the toys you ever had and collected them here. They've been waiting for you to come by. Take a look at all of them. Remember playing with them. Write about

> *"The purpose of art is the lifelong construction of a state of wonder."*
> —GLENN GOULD

them. How does it feel to see them again? The Lincoln Logs, the Creepy Crawlers, Parcheesi ("the Royal game of India"), Sorry, Life, Chutes and Ladders, Chinese checkers, Legos. Who are you playing Clue with? What are you all talking about?

I, ME, MINE. What are your tastes in music, in literature, art, sports, cars, foods, beverages, movies, plants, furniture, houses, politicians, magazines, appliances, friends, television shows? (That should take the rest of the day.) Have your tastes changed as you've grown?

Describe what you remember of your childhood prior to beginning school. Do you remember your bedroom? Describe it. Where did you play when you played outside? What is your earliest memory? Write about that. I've had people tell me they remember being in the womb. Other folks have said they can't remember anything before they were six or seven. Why do you suppose that is?

Discuss three events that have caused you to be profoundly unhappy. And it's not always the obvious events that make us the saddest. Now, what is the best thing that has happened to you in your life? The worst? (Just a reminder: There are no right answers. Do this again next week, and you'll likely have different responses.)

When do you feel most at ease and comfortable? And where? And what are you doing when you are at this ease? Are you alone? (Why is it that we can stare at the ocean or at a fire in a fireplace for hours? What is the comfort we find there?)

Now that you're blissful, and since I brought it up: How do you think you'll die? How would you like to die? *Like*, I suppose, is the wrong word. Imagine your own funeral, your wake, the gathering after the burial. (This is your only chance to be there.)

Describe some silly, foolish thing you've done. What does it feel like to remember this? How did it feel then?

What are your attitudes toward the opposite sex, love, money, insanity, suicide, abortion, violence, family life, animals, and poverty? Remember that our attitudes are seldom simple, often ambivalent. Be honest with yourself. Maybe you're a liberal and a feminist and believe in a woman's right to choose, but you're not sure what you'd do if you were confronted with an unwanted pregnancy.

What would you like to change about yourself? Why haven't you done it already? When will you start the change? Wanting to write starts today.

What are the motivating forces in your life? What are your ambitions? Describe your life in ten years as you want it to be. How would you live if you could have anything you want? What do you want?

Describe any jobs you've had. Talk about the people you worked with.

Have you had any mystical experiences? What were they?

What did you want to be when you were five? When you were ten? Why aren't you that person you dreamed of being? Do you still long to be that person? What's stopping you?

Write about all of the places you have ever lived. Describe each house in great and loving detail. Recall if you were happy or unhappy in these places and why. Describe the kitchens, the yards, your bedrooms, the neighbors, the views, etc.

Remember the worst part of being a child. Dramatize it. Remember the best of it and dramatize that.

FEAR AND LOATHING. You knew we'd get around to fear. We think of phobias as abnormal and irrational, but they still count. And not all fears are irrational. I've had friends tell me they aren't afraid of death. I don't believe them. I'm with Louis-Ferdinand Céline, who said, "If you have no imagination, death is nothing. If you do, it is too much." Give examples of your fears and try to trace the fears back to childhood incidents if you can. Maybe you're afraid of the dark for a good reason.

This morning we got a call from our friend Kimberly, who has a pathological fear of geckos, anoles, skinks, and all the other lizards we have here in South Florida. She called to say she was trapped upstairs in her house because she'd seen a lizard in the kitchen. Her husband, Jeremy, was off at work, I think. Cindy offered to drive over and catch the critter (or at least tell her she had), and I was thinking, How can I use this? And here it is, a few hours later! Kimberly's afraid of lizards. I'm terrified of heights as well as some more significant things like abandonment, death, failure, illness—actually it's quite a long list. What are you afraid of? (Your characters may share your fears.) Who are you afraid of? Who are the people in your life who have frightened you? They may be friends or strangers, teachers or coaches. The list might include yourself. See if you can trace the source of these rational or irrational fears. Write about your first recollection of the fear. How has the fear changed over the years?

IN MEMORIAM. Write now for a half hour. Minimum. Write more if the spirit's with you. Time yourself. Once you begin to write, don't stop for *any* reason. Door locked? Phone off the hook? As you write more and more, you'll see that writing doesn't work well in fits and starts. You need to find a flow, get into a groove. It's simply more efficient. Your writing mind is not as rational and analytical as your working mind. So don't interrupt it. A half hour, then. Make sure your pen is inked or your computer fired up. All you have to do is write. It is not a story or a poem or a scene unless you want it to be. No one needs to read it. Perhaps some of what appears will wind up in the novel you're beginning—beginning right now, in fact. But nothing here needs to show up later. Here are your first two words: *I remember* . . . Now you do the rest. Don't think very much. Let the words and the images and the memories carry you. When you feel jammed, write *I remember* . . . And continue. There is no right or wrong way to do this exercise. Relax and write. One half hour.

MORALITY PLAY. You have to have a vision of the world in order to write a novel. And you do have one, but you might not be in touch with it. So let's begin to think about it. What is it that you care passionately about? Your family? The environment? Write about those and about your other moral beliefs. What do you think makes the world a better place to live in? What makes it a more difficult place to live in? Is there evil in the world? Are people basically good or basically bad or neither? What are your own prejudices? Where do they come from? If you were elected president (or mayor or head of the neighborhood association), you'd make what changes in the status quo?

MENU AS MEMOIR. Remember your meals at home growing up. Make a week's worth of supper menus that your mom (or whoever) cooked for you or that you cooked for yourself and the family. Describe the meals and mealtimes. Use all of your senses. Don't forget dessert.

STOP-TIME. What are the moments in your life when you wanted time to stop? If we (or I) could just stay like this, you thought, right here, right now, forever, life would be bliss. Write about those times in great detail. Where were you? With whom? Describe and dramatize these transcendent moments. Use all of your senses.

LOOKING FOR TROUBLE. There are eight million stories in the naked city, and they are all about the same thing—trouble. Your novel will be about trouble. We're not interested in reading about anything else. So let's think about trouble right here in River City. Write about the troubles in your own life. The big dramatic troubles like the divorce and the arrest and the death of a friend and the smaller, no less significant troubles like chronic illness, like emotional exile,

> "I think if I get into the habit of writing a bit about what happens, or rather doesn't happen, I may lose a little of the sense of loneliness and desolation which abides in me."
> —ALICE JAMES

like fear, and so on. Write about them and try to understand where they came from. What is the worst thing that could happen in your life? Has it already happened? What is the worst thing that could happen to anyone? The death of a child? Accidentally killing someone else? Being tortured? Paralyzed? We all have our nightmares. Write about them.

YOUNG LOVE. Recall your first love. Try to remember the person and the emotions of the affair. Try to remember your own compulsive and odd behavior. Your entire world and all its priorities were changing. Recall your big date, the first one, the prom, whatever. The one that just came to mind is probably the right one. Write about it in loving detail, from the time you left your house for hers until you dropped her off at her door and took the bus, the car, hitched a ride, or walked home. Remember touches, smiles, caresses. Remember her smell—Ambush, Ivory, gardenias, Prell. What did you talk about? Was there a song you two heard? Do you recall the lyrics? What is it like remembering all of this? Do you perhaps have a sense of loss, sadness? Or is this a pleasant reminiscence? A sense of loss is perhaps natural and inevitable since one of the losses is your youth, your innocence, and all they stand for.

Now imagine you married this first love. (Or if you did, that you didn't.) You did not break up because you met someone else in the cafeteria, or she said she actually liked the *Forrest Gump* movie, or he told you what he really thought about Bob Dylan. You worked through the difficulties instead, and you stayed together. So imagine your life with her now. Picture your house, your apartment. Look around at your things and at hers. Walk into every room and out into the yard. Use your five senses. You can smell supper cooking, hear music on the stereo. Who exactly is living in this house? Are you happy here? Is everyone else? Are you doing what you want to be doing? What do you do? How is it different from the life you have been living these many years? Not better or worse, just different? Now it's night, and everyone's in bed. You sit in the living room and relax. You imagine how life might be different for you. You think of how you might want to change your life. Write about that.

SECRET AGENT. In his remarkable story "The Lady with the Dog," Anton Chekhov writes of his hero Dmitri Gurov: "He had two lives: one, open, seen and known by all who cared to know, full of relative truth and of relative falsehood, exactly like the lives of his friends and acquaintances; and another life running its course in secret. And through some strange, perhaps accidental, conjunction of circumstances, everything that was essential, of interest and of value to him, everything in which he was sincere and did not deceive himself, everything that made the kernel of his life, was hidden from other people; and all that was false in him, the sheath in which he hid himself to conceal the truth—such, for instance, as his work in the bank, his discussions at the club, his 'lower race,' his presence with his wife at anniversary festivities—all that was open." We all have a public self, a private self, and a self we may not even be fully aware of. Let's begin to examine that private self. You have a secret that nobody knows, not your spouse or your parents or your children. (Your characters will all have their secrets too.) What is this secret? (It remains a secret until you show your notebook to someone else.) It doesn't need to be incriminating; in fact, it may even seem silly when you write it down, and you might wonder what all your secrecy has been about. Why have you kept this secret? In keeping the secret, are you being prudent or afraid, selfish or noble? All of the above? Does the secret concern only you or is another person, are other people, involved? What will happen if you reveal the secret? To you? To others? What will people think of you? Will someone be hurt? Will that someone be you? What other secrets have you kept in your life? What are the secrets you share with another person or a few people?

THE TOP TEN LISTS. Your characters make lists just like you do. (How else will they remember what to buy at the market or whose birthday is coming up or what errands to run before work?) You don't make lists? Well, here's your chance to start. What are your top ten favorite movies? One or two will no doubt pop right into your head—but not all ten. You'll have to make some decisions toward the bottom of the list. (Your characters go to the movies—do they like the same movies that you do?) Your ten favorite foods. Your ten favorite songs or albums or musical performers. Ten favorite TV shows of all time. The ten best friends you've ever had. Ten best experiences of your life. (This is going to take a while.) The ten worst experiences of your life. (This is going to hurt.) Ten favorite places. (Paris? Your little office? The corner booth at the diner? Greenland?)

———

ALL RIGHT. You've written for two weeks about yourself, and you've filled pages and pages in your notebook. You've been writing easily, serenely at times, energetically at others, without pressure and without block. Nothing to it, really. Writing is easy. Writing a novel, not so much. But still, it's writing, and you've proven you can do that. And you've also proven to yourself that your own life is a rich source of images and scenes and themes and drama and characters and settings and everything else you need to write stories. Secrets and lies. Betrayal and redemption. You've lived it all. Love and loss and birth and death. Sex and drugs and rock 'n' roll. What else do you need?

Weeks 3 & 4:

Desperate People; Desperate Measures

I would never write about someone who
was not at the end of his rope.
—*Stanley Elkin*

Y OU'RE WRITING A novel, and a novel is about people. It's
not about ideas, or it's not only, or not principally, about ideas.
Don't start your writing with an idea or an emotion if you can help
it, no matter how important that idea may be to you. If the idea is
so urgent, and you have something to say about that idea that you
think we need to hear, then write an essay. Or write an editorial,
write a manifesto, write an ad, write a poem, write anything but
a novel. We read novels for the people in them, not for the ideas,
although we do expect that those people will have ideas. When we
remember our favorite novels we remember the character who won
our hearts. Thomas Mann's *The Magic Mountain* was a grand novel
of ideas, but when I remember the novel, I recall Hans Castorp,
sitting on a bench outside the sanatorium, listening to Herr Set-
tembrini and longing for Clavdia Chauchat. We read to understand
character because we're reading to learn about ourselves.

I usually begin my novels with a character, someone who intrigues me for some reason or other, the way he looks or talks or the way she lives her life. I find a person, and then I give that person some trouble, and then I ask that person what she wants to do about the trouble, and then I put some obstacles in her way and then more obstacles (writing a novel is taking the path of most resistance), and I see what she does about the obstacles, and I write down what she does. Something like that.

Where do these people in your novels come from? Well, they come from out there and from in here. Out there in the world and here in your heart and mind. Potential characters are not in hiding. They are all around you. You only have to pay attention and take notice. Writers see what no one else sees or takes the time to see. (Writing is all about taking time, and writing a novel is about taking a lot of time.) You can't, and you wouldn't want to, take a character whole cloth from life. You don't necessarily want to know very much about the real-life model for your character, in fact. Instead you steal an articulate gesture from the person who sat across from you on the bus, a turn of phrase overheard at the Laundromat, one woman's statuesque posture, a gentleman's limp (and you think, Yes, every scar tells a story), an engaging smile here, a curious tic there, and you build a character around it. You take a hairstyle from this one, a breathy voice from that one, a remarkable event from one guy's life, a childhood trauma from another's. (You learned about said remarkable and grisly event [the narrator's brother was scalded with boiling water, and the burned skin eventually slipped off the brother's fingers like a chicken-skin glove, and so on] while you were having lunch at the Japanese place on the boulevard [crispy bok choy and yakiniku steak], and you were eavesdropping on the hushed exchange coming from the booth behind you and writing it all down on a napkin with the pen you borrowed from the waitress—and what's her story anyway? She [the name tag says COSETTE] sat across from you when she took your order, said she had to rest her aching feet [her "tired puppies" was how she put it], asked what you were reading, and when you showed her the cover of *The World as Will and Idea*, she rolled her eyes and asked you if you really had time for pessimism, and you wonder now whom she goes home to after her shift and what she finds there and what she doesn't, and you realize you've discovered another character.)

You can't ever really know a person in real life. You can speculate about what he's thinking or feeling, but you can't be certain. You can never know why she's doing what she's doing. So when you base a character on your dad, let's say, the character is not your actual dad. You can know a person in a novel better than you know yourself. In her book *Reading Chekhov,* Janet Malcolm writes, "We never see people in life as clearly as we see them in novels, stories, and plays; there is a veil between ourselves and even our closest intimates, blurring us to each other." *Homo fictus* can be understood completely. And that's why we read fiction—can't do that with memoir. And because we can know fictional characters in full, novels suggest, to paraphrase Maupassant, a more comprehendable and so a more manageable world.

Let me give you an example. Real life and then fictive life. Let's say in real life a man sits at home listening to talk radio. He's writing what seems to be a letter, and in the letter he's writing directions to his house. He puts the letter in an envelope, puts his coffee cup in the sink, gets his work gloves and his tools, and heads out the door. That's it. Behavior awaiting significance. You see that few minutes (in your head, if not in your kitchen), and as a writer you wonder what it was all about, and in the wondering, you imagine what it was all about—you look over the man's shoulder and read the letter, and you peer into his thoughts, and in your novel, you write this:

"Richard's listening to WTAG, talk radio, and a caller from Grafton Hill wants to know why he should have to pay for parking at the Galleria. He has a point, Richard thinks. Why should you have to pay to spend money? Richard's writing a letter to Ed McMahon with the directions to his house. It's not so easy to find. *And when you get here, go around to the back (the landlady hates for anyone to use the front), go past the bulkhead, and come on up to the third floor. Don't mind the mess in the hall.* This just in case he does win the Publishers Clearing House Sweepstakes. He probably won't, but it would be wicked sick to win, and then they can't find you, and the money goes to some runner-up from New York. Richard puts the letter in an envelope, puts his coffee cup in the sink, the jar of Folgers Instant in the cupboard. He leaves the radio on for the cat."* And then you wonder where he works. They looked like garden tools, didn't they? He's not going to work at all, you realize. He's going to groom his mother's grave out at Hope Cemetery. And what's the cat's name? Neutron. Richard calls him Nootie Kazootie. The map gave Richard the most trouble. He couldn't figure out how to draw the house so it didn't look like it was lying down beside the street.

In our daily lives we look at people, note their expressions, observe their behaviors, and we then speculate on their thoughts and feelings. We work by inference. You're driving along Alligator Alley with your spouse, and she just stares out the window and taps her foot a mile a minute. You lower the radio and try to start up a conversation, but all you get are monosyllabic answers, and she never turns to look at you. You might surmise that she's angry about something. Or maybe she's just sad. No, she doesn't drum her fingers like that when she's sad.

When we write a scene we often work in quite the opposite way. We want the wife in this scene we're building to be angry, and we

---

*This is actually part of the opening paragraph to a story called "Congratulations, You May Already Be" in my collection *Johnny Too Bad*. And it came to me quite like this.

know we have to show the anger, not simply report it. We want the reader to feel what the characters feel. So when hubby walks into the kitchen and says good morning, she slams the cabinet door, and when he touches her, she stiffens, and when he asks her what's wrong, she walks out of the room. And we never have to mention her anger once. We work with evidence.

We also build characters, as I said, from within. We use the events of our own lives and our emotional history as well. We may never have suffered through a divorce the way our central character does, but we have suffered loss, perhaps profound loss—the death of a parent or child or sibling or friend, the drying up of a dream. We can apply our own emotional memory of loss to our aggrieved spouse. In the conversation between the couple driving across the Everglades above, I used my own emotional response to perhaps a similar provocation in my

> "My imaginary characters take on my shape, they pursue me, or rather it is I who am in them. When I wrote about Emma Bovary's poisoning, I had the taste of arsenic so strongly in my mouth, I was so thoroughly poisoned myself, that I gave myself two bouts of indigestion."
> —GUSTAVE FLAUBERT

past (or a hundred similar situations) and gave them to my driver, you. He started the conversation up for the same three reasons I have, or would have, or will. First, to lighten things up, to break the tension. Second, to make himself (myself) appear to be interested and reasonable. No use responding to her irritating behavior with more irritating behavior—that would be childish. Third, for information—to find out what actually is bothering her while hoping it's not something he (I) did (although this is not his/my first priority). And I gave the rankled passenger a part of myself as well. She's irritated at something (of course it's something he did or more likely didn't do), but she is being indirect and passive-aggressive about it (like I tend to be) and no doubt making the situation even worse. That son of a bitch is going to pay! Every character in the novel may have a part of you in his or her makeup. Richard's cat, by the way, is one of my cats, the frenetic one, the lovable thug. Poor Richard.

So you find your characters by attending to the world and to yourself. How do you develop them, and what are they like? Creating compelling and convincing characters whom the reader feels strongly about is your most important job. The plot, which we'll discuss more about later, will help you do that. The plot is the course of the central character's struggle. You make him want something intensely, and then you put obstacles in the way of his getting it. Plot ought not to be imposed on the novel; it ought to grow out of the desires and struggles of the characters. But when you begin the novel, your central character is someone you've just met. How are you supposed to know what she wants, never mind why? How will you know what she'll do when confronted with the knowledge that she has been betrayed?

So you have to get to know your characters, all of them, of course, but let's stick with your central character for now. You get to know your central character in the same way that you get to know a friend: you spend time with her. That will happen quite naturally in the course of writing your novel. And very likely you'll know him so well by Chapter 30 that you realize he would not have said what you coerced him into saying in Chapter 3. And now you'll have to go back and change it, and that change will necessitate others, and as you make the subsequent changes, you'll be learning even more about your character. Jeez, she's afraid of certain words, can't stand to read them or hear them. Who knew? You didn't know that till she closed her copy of *Harper's* and started humming, and you asked her what was going on. I feel like I'm going to explode through my skin, she said, and my heart is racing a mile a minute. What's that all about? you wonder. Where did this lexical aversion come from? Her reading life must be an excruciating one. (So why did she become a librarian?) You're glad to hear she has soothing words too. *Hemline* calms her right down. *Susurrus* smooths away the rough edges of her gray matter. And when you reach the end, or what you think is the end, of your novel, you realize that so much of what the character may have done early on now rings false. Sure, it's false, but it served its purpose. Got you moving forward. Now go back and fix it. Thoroughly imagining a character is surrendering your own ideas and control. You give up what you thought was going on, and you are pleasantly surprised at what does go on. It's the Zen of fiction. You aren't trying to learn; you are learning.

As a way to get to know your character in the early stages of writing your novel, have her do all of the memory exercises that you did in the first two weeks. Keep her responses in a file you've created for her. (You have a file on every important character.) Find out about her habits and rituals and tics and routines, her likes and dislikes. Ask her whom she voted for in the last presidential election and then ask her why she did. Ask her to tell you something about herself that you don't know. Find out what her secret life is all about. See what she does on Tuesday evenings, on Sunday mornings, at lunch, in the car, when she has a moment's peace. Character is action. The exercises at the end of this chapter will help you as well. And don't think about creating a character, which might, in fact, result in creating a caricature; think about getting to know, think about creating, a person. Your fictional characters must breathe and bleed and ache and must convince the reader that they live and are just like the rest of us. More on that in a minute.

So when do you know that you know your central character well enough? Maybe that happens when you fall asleep thinking about him, wake up wondering what he's up to, when you dream about him. Maybe it happens when he does something on the page that you didn't expect him to do, didn't know he was capable of doing, or he says something surprising. And now you can be sure that he is no longer your puppet. He has a mind and a will of his own. He will refuse to do your bidding, and you can trust in him and follow him around and write down what he does. To this point, André Gide wrote, "Characters in a novel or a play who act all the way through exactly as one expects them to . . . This consistency of theirs, which is held up to our admiration, is on the contrary the very thing which makes us recognize that they are artificially composed."

What are the characters in novels like? As I said, they are like us. And what are we like? "People are humble and frightened and guilty at heart, all of us, no matter how desperately we may try to appear otherwise. We have very little conviction of our essential decency and consequently we are more interested in characters who share our hidden shames and fears." Tennessee Williams said that. Characters in novels have aspirations and regrets; they have attitudes, memories, and secrets. They've had traumas in their lives. They have friends (never enough of them) and enemies (always too many). They hurt and they feel joy. They have senses of humor and wonder, which they cultivate or not. You're creating three-dimensional people, and you may not always like what they do, but you have to try to understand why they do it.

> "I like looking at people's lives over a number of years, without continuity. Like catching them in snapshots. And I like the way people relate to the people they were earlier. This is the sense of life that interests me a lot."
> —ALICE MUNRO

Every man has his reasons, and the heart has reasons that reason cannot know. Blaise Pascal said that. Your job is not to judge your characters but to witness what they do and to write that down. A character is what he does, what he means to do, what he thinks and what he feels, but mostly what he does. We believe what we see, not what we're told. Actions, we know, speak louder than words.

Put up or shut up, we tell the procrastinator. The proof is in the pudding. A picture is worth a thousand words, and all that. Love is a behavior, as we understand it, not an emotion or a platitude.

And the characters are also like us in that they are not victims or villains. Some people may act villainously, and others may be victimized, but this behavior does not define them. Life is not black and white. We are each of us saint and sinner. (And, of course, we're not talking about children who may be perfectly good and terribly victimized.) As I read my handwritten notes there a moment ago, I read "saint and sinner" as "sauté and simmer." And that misreading* might lead somewhere, I suppose, to some culinary approach to character development, but I'll spare you for now. Where was I? What the characters in novels are not—they are not passive. They want something intensely and they go after it. (If we tried to act like compelling fictional characters, we might get more done in our lives.) They are not mouthpieces for the author or for an ideology. We have enough of that miserable proselytizing in real life. They aren't types or clichés; they are unique individuals, unlike anyone we've ever met. They may march to a different drummer;

---

*Mishearing is even more interesting and more common than misreading. We can see words on a page discretely separated, but we can't always hear them discretely—if you've tried to learn another language, you know that. Where does one word stop and the next begin? And if you listen to pop music much, you've no doubt confused the lyrics. These mishearings are called mondegreens, from the Scottish ballad "The Bonny Earl of Murray," whose line "And laid him on the green" was misheard by some as "And Lady Mondegreen." The poet Henry Taylor wrote a delightful poem called "The Parrot Bath" on mishearing the word "paragraph." On a book tour a few years ago, I sat with my driver Frank at a sidewalk café in Berkeley waiting to do an NPR radio show around the corner. Frank told me that he was into media rights, and I wasn't sure what he meant. He said he collects them, buys them on the Internet. I smiled. He's got twelve of them on his bookcase gathering dust. I realized then that he meant *meteorites*. He's investing in meteorites. I had a whole other story going on in my head. There are actually a few words, perhaps many, that came into the language as mishearings. Asparagus is a mishearing of "sparrow-grass." "Buttonhole" was first "buttonhold."

they are not always heroic, but they are willful and vulnerable. We don't believe in superheroes. Our characters are marvelously flawed. We relate to failure because we fail so often ourselves, and often what we've come to call success is just a grander failure. And characters are likely to be in pain, in doubt, in love, and in misery. Anthony Burgess wrote this about fictional people: "A character, to be acceptable as more than a chess piece, has to be ignorant of the future, unsure about the past, and not at all sure of what he's supposed to be doing." Perhaps it goes without saying, but your characters must change by the end of the novel. The change can be psychological or emotional, can be subtle or dramatic. As a result of his struggle, he has come to some understanding that he didn't have when he started his journey. And when you want us to see your character or when you want to see her, don't describe her, give her something to do.

In your novel you'll have central characters and minor characters. (And perhaps a few spear-carriers as well.) E. M. Forster called them round and flat characters. We've been talking about the round characters mostly. And the test of a round character is that she can surprise us in a convincing way. A flat character in his purest form, according to Forster, is "constructed round a single idea or quality." The loyal sidekick, the hard-boiled killer, the furtive underling, the gruff boss, and so on. But even then, I think, you want to suggest that the character has a fuller life. Every character is the central character in his own novel. For example, you may have a character who's at your hero's house (we'll call your hero Preston) installing the cable TV, and she (we'll call her Denise) notices that Preston has the Alan Price soundtrack CD to the Lindsay Anderson film *O Lucky Man!*, and she tells Preston that they've just released the film on DVD, and she has a copy, and she could burn him a disc if he would like one. Sure he would. And then we learn that Denise is a film lover and has over three thousand DVDs at home and spends her vacations at film festivals all over the world. And then she's finished, and Preston signs the bill, and she's off—out of his life and out of the novel. Except that a week later Preston gets the DVD in the mail. So much better than an anonymous cable gal.

And by the way, when you stop to pay attention to what you are thinking of as your minor characters, some of them may surprise you. In *Louisiana Power & Light*, I needed to get my newlyweds from a restaurant back to the motel and to their wedding reception. Luckily, a waitress at Marianna's pointed out a cabdriver at nearby table. His name was Hotson Taylor, and his only function was to drive the couple the two miles. I noticed he kind of looked like Roy Orbison. He was trying to quit smoking but had a cigarette tucked behind his left ear. He had a pile of socialist magazines in the backseat of the cab for his customers to read. His company was called At Your Service Cab Co. I thought maybe I should have him hang around a little longer. He ended up being around until the last page.

Let's get writing and see who we find. The first week we'll look for some likely leads, and the second week we'll learn more about them.

YOU OUGHT TO BE IN PICTURES.

"The capacity of photographs to evoke rather than tell, to suggest rather than explain, makes them alluring material for the historian or anthropologist or art historian who would pluck a single picture from a large collection and use it to narrate his or her own stories."
—*Martha Sandweiss*

And I would add "for the fiction writer." I love photography. Snapshots included. I have a gallery of tintype portraits in our guest bathroom. Yes, I tell the guests, they are my ancestors. I have a basket of occasional photos up in the guest room of weddings, baptisms, graduations, and so on. As much as I love and admire the great landscape photographers like Ansel Adams and Eliot Porter, photographs of nature don't move me in the same way that photographs of people do. They don't move me to story. They don't open the world. I think of a nature photo as a lyric poem, I guess. It's evocative enough and personal and insular. My attention stays fixed on the image.

Photos of people at work and at play, at rest and in motion, their hands, their backs, their eyes. This is what I think of as narrative photography. And I'm a fiction writer, so I'm looking for story. These photographs provoke my imagination and release my attention. Finding a character is much easier if you can gaze on the subject's face, if you can look at her hands, note her posture. It occurs to me that besides photographs of people, photographs of abandoned homes provoke stories in me. Each derelict construction a dream dissolved, each a failure, a loss, an emptiness, and each a place I might want to have lived in or worked at, and each resonant with echoes of the life once acted out within.

Diane Arbus said, "A photograph is a secret about a secret. The more it tells you, the less you know." Stories are all about secrets; nothing is what it seems to be. Secrets and lies. Who are your favorite photographers and why? Go back to their photographs and ask yourself why they compel you to stare at them.* (Stare at a pho-

---

*In *Camera Lucida*, Roland Barthes wrote that there are two elements involved when looking at a photograph. The first he called the studium, a term for the interest which we show in a photograph, the desire to study and understand its meanings. It's a kind of general, enthusiastic commitment to the photograph, but without any particular keenness of perception. It's interesting and informative. The second element Barthes called the punctum (from the Latin for "a point"), which is more about the sudden and unexpected recognition of meaning, an epiphany, as it were. It "shoots out of [the photograph] like an arrow and pierces me." It's the punctum that draws you into the object. *The Ongoing*

tograph long enough and it stares back at you.) I especially admire the work of Walker Evans, Dorothea Lange, Paul Strand, Ralph Eugene Meatyard, Sebastião Salgado, and the studio portraits of Joe Steinmetz. Photographs of people being themselves offer the viewer character, setting, mood, tone, mystery, event, and may even suggest plot. What more could a writer ask for?

GO TO THE library or the bookstore and head for the photography section. Or get online. Choose a photographer whom you admire and look through her work until an image seizes you. Or go to your own attic and leaf through the family photos until a picture of someone you don't even know intrigues you. Now study your chosen photograph for a few minutes. Look at it closely. Note the composition, the light and shadow, the expression, the subject's hands, and so on. (George Eastman: "Light makes photography. Embrace light. Admire it.

> "Passing judgment on people, or characters in a book, means making silhouettes of them."
> —CESARE PAVESE

Love it. But above all know light. Know it for all you are worth, and you will know the key to photography.") Now give the photograph a title. Even if it has one, give it your own. Okay, now what does the title suggest? Write about that. Do you detect thematic material already? Forget the visual image for now and just write about the title for a few minutes. Or for as long as you'd like.

Look at the photo again. It will suggest a mood or perhaps an emotion. This might be, in fact, what originally attracted you to the photograph. Write down that mood or the emotion on a blank

---

Moment by Geoff Dyer is a brilliant study of photographs and how they attract our gaze and about the obsessive themes that run through the art.

sheet of paper and freewrite on that mood. (That is, write without thinking or stopping for five minutes, let's say. Use your stopwatch because you don't want your eyes leaving the paper.) Once again, forget the photo while you're doing this. The emotion or mood is what is important now. Don't let yourself think about it, write as quickly as you can.

Back to the picture. Where are we? And when, what year? What season? What time of day? Write about this place and this time. Give the place a name and a population. Be as specific as you'd like to be. Bewilderment, Arkansas, population 310 or 311. West Eighty-fifth Street between Ninth and Tenth, population 310. Give us the details of time and place, the way you might on the back of a photo: 9:20 A.M. *July 2, 1979, Everlasting, Utah*. Take a walk down the main street, whatever it's called. Look at the buildings and the businesses there, the folks out on the sidewalks. Write about this place. Take your time. Use all five senses. When you're done . . .

Look at the photograph again and decide whose story you want to tell. Give this person a name. This exercise is easier to do if you have people in the photograph, as I said, but it works as well in photos in which the presence of people or their absence is palpable. For example, the cover of my novel *Louisiana Power & Light* is a brilliant photograph by Patricia McDonough, and when I first saw it, even though I thought the book was finished already, I was moved to write a scene in the book in which my central character looks on the scene rendered in the picture.

So now we have a central character with a name and a place with a name. And names can tell us so much about a person or a place all by themselves. (Lamar "Babbo" Godbehere III, Dirge, North Dakota.) We have a title, a mood, a setting. Now let's consider plot. (Plot is all about character.) This central character must want something. What is that? Why does she want it? The motivation should be fairly intense. There must be something at stake. Who or what is in conflict with the central character? In other words, what are the obstacles in the central character's way? What will prevent her from getting what she wants? How will she struggle? Will she get what she wants? What are the moments of complication? Climax? Think and write. And don't be afraid to digress and wander. You might find something wonderful. Your hero can't keep up with the kids and the waitressing job and the trying to wrest some child-support money from her sorry-assed husband, and now she finds out her cousin Babbo and his new bride are driving down from Dakota with two Portuguese water dogs, a colicky baby, and his boy from the second marriage, the one with snaggled teeth and the foul mouth, and they're planning on staying for two weeks.

Now select a point of view from which to tell the story. Let the central character tell his story or have a third-person narrator tell us what's going on. Now that you know who's talking, have the narrator make a statement about the central character (about himself if it's first person). It ought to be a secret, something you didn't know about the character. And then ask the questions suggested by the statement. Begin with the general reporter's questions, *How? What? When? Where? Why?* and then get more and more specific. Why did you think you could get away with dumping a load of cement in your ex's T-Bird? Where did you get the cement truck? So when you figured out you couldn't drive a stick, who did you persuade to drive the stolen cement truck? Ask the questions, and answer them. The answers will lead to other questions and other answers. Write some more. We're just collecting information here and getting ready to write.

All of these questions of plot, character, point of view, do not have to be answered immediately. In fact, you probably want to avoid thinking overmuch about what happens in the story just yet. You don't want to tie your characters into behavior that is something you want and is not what they want. The point is that now you have a lot of raw material in which to begin the construction of your story. And all in a very short time.

Before you move on, try this. Think about the photographer. Who took this picture and why? What was in his mind as he looked through the viewfinder? What happened just before he took the picture? What or who is just outside the frame? What happened just after the photo was taken? Did the photographer and the subject speak? About what?

LET US BUILD US A TOWN. You look at a map, see a dot and a name, and you wonder what the place looks like, and what kind of people live there. (You do that, don't you?) Well, that's what we're going to do. We're going to get a story under way, and we're going to do it by thinking about a place. And the place is going to get us to character. Well, many characters, we expect. *Louisiana Power & Light* began this way. I wanted to write about Monroe, and I did so for months—in my notebook. Just jotting down sights, sentences about flowers and critters, lines overheard. But being a fiction writer, I needed characters to live in the town in order to write about it. I found one on the nightly news—a man who had kidnapped his boy from elementary school. I was off and running. But it all started with place.

I wrote a novel called *Requiem, Mass.*, and in the novel the narrator/writer imagines a town where, unbeknownst to himself, he will one day go. He does what we're about to do. He looks at the map and finds a vacant place and sets down a small town. He calls it Livia. It's in northwestern North Dakota, so *small* goes without saying. He imagines the main street: ". . . a row of empty storefronts, a Rexall drug, a Lutheran church, a line of diagonally parked pickup trucks, a feed store, a boarded-up Rialto movie theater, a gas station/bait shop, and several poplar-lined blocks of Craftsman bungalows, I watched the house catty-corner to Dell's Diner, the blue house with white shutters and a light on in the kitchen, waiting to see if someone would step out onto the front porch and walk to the steps, stare up into the starry spring sky, and inhale the cool air rushing down from Saskatchewan." And when someone does, he sets in to writing. Which is what we'll do.

Okay, you're going to write about an American town, and it's in the Southwest or in the Dakotas or in some New England valley or wherever your imagination takes you. This is a town that doesn't exist on the map—you're putting it there. It's unfamiliar to you right now. In fact, you might open your road atlas (which is what my narrator did in the novel) and find an empty spot in the region you'd like to visit and set the town there. Maybe it's by Stevenson Lake in western Nebraska, thirty-five miles to the nearest town. And it's called, what? Prague. Settled by Czech immigrants. Or it's in the Black Rock Desert of northwest Nevada, and it's called Alkali. Make this a place you'd love to live— you're going to be spending a lot of time there. See your town. Give it a name. The name may suggest something about the history of the town, about the landscape, the commerce, the hopes of the settlers or their nostalgia for the old country, as in my little town of Prague. The name will become a magnet, you'll see. Significant details will attach themselves to it. The name of the church in Prague, Nebraska, is St. Vitus, after the cathedral in old Prague, in the Czech Republic. The Czech-American Club holds Saturday night polka dances. And at Nita's Dumpling House you can order a three-course meal of *drstkova*, *teleci*, and *kolak* for eight bucks. You also want to consider what year it is. To know a place we may need a map, but we also need a calendar. Alkali, Nevada, in 2009, population thirty-five, is nothing like the Alkali back in the thirties during the boom days when the gold and opal mines were running full tilt, and there were eighteen saloons and fifteen houses of ill repute right there on Washoe Street.

Now I want you to walk down the main street and describe it in great detail. If you'd rather drive, go ahead, but drive slowly, pull over occasionally and take notes. Name the businesses, the churches, the institutions. (It's not the drugstore; it's Lee Bros. Drugs & Sundries.) Describe the buildings. (And maybe this will convince you to buy a field guide to architecture.) Look at the people on the street. How are they dressed, and how is that different from how folks dress where you live? (And you thought the whole clog thing was over, didn't you?) What time of day is it? What season? What's the weather like? Describe the flora, the fauna, the cars or other conveyances. What does it smell like here? If there's a paper mill nearby, by God you'll know about it. What are the sounds you hear? If you're

"I have to watch my characters crossing the room, lighting a cigarette. I have to see everything they do, even if I don't write it down. So my eyes get tired."
—GRAHAM GREENE

a decent artist, you might want to paint what you see. If you're like me, however, you'll have to settle for a rudimentary map. Walk down that street and spend as long as you need to in order to capture it all. Look for the vivid and surprising details. You're new in town, so you see what the locals are blind to. When you've done that, we'll go on to the next task.

Now I want you to choose one of those buildings you described, and I want you to walk inside. Look around. Sniff the air. Listen. What do you hear? Write it down. Touch the walls. Describe the interior in as much detail as you can. Once again, take your time. What shade of green are those walls exactly? (Make a note to visit the local paint store and take all the color sample brochures. You won't believe how many shades of green!) Walk into every corner, every room, every closet. You're looking for the revelations that lurk in details. Every particular tells you something about this town. So do that. Write about this building and the businesses or business inside it. When you've finished, we'll go on to the next step.

Maybe you thought you were alone, but now you notice that there's another person here besides you. This person is troubled, you think. Why do you think that? Something in the way she stands? The look on her face? Write about her. Or maybe there are several people here. It's a bank or a restaurant or a bar or a hardware store. If so, your job is to choose one of these people, the one who seems troubled, preoccupied, and describe him or her and what he or she is doing. Give the person you're writing about a name and address. The address must be in this town. (Now you're going to have to go out and look at the street signs.) Imagine what's going through his or her mind. What does this person want? What's stopping him or her from getting it? If you aren't sure, walk right up and ask. You are an author in search of a character. You want to write this person's story. There has to be trouble, big trouble, in his life. Write about that before you continue. Give the person a voice and let her tell you her story. Buy her a coffee, a drink, sit down where it's quiet, listen to her, and write it all down.

All right, so now you have a town and a person in that town who's troubled. And if you're lucky, you've learned about several other characters involved in your hero's life. She told you how her husband's been cheating on her with their daughter's fifth-grade teacher, let's say. Her daddy, the judge, never trusted his son-in-law Phil anyway. What you want to do now is to follow your central character home. You've given her an address, remember. Now describe the house, the trailer, apartment building, whatever it is. Walk around—you're alone. No one's home. Describe the yard and its maintenance or dilapidation. Look closely. Does the home tell you anything about the character? What does it tell you? When you get done with the exterior, we'll go inside.

Now we're in the house. Look around in each room. (Might as

well draw a diagram of the house.) What's there? What's missing?
In the kitchen: any pet food bowls? Has it been cleaned up or is it
messy? Dishes in the sink? Dead coleus on the windowsill? Describe
the kitchen. (Last night I went to a dinner party. The hostess and
I shared last names though we are not related, and she had in her
kitchen a glass-front refrigerator about seven feet tall and fifteen
feet wide.) Open the fridge and see what's inside. Who's on a diet
or who needs to be? Batteries in the vegetable drawer? Check way
in the back for the half-empty bottles of things that never get used.
(When I grew up we always had the same bottle of green label
Brer Rabbit molasses on the top shelf of the Hotpoint right next to
the can of bacon fat and the bottle of Karo syrup. I liked the label
of the rabbit in a red jacket carrying a plate of pancakes. But my
mother never seemed to use the molasses. Maybe once she made
gingerbread, and I've forgotten.) What else is unusual in the fridge?
Medicines? Might they have something to do with the character's
problem? Check the freezer, too. Frozen fast-food burgers still in
their waxy paper? What's that about? Open the junk drawer. We all
have one. Bottle openers taken from restaurants? String, twistees,
measuring tape? Go through the drawer. Being a fiction writer is
being an archaeologist. You're looking for clues to these people.
(Interesting—*people*! Who lives here besides our hero: husband
Phil and their daughter Phyllis? [Phil wanted a boy.]) Look through
the cabinets, under the sink and all. There's a pile of mail on the
kitchen counter. Go through it. Let's see who our character owes
money to, what magazines she reads, who is corresponding with
her. Now go nose around in the bathroom. Check the medicine
cabinet first. Prescription drugs? What else? What kind of soap is
there? Shampoo? Creams? Be just as thorough in the living room,
the den—open the desk drawer—the dining room and bedrooms.
Let yourself be surprised by what you find here. Not every detail
will spark your brain, but some will. Look from floor to ceiling, and

look closely. Check in the closets, too. If there's a cellar or an attic or a garage, go there. What has your hero or this family stored in these places? What are they saving from their pasts and why?

You've been here awhile, but it's only now, as you're getting ready to leave, that you notice Post-it notes stuck to the walls, to the fridge, the ceiling, mirrors. Stop and read them. What do they say? They seem rather cryptic, don't they? What do they have to do with this character's problems? Her developing story? Who wrote them and why? Follow the tangent for a few minutes.

Begin to write the story. What does he or she want? Why does she want it? What's stopping her from getting it? How will she struggle? Will she get what she wants? And in writing you'll be getting to know her.

FOUND CHARACTERS. Everyone has a story, and the writer can find them if she looks. As Picasso put it, "I don't seek, I find." The writer with her senses alert finds stories everywhere. The term "found poetry" is used to describe a text lifted out of some original context and arranged to give the appearance, form, or sound we associate with poetry. It must be found somewhere among the vast sub- or non-literature that surrounds us. It must be taken from an innocent or naive context, from advertising, say, newspaper reports, police logs, menus, billboards, memos, and so on.

The rules are a bit different for the found fictional character and his story, since we probably won't lift the text itself, or at least not all of it. What we're looking for is character, perhaps, situation, the kernel of a narrative that we can spin. It's important that the found story isn't art. Our job is to make it so. It could be a human figure we see in a medical text with his musculature identified by arrows and terms. Donald Barthelme was perhaps so inspired to write about "the amazing Numbered Man" in his wonderfully comic story "The Flight of Pigeons from the Palace." Lewis Nordan writes about his character's mother telling him stories about the people in the Sears, Roebuck catalogue. The woman there by the Coldspot refrigerator on page 311 is worried because her husband's late. He's the dark-haired guy in the mohair suit on page 223. He's in sales. Covers the whole eastern part of the state. He's stopped at the Dew Drop Inn after a lousy day. He knows he should call Helen. He looks at his watch. He'll just have the one more beer and then head home. So let's stay with him a minute. He orders the beer. He can't get the Neely account of his mind. If he loses this one, Larry Shank will have a conniption fit. While our salesman's been lost in thought, a young woman has taken the seat beside him. She sniffles. She looks like she's been crying. Let the scene continue. What does our salesman do? (What does he say? Think of saying? For that matter, what does he sell? What's his name? How long has he been married?)

Today you might try opening a catalogue of your own and finding a couple of characters. You already know what they look like when you find them. Here's a guy in the Orvis Holiday 2000 catalogue. (I save old catalogues, and not only to find characters but to clothe them and feed them and furnish their houses.) He's lounging on a patio chaise reading *The New York Times*. He's wearing his polo shirt, pressed khaki slacks, sand-colored socks, and shiny penny loafers. His hair is perfect, his belt is braided. His name is Todd. Actually, Todd's not reading the paper; he's thinking about the pretty young gal over on page 86. She's in a red cotton pullover, a plaid pull-on skirt, black riding-style boots. Her hair is thick, long and curled. She's Linda from the club. Steven's wife. How did she end up with Steve Yablonski? Todd's wife's the woman to the right, on page 87, the woman with the short blond hair, wearing the black trimmed boiled wool jacket, the white wool turtleneck. Debbie. She likes the needlepoint flats on page 81. Todd finds them impractical. So what's the trouble in the marriage? Why is Todd so taken with Linda?

Or try something like this. Find a room in a catalogue and note the details. What do the details of the place tell us about the people who live there? Like this kitchen featured in the Christmas 1998 Pottery Barn catalogue. Stainless steel gas stove with a vent and pot rack above it. White counters and cabinets. A large window and French doors curtained in white lace. In the center of the room a metal-topped breakfast bar surrounded by chrome-plated steel barstools covered in black vinyl. A rattan area rug on the hardwood floor. There's an easel with a reproduction advertising print for Cinzano, featuring an equestrian on a spirited red horse. Whose idea was that? If they had kids, that would be impossible, wouldn't it? It would be getting knocked over every day. So maybe they're an older couple—second marriage for both. She used to paint. Gave it up when Husband #1 needed her help with his real estate business. She's always thought that this would be her dream kitchen—light, spacious, airy. But now she's thinking she'd like something more serviceable, something like her grandmother's kitchen. A bit cluttered, cramped, and cozy. Enamel-topped table, white Tappan range, floral bread box, and matching canisters. But how to tell Russ? What does this mean, her dissatisfaction for the modern, stylish kitchen, her desire for another?

> "I always begin with a character, or characters, and then try to think up as much action for them as possible."
> —JOHN IRVING

ALL IN THE FAMILY. You can count on this: Your family is full of stories. Some families may be more colorful than others, but maybe some are just more closemouthed about their crimes and eccentricities. With your parents' help or your grandparents' or a professional genealogist's, make up a family tree. And then find out everything you can about each of the people there. And then, with that information to go on, imagine the rest. That's the fun part.

Write an anthology of family stories. Write about your cousin Billy who—oh, that's right, you're waiting for Billy to die before you can tell that one. Write about your uncle Gino, then (but change his name), who left home at sixteen, became a carpenter out West for a while, and the next time you saw him he was on TV holding his baby hostage with a pistol aimed at her head. This after his wife left him. Write about your aunt Randeane, who smuggled rum from Barbados to Key Biscayne in the twenties; your cousin Weezie, who went to L.A. in the fifties to make her fame and fortune in the movies and married a page at NBC, who left her and went on to became a well-known TV star. Talk to your family and find out who were the relatives they admired or despised. Dig through photograph albums, family Bibles, whatever you can find.

EVERYDAY PEOPLE. William Butler Yeats has said that we should write about ourselves when we are most like ourselves. We're going to try that now but with the knowledge that fiction can only be about trouble. Most of us are not spies and detectives and dashing young attorneys with the mob or the CIA after us. We don't go looking for trouble, in other words. But still, as we know all too well, trouble may seek us out and find us when we least expect it, when we are least prepared to deal with it. This exercise is designed to surprise ordinary people, going about their daily routine, surprise them with potentially difficult but interesting problems.

Write a sentence in which a person is involved in an ordinary situation. For example: A stock boy at the supermarket is stacking canned goods on shelves. Or: A young woman is waiting for her soldier boyfriend to return from the war.

Now add a complication. The complication can come in the form of a person, a thought, a behavior, can come from the present or from the past. It can seem fairly innocuous, or it can be boldly foreboding. For example, in the case of our stock boy: In walk these two girls in nothing but bathing suits. For our young woman: She sees in the newspaper that her boyfriend has married another woman. You may recognize these two situations as the beginnings of two brilliant short stories: John Updike's "A&P" and Alice Munro's "Carried Away."

Try the exercise this way. List as many random and ordinary activities as you can in five minutes. Tossing out the trash, brushing your teeth, walking on the beach, driving to work, riding an escalator, shopping at the market, eating at a restaurant, etc. When the list is finished, go back and include a specific character performing each of the activities. A drifter eating at a restaurant, a child riding an escalator, and so on. This will be your opening sentence. Now add a sentence of complication. The drifter has no money; the child's shoes are untied.

You might ask yourself, "What if?" and let the answers guide you. What if a bridge tender, smoking outside his hut, hears a scream and then a splash? Here are some examples of openings that could provoke stories, given some imaginative attention:

1. A gardener tends her rose garden. She opens her sack of mulch and discovers a severed human hand.
2. A professor is lecturing his class on Dante's *Inferno* when the class disappears in a blur. He blinks his eyes. He can't see his notes.
3. An eighty-year-old woman looks up from her puzzle and sees a man she thinks she may know. He's crying.

Ask the questions suggested by the situation. Answer the questions and begin. Don't think of writing a novel just yet—only a scene. You want to know who these people are.

Four Gates into the City

There were four gates into the city, one at each point on the
compass, with outer protecting gates, and the fortifications
were surrounded by a deep moat.
—Jung Chang

If you can write this sentence, "It is a truth uni-
versally acknowledged, that a single man in
possession of a good fortune, must be in want of a wife,"
then you might have what it takes to become a famous,
respected, and handsomely remunerated novelist. Act
now! Send for the **Famous Novelists Aptitude Test.** If
you score well or show other evidence of writing talent,
you may enroll in **The Famous Novelists School, Inc.**
Write in your spare time and in the comfort of your home!
Writing novels today offers a life of financial reward, personal recognition, and the freedom to live as you please!
Send for your **FNAT** now! Famous Novelists School, Inc.,
Box 021, Dania Beach, FL 33004.

LET'S ASSUME THAT you've scored remarkably well on the
rather grueling Famous Novelists School, Inc., Aptitude Test,
sent along your stunning opening sentence, and I've graciously

accepted you as a matriculating student at FNS. Ready? Let's write that novel! Let's open four gates into the forbidden city of the novel and spin out plot outlines at each.

FNS. WRITING THE NOVEL 101

Lesson #1: "Four Time-Tested and Highly Effective Methods for Finding a Plot and Using That Plot to Think About and Develop Your Novel!"

A few preliminaries. Before you begin, you'll need a pen and some paper or a keyboard and screen. A writing surface. Desk, altar, dining room table, lap, it makes no difference. (Robert Frost: "I never write except with a writing board. I've never had a table in my life. And I use all sorts of things. Write on the sole of my shoe.") Easy enough. You'll need words. Fortunately, you have all the words you'll ever need in the dictionary. You want one that's too heavy to lug around. You want the OED, but you can't afford it. So you get *The American Heritage Dictionary of the English Language*, which is my favorite, or you get the *Webster's Third New International Dictionary*, favored by my publisher, at least with reference to spelling. Actually, here's what Nancy Palmquist at Norton had to say: "We use *Webster's Collegiate 11th Dictionary* for basic spelling and treatment of words and terms. If something is not in that one, we go to the huge *Webster's Third International Dictionary*. (Not the second edition, because that has some weird hyphenations, and definitely not *American Heritage*. [Should I be offended?]) The big *Random House Dictionary* is very useful also; and *Webster's* online stays up-to-date with new words and terms, especially computer language."

And you don't just need words, you need the precise words, the exact, accurate, correct, unerring words, and so you get yourself

Rodale's *The Synonym Finder*, the best inexpensive thesaurus, the finest handy treasury of like-minded words, now available. And you might also want *Roget's International Thesaurus* (Harper-Collins) because *Roget's* groups the words according to ideas and concepts (1,075 of them), like "continuance" and "vulgarity." Under "restraint" at number 4 is *shackle*, followed by its synonyms *restraint, restraints, fetter, hamper, trammel, trammels, manacle, gyves, bond, bonds, irons, chains, Oregon boat* (Oregon boat!), and a couple dozen more, including *bilbo, spancel, camisole,* and *iron hand*. It's like reading a fossil poem.* Oh, and get *Bartlett's Roget's Thesaurus* (Little, Brown), which has a lot of extras like the French Republican Calendar, a list of multicultural deities, and, as you would expect from Bartlett's, quotations. Jules Feiffer on color: "Artists can color the sky red because they know it's blue. Those of us who aren't artists must color things the way they are or people might think we're stupid."

A synonym, by the way, is not another word with the same meaning. If that were the case, we wouldn't need the other word, and we certainly wouldn't need a thesaurus. The meanings are *similar*, not *the same*. And that makes all the difference. The choice of the exact word is all about nuance, connotation, music, and rhythm. Why *valiant* in this sentence and not *heroic*? Why *dish* and not *plate*? Why *crimson* here instead of *scarlet*? And as long as we're on the subject of books, know that you'll need not only the words, but their attendant punctuation as well, and you'll need to know how to arrange those words comprehensibly, efficiently, and elegantly. So you'll need a style book of some kind, and the best for the fiction writer is *The Chicago Manual of Style*. Writing is like carpentry—it's a craft. You learn it through a long—in this case never-ending—apprenticeship. You begin your journey to accomplishment and to art by first learning how to use your tools. Your reference books are

---

*James Merrill: "[The] collective unconscious of the race is the OED."

some of your basic tools. Don't go to work without them. You can't build a house without a hammer. You can't build a novel without a dictionary.

Okay, we were talking about what you'll need. The pen, the paper, the books about words. You'll need a quiet place to write. A place where you will not be interrupted. Not by visitors, not by the phone. No distractions. And you'll need lots of time. A novel isn't built in a day. Don't think you're going to finish anytime soon. Blaise Pascal wrote in one of his provincial letters, "I have made this [letter] longer because I have not had the time to make it shorter." Brevity takes time. Less is more time-consuming.

You're going to need a plot (and perhaps subplots), a beginning, a middle, and an end, conflict and resolution.* You're going to need at least one, preferably two or more characters. A setting. You're going to use the tools of narrative, and you'll need to know what they are: point of view, voice, scene, place, and so on. And before we get started, something you should know. You have to have read a lot of novels in order to write good novels, and if you aren't in the habit of reading novels, why on earth would you want to write one, want to do something that doesn't interest you? If you haven't read a lot of novels yet (just some few that mesmerized you, perhaps), but still want to write one, then start in earnest reading novels today. You'll learn more about writing novels from reading the great writers than you will in a book like this or in a semester's creative writing class. Of course, it'll take longer. (And why not start with the greats, those writers your English teachers were always telling you to read, like Leo Tolstoy, like William Faulkner and James Joyce, like Thomas Mann and Jane Austen?)† And read your con-

---

*Cesar Pavese: "If immoral works of literature exist, they are works in which there is no plot."

†Here are some other novelists you'll enjoy and learn from: John Berger, Emily Brontë, Charles Dickens, George Eliot, Ralph Ellison, Henry Fielding, F. Scott

temporaries as well. If you're particularly interested in a specific genre of novel, say legal thrillers, then you'll also want to read the best of the novelists working that territory. Scott Turow, Lisa Scottoline, and Barbara Parker come to mind.

We make sense of the world and of our lives by telling stories. We love telling stories. We can't stop ourselves. It's what we do at the bar with our friends. ("So I'm sitting there at Starbucks minding my own business when in rolls this homeless guy in a wheelchair, and he's waving a service revolver over his head . . .") And it's what we do on the couch with our shrinks. ("I remember watching the child out there in the middle of the ice, screaming and struggling for purchase, and there was nothing I could do; I was afraid and ashamed at the same time, so I . . .") We construct a coherent story. A novel is a long, coherent story. It's at least that.

Anecdotes are not stories; jokes are not stories; chronology is not story. Your life, as interesting as it may be, is not a story. Plot, that necessary and key ingredient in your prospective novel, the gravity that keeps it from flying apart, is not about one thing after another. It's about one thing causing another thing to happen. There is an architecture to stories, to novels. They have plots, as I said. Plots give the characters something to do and engage the reader in the tale—the reader needs to feel assured that a middle will follow the beginning, and an end will follow the middle, that the problem laid out at the start will be resolved, that we are on a cruise to somewhere. And, yes, there is probably a perverse part of ourselves that wants to write a novel that will be as plotless as our lives. (Why should I resolve the character's problems when mine never seem to go away?) Resist this impulse, at least for now, at least until you

---

Fitzgerald, Henry Green, Knut Hamsun, Ernest Hemingway, Henry James, Franz Kafka, Gabriel García Márquez, Herman Melville, Toni Morrison, Vladimir Nabokov, Marcel Proust, Philip Roth, Stendhal, William Trevor, Virginia Woolf. And the list goes on.

learn the basics of plot. Remember that the reader wants to know about the lives of the characters, not about your life. Plots allow us to get below the surface, which anecdotes do not. Plots explore the human condition, examine values and motivation. Plots open up the lives of our characters, who are at the heart of stories. We want to know why these people do what they do.

I usually begin a novel with a character, someone I'm intrigued with for whatever reason. And you might start there as well. (Where do you find this character? you may well ask. They're all around you. See a person who looks troubled? Ask her what's going on.) And then I give this character some trouble—every novel is about trouble—and then I muddle ahead and see what happens. I don't need to know where the novel is going—I don't want to know, in fact. Part of the joy of writing is discovery. I do know that characters must act, must do something, must struggle. I trust in the plot to carry me to the resolution. And every plot boils down to this: A central character wants something, wants it intensely, goes after it despite obstacles, and as a result of a struggle comes to a win or a loss.

Here are four ways we might begin:

1. With a Person in Trouble

Let's try getting started in the way that seems most natural for me, although it may not be for you. You'll find out what works best for you by experimenting. Let's say our central character, then, is a sixty-year-old man, let's call him Donny, whose only child has just died. That's trouble enough, certainly. He's an ordinary guy, and perhaps we'll learn that he has extraordinary qualities before the novel is over. How will Donny manage? What does he want? How can he deal with his sorrow? Well, what he wants immediately is to talk about his son. Doing so will help him make sense of the senseless and unnatural death, put it into perspective. And it will immortalize his son a bit. Someone else will know the boy's story. That sounds easy enough to do, doesn't it? Talk. Talk is how we find our solace, after all. But to whom does Donny tell his grief? Let's say he lives alone—has no wife, and now no family. He keeps to himself. If he were a churchgoing man, he'd tell his priest. Does he tell the people at work, then? None of them are what he would call "close."

On the ride to work, he takes a seat on the bus by a woman who is reading her newspaper. Her face is blank and calm as a pond. Women, Donny thinks, are easier to talk to. He smiles, coughs, rustles his body until he gets her attention. She smiles. He tells her that his son has died. She looks up, says she's sorry to hear that, stares ahead a few moments, and then goes back to reading her newspaper. Donny considers how best to tell her the story. He'll show her Gregory's photo. Words are a clumsy way to capture real people. With a picture, however, you see the nature of the person in an instant. He leans to his left, reaches for the wallet in his back pocket. His shoulder touches her shoulder, and she stiffens. My son Gregory, he says. He holds up the photo. The woman pulls the bell cord and excuses herself. Donny stands and lets her out to the aisle. A missed opportunity.

> "In a utilitarian age, of all other times, it is a matter of grave importance that fairy tales should be respected."
> —CHARLES DICKENS

The bus passes by Grafton Street Grammar School, which Gregory attended from kindergarten through sixth grade. Donny turns his head and looks away, across the street at the lot where Arrow Cleaners once stood. He remembers the neon sign over the parking lot with the Indian shooting an arrow into a target, how the flaming red arrow moved in jerky increments from bow to bull's-eye. If he looks at the school building, Donny knows he'll remember Gregory's first day of school and how he held Gregory's little hand

and how they both cried. He doesn't want to do that now, doesn't want to weep in public this morning. You can't tell a proper story while you're in tears.

Donny wonders where the story should begin. When the boy collapses at the kitchen table, dead, they say, before his head hit the plate? Or earlier? Should Donny begin way back when, with his own unbounded joy at the birth of his son? He shivers when he sees the full span of his son's life played out in this instant—born and dead in the same moment. Over with. Gone.

If Gregory had died in Iraq, then people would be interested. Donny would be interviewed in the newspaper; he'd get to tell the story meticulously. *Meticulously* would mean talking about the divorce, of course, and of Gregory's subsequent and unresolved estrangement, the agonizing gulf that separated father and son. But Gregory did not die a hero. He died rather undramatically of a congenital heart defect that no one even knew he had. People don't want to hear about what might be at work in their own bodies.

Later, on lunch break at the factory, Donny sits beside a group of men playing kitty whist in the canteen. He chews his bologna sandwich, watches the game, sips his 2% milk from the carton. The men seem happy, slapping trump cards on the table, happy not to be out at the extruding machines, happy to be off their feet for a few minutes. Donny tells the men that his son has died. Oscar from shipping asks him how old the boy was, and he tells them all that Gregory was thirty-one. The dealer shuffles, says we all die. Donny is trying, is struggling, albeit unsuccessfully, to get what he wants. He wants to tell Gregory's story. He wants sympathy, too, he now understands. He wants recognition. He wants the world to know that he has suffered, is suffering still, will never get over the loss of his boy. There's dignity in suffering. Imagine that.

That afternoon, as he sits by the extruding machine and strips excess plastic off toy bowling pins, Donny wonders if he should call

Gregory's mother. He and Vera share this grief, this loss. He could talk with her. If he had known in time, he could have made it to the funeral. Pennsylvania's not so far. He stops off at Gleason's Luncheonette for coffee and a honey dip doughnut on the way home, as he does every day. Home is such a quiet place. Ray's behind the counter. Donny tells Ray his boy is dead. Ray says, That's a bitch; sorry, Donny. I didn't know you had a kid. Donny snaps his fingers. Heart went, just like that. Ray would like to listen, but he's in the weeds here. Got a rush.

Donny buys a paper and walks home. He slides a TV dinner into the oven, collapses in his easy chair. He taps his pocket for a smoke, remembers he quit smoking three years ago. His cat leaps to the arm of the chair. He strokes the cat, says, Ah, Molly, our Gregory . . . he's dead. The cat purrs and runs her length against Donny's arm. She sits. And he tells the little cat the whole story. So Donny gets what he wants today, but maybe not all that he wants. He gets to tell Gregory's story, but doesn't get a human response, doesn't tell it to someone who will remember it, consider it, sympathize with him.

And that's how to begin a novel, to begin to shape a plot, with a character who has significant trouble. You give him the difficulty and make him want to do something about it. Make him want whatever it is so badly that he'll act, he'll go after it no matter what gets in his way. And then you muddle ahead and see what happens. Follow him around and write down what he does. Our novel is under way; the opening chapter is finished. Well, it will be when we write the scenes and revise, when we get the vivid and telling details in place, when we get the words right, when we get to the end of the novel and see if the promise of the opening lines is fulfilled.

2. Begin at the End

This is what Tolstoy did, remember, with *Anna Karenina*, with the news of her death, the death that would come at the end of the novel. You can find the seeds of plots and characters in the newspaper. Take a look at today's headlines. These days with the Internet, every hometown newspaper is your own hometown newspaper, delivered electronically to your door. All of the following situations (not plots yet) came from recent newspaper stories:

- A man kills his wife and takes up with another woman. (Sure, it's a familiar story until you decide as you write that the husband is the governor of your state and the other woman is married to the governor's richest campaign donor.)

- An elderly woman dies; her son and daughter-in-law toss her body in a roadside ditch.

- A man has been missing for three years; his brother finds his body stuffed in a kitchen freezer.

- A baby is found buried alive in a dump.

- A six-year-old boy lives for a month alone in his house with the corpse of his mother.

- A bride gets drunk, busts up the reception hall at her wedding reception, and gets arrested.

You can begin your stories at these moments, of course, but often the situations we find in newspapers present us with climactic events, suggest the culmination of a struggle, an inappropriate, perhaps, resolution to earlier trouble. We see an elderly woman holding a 7-Eleven clerk at gunpoint. What does she think she's doing? What led her to carry out such a desperate act? We ask ourselves what could have led up to this moment, and we work our way back to the beginning of the story.

Let's take our inebriated and tempestuous bride as an example. Here's Brenda on what should be the happiest day of her life thus far. She has married the man of her dreams. She has invited all of her friends and her family out to the Olde Mill Restaurant to witness her commitment, to celebrate her sunny future, to share in her happiness. What went wrong? Why did she do what she did? And what exactly did she do? (She argued with her new husband in the parking lot, then came back to the reception, threw the wedding cake to the floor, and smashed the vases of flowers. She stormed out of the club and walked down the highway, ignoring the friends who had come to calm her down. We'll say that because that's what we read in the newspaper article. Maybe we'll change some of the details as we write, but this gets us going.) What led up to this ruinous and humiliating business? This is what fiction writers do—they ask questions.

> "I chart a little first—lists of names, rough synopses of chapters, and so on. But one doesn't over plan; so many things are generated by the sheer act of writing."
> —ANTHONY BURGESS

Not five minutes before the outburst, Brenda had seen her new husband making out with the maid of honor, the slut, right there at the bar. It didn't mean anything, my ass. Combine that revelation with a few cocktails and you get combustion. So the discovery of the infidelity, let's call it, was the precipitating event to the climactic scene (which we understand might be followed by a denouement at the police station involving a hangover and perhaps Brenda's realization that, yes, she may have lost her dignity last night, but she just may have saved her emotional life and preserved a benevolent future in the process. The marriage is thankfully over [annulment] before it started.) But that was only the last scene in the final act. What led up to all this storm and stress? Where does our story begin? Let's back up.

Brenda is the holdout—the last of her gang still single. Maybe we open with her at the wedding reception of her close friend. She's moved to tears and suddenly feels old and alone. And maybe she's feeling a little pressure from the parents and from herself to tie the knot and let the breeding begin. That's how she thinks about it. She's tired of living alone, to be honest, and tired of eating alone at restaurants, but who has the time to conduct a proper courtship? She's got the career (she's an optometrist with one of the chains); she's got family and civic obligations (the Rotary Club, the Lions Club, the Young Democrats). The only guys hitting on her these days are the happily married Rotarians.

Brenda loves to travel and enjoys throwing her money away a couple of nights a month at the casino. The blackjack table is where she meets Dario. She's his lucky charm, he says. He buys her a dinner at Tequila Ranch. One thing leads to another. It's easier to fall in love than she remembered. Dario's considerate, witty, attentive, and affectionate. He's so charming and adorable that even we fall in love with him. He has two boys, Caden and Cole, from a former (well, not quite former) wife. He has the boys every other weekend and seems devoted to them. In fact, he tells Brenda that she has to understand that his kids come first in his life, a sentiment she both admires and resents.

Dario hesitates in getting the divorce. Brenda is disappointed when Dario goes through with his planned fishing trip with his pals on her birthday. But Brenda is in love and will not allow these frustrations to get in the way. She pursues Dario with all the grace and charm she has. She allows herself to be unguarded and susceptible. That's how you have to be when you've found the one.

One weekend when the boys have joined her and Dario at her

place, Cole comes down with a stomach virus. Brenda calls Penny, the mom, by now Dario's ex, and lets her know Cole's situation. He's up watching TV and eating chicken soup. Penny tells Brenda she'll buy her a drink when Dario drops her.

Oh, I know he's not perfect.

He's not even who you think he is.

Meanwhile, there are other difficulties in Brenda's life. Her dad is ill, and her mom is falling to pieces with worry. The optometry chain Brenda works for is closing the local branch and wants her to transfer to a Midwest location. There'll be a sizable raise included. Dario, of course, can't leave the area, what with the boys and all.

She and Dario have their most serious disagreement over children. He doesn't want another one. She desperately wants a child. Nothing is settled, but Brenda figures she can make a pregnancy happen. Dario stops by the casino some days after work, but doesn't like going with Brenda anymore. And he doesn't like her going on her own. It doesn't look right, that's all. He can be pretentious and has turned off her friends with all his pontificating about wine and cheese. Some days Brenda worries if this struggle isn't all too much. She feels like her own life is on hold sometimes. But then she remembers that night.

They're snowbound in a cabin in Vermont. No power, no phone service. The drafty windows rattle in the wind. So they snuggle by the fire, sip brandy, and talk into the night. He tells her about his childhood, about his dad's abandonment of the family, something he never really got over, how he misses his dad and resents him at the same time. He tells her about his dream, and he sits up and stares into the fire when he does, like he's almost afraid to look at her when he speaks. He sees himself—"I mean the two of us"—on an island off the coast of Maine living a simple and bountiful life. "We're together and we have very little, but we're rich in love." She tells him they can make that happen. And they make love by the fire, and he does not turn away when they finish. The memory and promise of that night are reason enough for her to overlook the little annoyances.

And so she takes the severance offer from the firm and decides to worry about her next job after the wedding. Maybe start her own business. And she busies herself with plans for the ceremony. And so on. Which carries us to what had seemed at first our chaotic and destructive climactic scene, which, we now realize, was not crazy, but liberating, and we consider rewriting the scene and toning down her drinking—she hasn't drunk at all, maybe. It's so much more interesting if she's cold sober when she bursts into flames, when she sees Dario in action, and recalls the supposedly vacant condo, his stops at the casino, the lipstick case she found in his pocket and assumed was the ex's—it's all been a lie. We have an outline, a draft, of our plot and we're ready to do the real work of writing and dramatizing.

3. Steal the Plot.

That's what Shakespeare did. That's what I did in our first example above, Donny and his dead son, in case you didn't notice. I stole the plot from Chekhov. I took his story "Misery," set in Russia at the turn of the last century, and set it in contemporary urban America. You can steal plots, too, of course. Take a favorite story or play or folk tale or epic or myth and use its structure as a model for your own story. Let's say we want to write a novel based on "Hansel and Gretel." We can do this quickly, in twenty minutes or so, and then have the outline for a novel that we can spend the next several years writing. What we'll end up with is our own plot, but with allusions to a classical work. The way, say, *West Side Story* is not *Romeo and Juliet*, but certainly owes a debt to the play

> "The last thing one knows when writing a book is what to put first."
> —BLAISE PASCAL

Hansel and Gretel. First of all, change the time and place. So let's say it's contemporary America. Let's say in Miami. Already we're thinking about where to set the scenes, how to use the beauty—and the ugliness—of the city. The ocean, the river, palm trees, art deco hotels in South Beach, Calle Ocho, the alleys and slums, and so on, and, of course, the Everglades, our "woods," where the children (we'll steal their names from Shakespeare, from *The Tempest*), Adrian and Ariel, might be abandoned. (Perhaps one or both of the parents loved or loves Shakespeare.) It strikes us that we might be better off reversing the direction of the story here. Not abandoning the kids farther from civilization, but abandoning them farther into civilization. We know that wolves and the other dangerous and cunning predators live in the city these days, not in the wilderness.

> "A bad beginning makes
> a bad ending."
> —EURIPIDES

We know that the family lives in extreme poverty. So let's say they are squatting on public land in the Everglades. They live in tents without plumbing or electricity. The kids don't go to school. Let's push it even further. The parents, Dad and Stepmom (Mom died giving birth to the twins), are survivalists, wanting little to do with the government. No Social Security cards, no driver's licenses. They live off the land, fishing, trapping. It's a tough life, but the children are happy and well cared for. (Of course, we don't need all the days of happiness and tranquillity in our novel—we want to start as close as we can to the trouble.)

The father becomes ill. He's unable to trap or fish. The kids and stepmom try. But Dad is getting worse, and he is irritatingly fatalistic—won't go to a hospital. If it's my time, it's my time. His wife treats him with natural remedies. The parents decide that the children are suffering and are in danger of malnutrition and worse. They figure that the kids would be better off in foster care. And we might well agree. We realize that they need good nutrition and proper health care and an education and the company of other children. Ariel and Adrian overhear the whispered plan. Mom will walk them into the city and leave them at a hospital or at a police station, the welfare office. And maybe that's where the novel begins.

Before we get ahead of ourselves, however, let's take a look at our fairy tale itself and use it to plan our novel. Since we know the story already, we might borrow a technique from screenwriting and establish four important scenic moments and use them as a scaffold for building our plot. (1) The opening scene; (2) the plot point at the end of Act I; (3) the plot point at the end of Act II; and (4) the end of the novel. We might think of the opening and the ending as two sides of the same coin. The opening will echo in the ending. So let's decide we'll end with the reunited family, and we won't even kill our somewhat benevolent stepmother. The family's together and the future's so bright they have to wear shades, as the song goes.

We might open with the kids bringing food to Dad, who is laid up sick. That gives us immediate trouble. We'd see the warmth and love and also the precarious lives being lived here. With this opening in mind, I Googled *edible food in the Everglades* and learned in the first hit that most of the fish there are contaminated with mercury, a toxin which will do you in with a vengeance. And now we know why Dad is ill, and now we know that they are all in danger. The effects of mercury poisoning: difficulty walking and speaking; tremors; fatigue and weakness; impaired vision and hearing; headache and trouble concentrating; coma; death. And now we have a subplot and certainly a theme if we want it. The deteriorating wilderness, the destruction of the earth. People go back to nature for spiritual peace and bring physical devastation to themselves, a dramatically appealing, if tragic, irony.

So we see them all eating the fish that the kids caught. Drinking rainwater. (Yes, there are ample poisons in rainwater, too, but let's not go there just now.) Dad expects to be well shortly, but we can see he's having a hard time speaking, remembering. The kids snuggle with him after dinner by the campfire. Stepmom sings a lullaby, the kids fall asleep. Cut to Ariel, our central character, as she hears the parents talking about leaving her and Adrian in the city. She wakes her brother. They listen. What will we do? And all of that in the first few pages of the novel. So now we know the central character, the dramatic premise—the kids have to get home—and the dramatic circumstances surrounding the story: poverty, illness, helplessness, alienation from society, etc.

So we have the opening action, but what's our initial image? What is the first sight our reader will see? What's the first sound she'll hear? We're putting the reader in a frame of mind to read the novel. This is, we know from the fairy tale, a story about family bonds, about home, about the courage of children and their betrayal by adults. Can we show some or all of that and show our central character visually? How about this: We see Ariel flying through the air, arms thrashing, obviously frightened. She hits the water; we hear a splash! A scream. Her dad has tossed her in the water to teach her to swim. She can't. Adrian rescues her. Dad says, You have to learn sometime, sweetheart. Cut to the meal. And now we know that before the novel's over, Ariel will swim. She'll display that courage she lacks right now.

So we know the opening, and we know the ending will be a reunion. What about the action at the end of Act I that spins our story around and is the real start of the struggle? That's when whatever plan Adrian had to get them home the second time fails, and the children find themselves deep in the city, lost, frightened, abandoned, without hope. And at the end of Act II? The children finally find an adult they can trust through Ariel's efforts, someone who will carry them home.

Let's think of two other moments. The implementation of the

parents' plan. The children leave home and walk to the city with their stepmom. And now let's consider the children's lowest point when all seems hopeless and lost. It's when the children are hostages of some nasty character or characters. They are virtually enslaved and are in great danger.

So let's look at this framework we're building, a framework we have access to because we're borrowing the plot: (1) the toss in the water, the meal; (2) the walk to the city (which will be followed by a second walk); (3) lost!; (4) trapped and threatened! (5) Ariel finds the "angel"; (6) reunion. Now all we have to do is tie these together. Back to the opening sequence. The children overhear their parents plan. They talk. Adrian says they'll take Crab, their cuddly, delightful mutt. In the morning they convince Stepmom to let Crab tag along. They get his leash. They make it to the city. Stepmom tells them to wait on the steps of the police station while she runs inside for a minute. She leaves them. (Yes, we'll

> "Every thought tends to connect something with something else, to establish a relationship between things."
> —L. S. VYGOTSKY

have to work on her character, on her motivation.) We remind ourselves that we want to show the city and show it from the children's POV—so lots of noise, lots of congestion, confusion, and threats. Ariel and Adrian lie to folks who come to their aid. They've been told how many times never to divulge their father's location, or the government will take him away and they'll never see him again. We're waiting for our dad, they say. They sleep in a park. In the morning Crab leads them home. Cheerful reunion and all that.

The next time Stepmom'll bring them even farther into the city. Before she does, however, the children see that Dad is wasting away and needs a doctor. They aren't quite sure where you get a doctor. Maybe when they come back, they'll bring one. This time

Crab can't come along. Adrian's plan is to jot down all the lefts and rights they take on the trip. He can do this with pencil and paper. He'll draw a map of where they're going. But, of course, this doesn't work. He's written down lefts and rights but not the space between the turns, and they wind up hopelessly lost. Mom leaves them at a hospital. Had they stayed put, they may have been rescued, but they began to wander aimlessly. They huddle together in the bushes at a park and try to sleep. Ariel cries.

Act I is finished; Act II, the buildup, is under way. Here the children will struggle to find their way home. But first, they find their way to the beach and make camp in the sea grapes. Life is easy. They forage for food in the Dumpsters behind restaurants. They sunbathe, play in the sand, wade in the surf. They are even tempted to stay awhile. But then it rains. They find a community of homeless folks living under an interstate overpass, and they settle in. They are cared for by a few elderly women. It's okay there until a nasty crackhead tries to rape Ariel. Adrian stops him, smashing him with a brick, again and again. They are rescued by a religious minister who takes them into his home. They tell them their story, and he promises to get them back to their parents as soon as he can locate them. They ask him not to go to the cops. (Now we know he has a weapon to use against them. Do what I say, or I'll go to the authorities and sic them on your dad.) Life is great at first. They eat well—lots of candy and desserts, too—they clean up, wear new clothes. They no longer look like feral children. They see a doctor. They tell him about their dad, describe his symptoms. They tell the minister they want to go home now. He lies. Locks them in. Threatens their dad. He's trying to save their souls, it turns out. He thinks they are the emissaries of Satan. He tries to brainwash them in the ways of the Lord, and is making some headway with Adrian.

This, perhaps, is the midpoint of the novel. When Adrian says to Ariel, We'll be better off here—Dad is a bad man who does not believe in God—Ariel is in a panic. But she is determined not to lose her brother to this fiend. She finds courage. She drugs or in some other way disables the minister and she browbeats Adrian into leaving, and they make their escape. They go to the doctor they've met. He was so good to them. He's the only person they know and can trust. And besides, their father needs a doctor. The doctor will help them out, certainly. (Of course, we already know he won't.) The doctor calls the minister. Here we have another reversal in the proceeding plot. Ariel hears him make the call, and they bolt. They know they live west and they head off into the sunset.

Eventually, they leave the city behind and come to the 'Glades and don't know which way to go—but go they must, Ariel says. They can't stay here. They wade through the snake- and alligator-infested water, moving from hardwood hammock to hardwood hammock. Nothing looks familiar. Adrian twists his ankle and can't go on. They are stuck, hopelessly lost once again. Another reversal. Starving, tired, frightened. That night Ariel can't sleep. She's keeping watch and sees what looks to be a fire or some kind of light coming from a hammock, a mile, five miles away, she doesn't know. She marks the direction and in the morning leaves Adrian and heads off. Adrian is sick, vomiting, etc. She wades in the water and we see it rise to her chin. She swims. Alligators, snakes are in the water. She finally arrives at the cabin that was the source of the light she'd seen the night before. No one's there. She enters the cabin. Finds food, water. She sleeps. (We've slipped into "Goldilocks.") She's awakened by an elderly Miccosukee. And now, with the buildup finished, our payoff, our resolution begins. They take his airboat to rescue Adrian. She describes their camp to the old man. He knows where they live and carries them home. Once there, the hysterical and grateful stepmom, the old Indian, and the children load the unconscious dad into the airboat. Cut to hospital. We've got an outline for our novel.

4. Plottomatic!©

So you begin with a character, and you muddle ahead. Or you begin at the end, and you work your way back to the start. Or you steal the plot. A fourth choice available to you because you're a student here at FNS is Plottomatic!© Simply take one item at random from each column in the chart that follows. (A hat with pieces of paper numbered 1–26 will serve. Close your eyes; pick three numbers.)

PLOTTOMATIC! ©

1. Newspaper reporter	1. Wants to be happy again	1. Has a perfectly good tooth removed
2. Gift shop manager	2. Wants to save his/her marriage	2. Sends money to a televangelist
3. Heavy-equipment operator	3. Wants to start over before it's too late	3. Paints the kitchen at three A.M.
4. Architect	4. Wants to solve a crime	4. Writes an anonymous letter to the editor
5. Baker	5. Wants to earn his/her mother's/father's respect	5. Buries his/her face in spouse's arms
6. Dental hygienist	6. Wants to leave his/her spouse	6. Shaves his/her head
7. Stand-up comic	7. Wants to salvage a friendship	7. Listens at the wall as the neighbors argue
8. Jeweler	8. Wants to win the heart of X	8. Sleeps with a crucifix
9. Lifeguard	9. Wants to save his/her self-destructive child	9. Rips up the clothes in his/her closet
10. Florist	10. Wants to have a child	10. Washes hands over and over

11. Landscaper	11. Doesn't want to die this way	11. Digs a shallow grave
12. Used-car sales-person	12. Wants a secret life	12. Pretends to be blind
13. Priest	13. Wants to get over this heartbreak	13. Shoots the television
14. Bartender	14. Wants to understand the death of a child	14. Sings on the front porch
15. Postal carrier	15. Wants to find his/her real parents	15. Calls a radio talk show
16. Cabdriver	16. Wants to clear his/her name	16. Holds a flower to his/her ear
17. Tailor	17. Wants to talk about his/her child's death	17. Covers the mirrors in his/her house
18. Cable TV installer	18. Wants to make things right before he/she dies	18. Irons clothes at two A.M.
19. Exterminator	19. Doesn't want to be alone	19. Talks to a chair
20. Tollbooth attendant	20. Wants someone's respect	20. Calls a friend he/she hasn't seen in twenty years
21. Criminal defense attorney	21. Wants to write a novel	21. Cries in a restaurant while alone
22. Social worker	22. Wants to teach his/her mother a lesson	22. Goes to a fortune-teller
23. TV anchorperson	23. Wants to win a prize	23. Goes to the store and doesn't come back

24. Pilot	24. Wants to make a difference	24. Watches neighbors with binoculars
25. Emergency-ward nurse	25. Wants to cover up a crime	25. Lies to his/her therapist
26. Shakespearean actor	26. Needs to deliver an important message	26. Writes a suicide note for someone else

The first column lists characters by their occupation. The second column tells us what the character wants. The third column presents us with a scene that can either open or close your novel. In other words, we start at the beginning or we start at the end.*

Let's use this example: Numbers 2, 24, and 11. A *gift shop manager* wants to *make a difference*. He *digs a shallow grave*. Our gift shop manager is named Henry Perch. He's balding, in his fifties. When he speaks, threads of saliva connect his lower lip to his upper. He wears reading glasses around his neck on a gold chain. His nails are manicured, his shirts starched; his slacks are pleated. He lives alone upstairs over Perch's Cottage Gifts. This is the house he grew up in. This is the shop his mother ran for thirty-seven years before he took it over when her heart gave out. (Dad was someone he never knew.) This used to be a decent neighborhood, but it's been going downhill for some time. Henry's out in his small backyard burying his Jack Russell terrier, Curly. Imagine someone cruel enough to poison a dog. The dog's body is swaddled in a bath towel and zipped into a gym bag. Henry drops the bag and his little pal into the small hole in the ground by the rose trellis. He expresses some

*Plottomatic!© offers you the chance to work on 17,576 distinct situations, according to my math consultant, James Barret-Morison. And, of course, you can make up your own.

saccharine sentiment he's read on one of his bereavement products somewhere. He says, "Perhaps a life is a journey that leads us to the perfect home."

And now we're off and running. We've created, though we may not have known it, a character—by naming him and giving him something significant to do. We've established a setting, that cozy backyard in that decaying neighborhood. We've given our character trouble. Now what? We put things that we like in stories. So Henry's upstairs later that evening in his apartment. He pours himself a cognac (we like cognac), puts Mozart on the stereo (we adore Mozart), opens his collection of vintage postcards, and imagines himself in those exotic locations. Henry wishes he had lived in a more refined age and laments the recent corruption of civility. Here he is at the Hotel Minerva in Florence circa 1925. He imagines himself in the grand dining room, sees the frescoed ceiling, the bright morning sun streaming through the French doors, smells the aroma of fresh espresso and bread. He is not alone. He and his colleague have arranged for a morning excursion to the Boboli Gardens. Let's pause here a moment to note that we've established a few contrasts already. The present and the past; civility and barbarity; solitude and friendship. We've described a man who seems ill at ease in the modern world.

And now we put some things that make us nervous in the novel. Henry's distracted from his Tuscan reverie by his loss. He stares at the dent in the sofa cushion where Curly should be twitching in his sleep. Henry has never before thought of himself as a victim, but now he does, and he doesn't like it. Curly was killed in order to get at him, Henry thinks, but why? If he could prove that his neighbor was responsible . . . But does he even need proof when, in fact, he knows?

Henry understands that when you have excluded the impossible, whatever remains, however improbable, must be true. (He's remembered a line from his favorite literary detective, Sherlock Holmes.) And the murder of his dog by the criminal next door is not improbable in the least. When he finally tries to sleep, he hears the noise of rock music from next door. (We despise noise.) Not another party! He stuffs his plugs into his ears, closes the windows. He's hot, aggravated, overtired. He'll never get his eight hours this way. He calls the police, as he's done many times before because of this neighbor's loud music. We've written two scenes already. Novel's under way. What happens next?

To answer that question, let's put our character in a different setting so that we can learn more about him and more about his world. He's in the gift shop. *Henry looks across the counter past the display of mothers' birthstone necklaces, past the German glass thermometers, and sees the door fly open before he hears the bell ring* . . . And now we create a new situation. Here comes trouble through that door . . . *and sees the one they call Sledge walk into the store. Big smile on his sorry face.* And here we create the second character by giving him something to do, something to say. *Sledge picks up a Country Life Hummel—a girl and a fawn. "How's your dog, Perch?"* And now we emotionally charge the situation. *Sledge drops the Hummel. It shatters on the tile floor. "Oops!" Henry says. "You break it, you take it. That'll be two hundred and fifty dollars plus tax." Sledge says, "Wrap it up." Henry says, "I know what you've done." Sledge says, "You don't know the half of it." Henry says he's calling the police right now.* And here, perhaps, we charge the situation again. *Henry looks at the pistol behind the counter.* Is it loaded? Does he know how to use it?

A recap of what we've done so far. Created a character, a setting, put things in the novel that we like, put things in the novel that make us anxious, created a situation and a second character, intensified the situation, intensified it again. And now, perhaps, we add a small surprise. The surprise might be an unprecedented adjective modifying the noun. It might be the leap from one thought to the next; it might be an unanticipated spin to the plot. A novel should be unpredictable as it unfolds and feel inevitable when it's finished.

So now the doorbell to the shop tinkles, and in walks Mrs. Walsh. She lives over the dry cleaner's and works at Fisher's Pharmacy, has for forty years. Her grandson is graduating from high school, and she'd like one of those cards that you slip a bill into. She says hello to Sledge, asks him if he got rid of the rats in his attic. He looks at Henry and says he's working on it. And now we emphasize what has happened. *Henry sweeps up the Hummel, puts the pieces in a bag, and rings it up. "Is there anything else I can get for you, Mr. Smith?" Sledge tells Henry he's forgotten his checkbook at home.*

And so it goes. We ask ourselves, What does Henry, our central character, want? And what's stopping him from getting it? In the short run he might want to exact revenge. He wants this brute arrested. He wants justice. He's tried calling the cops. The cops have shut down the late-night parties at Sledge's apartment several times, but they have no proof that Sledge poisoned Curly. And they can't do a thing about threats to Henry that Sledge may have made. The officer Henry talked to told him that Sledge would have to physically harm him before they could legally intervene. *Sledge says, "Look, Perch, if I see a cop anywhere near me for the rest of my life, I'm coming for you. Got it?" Henry says, "I'm not afraid, Mr. Smith." "You ought to be."*

Maybe we look back at our Plottomatic!© prompt and remind ourselves that Henry *wants to make a difference.* He will move beyond the short-term goal of revenge to the long-term goal of neighborhood reform. Now he wants more than revenge—he wants a whole new civilized, cultured community, like it was when he was a boy. He decides, perhaps, that he'll start by cleaning out the riffraff. He decides to run for city council, where he'll champion civic reform. He forges an alliance with neighborhood associations. He announces his bid for a council seat. But he's gay and people tell him not to run. He's aghast at that. "Why? You'd rather live with scum?" he says. How badly does he want to make a difference? The only answer can be *intensely*. His motivation? The deteriorating quality of life in the neighborhood, the threat to his business and well-being, the killing of his dog. He runs for office and is handily defeated by the corrupt, do-nothing incumbent. He feels humiliated and more isolated than ever. His store is broken into, his merchandise destroyed. He goes after Sledge. He has that pistol, remember. *Sledge laughs and dares him to shoot. He shoots off Sledge's right index finger. He says, "Tell me about Curly." Sledge says, "Are you nuts? I'm going to bleed to death."* We know Henry's thinking his life is over; he's shot a man; he's going to prison. We're also thinking Sledge'll be going into shock soon, and maybe Henry ought to consider a tourniquet. And we think, Does Henry have some kind of gift item that could be used as a weapon? What about that broken Hummel? Or maybe that's not what happens at all. Henry tries to make a difference and is unable to, and he cannot face the future a broken man (broken like the Hummel). He walks out to the backyard, sits by Curly's grave, and uses the pistol on himself. We kind of hope that doesn't happen because we've grown to like Henry, to love him, and we know there is hope. So maybe . . . maybe what? Maybe he moves to Florence?

Well, you get the idea—we'll know what happens to Henry by the time we finish. And then we'll have black on white; we'll have a beginning, a middle, and an end, and then we can go back and make the story better in revision. And the changes will necessitate another revision. We're creating a world here. We'll take all the time we need.

Week 5:

Give Me a Place to Stand On

There are no shortcuts to any place worth going.
—*Beverly Sills*

YOU'VE GOT SOME people in your head and others on the pages of your notebook. You've thought about what kind of trouble they might be in or might be headed for, not unlike, perhaps, some of the trouble you've been in or seem headed for yourself. But before you can begin to tell their tale, you need to put your characters in a place. Nothing happens nowhere. You can't move the earth if you have no place to set your lever. Young writers sometimes tell me that they want their story's locale to be undefined and nonspecific; they want to leave it up to the reader, they say; they want their fictive world to stand for anyplace. These are writers, it seems clear, who are less interested in their characters than they ought to be. Their motivation to tell the story seems to be to deliver a message, a message that we likely know already: war is bad, nations must learn to work together, children should not be abused, and all of that. Those sorts of pronouncements are not truths, but truisms. Fiction is not about ideas; it's about people. It's not about sending messages. It's about exploring problems. It's not about answers. It's about questions. Fiction writers write about what they *don't* under-stand. Fiction is not about the author and his opinions; it's about the characters and their struggles, heartbreaks, and triumphs. Fic-tion is not a time to generalize. Understand that your novel will not be universal if your setting is not specific. *Universal* translates to vague, abstract, diffuse, immaterial, and unconvincing. We under-stand the general through the particular, not the other way around. Fiction deals with emotions, and emotions are evoked in the sen-sual world. Fiction deals with the concrete and with the palpable. Let politicians think globally. Fiction writers must think locally. So take your characters and plant their feet on solid ground, and you'll be grounding the reader in your world at the same time.

Eudora Welty wrote this about place: "Every story would be another story, and unrecognizable as art, if it took up its characters and plot and happened somewhere else. Imagine *Swann's Way* laid in London, or *The Magic Mountain* in Spain, or *Green Mansions* in the Black Forest. The very notion of moving a novel brings ruder havoc to the mind and affections than would a century's altera-tion in its time." Imagine *Absalom, Absalom!* in Minneapolis or *The Great Gatsby* in Orlando. Miss Welty also wrote that our feelings are bound up in place. So, too, are our characters' feelings.

There's a somewhat derisive term, *local color*, used to describe regional writing, which is seen as sketchy and nostalgic, quirky and quaint. But all writing is regional, after all, even if the region is the methane quags of Melmac. Even if the region is Midtown Manhattan.* You want the color of your place, and you want the

*You never hear of New York writers being described as regional writers, do you? Because it's the center of the world, I suppose. I, on the other hand, often think (I'm wrong, of course) that there are three literary regions in the US: New York, the South, and Everywhere Else. I grew up reading Southern fiction in New England and am always humbled and exhilarated when I see my books on the Southern Literature shelves at a bookstore. I went to school in Arkansas at the

flavor of it. And flavor suggests *terroir*, a word borrowed from the French, meaning *soil*, from the Latin *terra*, *land*. Terroir is a word used a lot these days when talking about wine. To oenophiles, terroir refers to the special characteristics bestowed upon the wine by the geography, the environment, and the qualities of a specific locale. The French phrase *gout de terroir* literally means a taste of the soil, the tang of the locale. Let me suggest this idea of terroir as a helpful metaphor when thinking about characters and place. Every city, town, every neighborhood comes with a unique set of characteristics that identify the people within that area. Call it *somewhereness*.* That's what we're looking for in fiction—a sense of somewhereness. We want our characters to smack of the soil from which they grew and/or in which they live. John Doe planted in Five Points, Georgia, will be a different man than the same John Doe planted in Butte, Montana. For one thing, folks around Five Points call him Johnny Boy. Folks in Butte, the guys he played ball with and now works the mine with, call him Big John. Oenophiles talk about soil, nature, appellation, and human activity. The fiction

---

oldest MFA program in the South with writers from everywhere, but we all loved the realistic short story like those by Mr. Faulkner and Ms. Welty, and others. We can recognize good writing when we see it, and it needn't be realistic, but we love the plotted story down here. After a performance of my play *Trailerville* at the Blue Heron Theater in Manhattan, I spoke with a woman in the lobby. She'd just seen the play and was irritated with it. She asked me why I wrote about people in Louisiana. She said, "I don't care about people there." I said, "Who do you care about?" She said, "People in New York." "That's it?" "That's it." I don't think you'd ever hear that kind of aesthetic provincialism in the South. (But maybe I'm wrong again.)

*A word coined, I've read, by Matt Kramer in his book *Making Sense of California Wine*. "Great wines taste like they came from somewhere. Lesser wines taste interchangeable; they could come from anywhere. You can't fake somewhereness. You can't manufacture it . . . but when you taste a wine that has it, you know."

writer can think of history, landscape, family, culture, and work. All of that shapes the character.

Think about your own terroir. You are who you are because of where you grew up and when and how you grew up there. The narrator of my novel *Requiem, Mass.*, addresses this notion. "I imag-

> "Every human event happens somewhere, and the reader wants to know what that somewhere was like."
> —WILLIAM ZINSSER

ined what my life would have been like if I had grown up here in Louisiana. I'd know boys with rifles, apparently. And girls who won blue ribbons. My backyard would go on forever. I'd be alone more often. If you were crazy, and you lived out in the country in Louisiana, would anyone even notice?" Place shapes us as surely as waves shape the coastline. As it shaped you, it will shape your characters. We are built to survive our environments. Some of us need space; others need to be bumping into people. Some places train us to be self-sufficient; others teach us to be reliant and trusting.

You can set your novel in the place where you live—even if you change the name and details of it, as I have done in *Requiem, Mass.* You can set the novel in a place you'd like to spend some time in and with which you might be familiar—the Pacific Northwest, some tranquil river valley. (A friend of mine once told me she was writing a novel set in Phoenix, and she didn't want to go there until she finished the novel. Very brave, I thought.) And that brings us to your third option. Set the story in an imagined town. We did that already in the *Let Us Build Us a City* exercise. Let's start writing by writing about our hometowns.

YOU CAN GO HOME AGAIN. Think about the place where you grew up, and, of course, the time you grew up there. How was that place different from any other place, than the place where you live now? And even if you haven't moved geographically, the place has changed, hasn't it? What were the local rituals that made it unique? Think about language, vocabulary, dialect, and accent. Think about foods; think about the work people did, the work they didn't do. Remember the annual events that everyone looked forward to. The schools, the architecture, the folkways, the history, the customs, the landscape, the flora and fauna, the styles of dress, and all of the native details that affect the characters. The town or the neighborhood legends. This could be the setting for your novel, remember. Walk around the town or the neighborhood and put your five senses to work. Stop and talk to the people you find there—the people from your own past. Think about the seasons, the light, the ground, the schools, the churches, the secret places you escaped to. Remember that when you write about your town it will not be *the* town, but *your* town.

WALKABOUT. "Before there was story there was place. landscapes are the archetypal containers of the lives of people. Narratives 'take place' as characters converge, act, and interact within the framework of a specific place and time."* And place can be character. Think of a story like Stephen Crane's "The Open Boat." Four men battle for survival against the indifferent, mighty, and unyielding sea. If place is to be a character, it needs to do something, to act on your central character, and/or react to her. If place is character, you ought to be able to render its personality, its makeup, mettle, and mood, its attributes and temperament. So let's see how place affects character and plot. Your central character goes for a walk. Seems innocent enough—until the place presents him with trouble. Write about that.

*I'm quoting here from "When Place Becomes Character: A Critical Framing of Place for Mobile and Situated Narratives" by Glorianna Davenport, which I found at the following Web site: http://mf.media.mit.edu/pubs/other/CharacterPlace.pdf

1. Right now it's twenty-two below in Barrow, Alaska, at two in the morning. (I just checked online.) Your character (give him a name) has just left his friend's house after an evening of drinking. Liquor is illegal in Barrow, but the guys find a way. Not so hard, really. He, let's call him Rob for now, needs to pee and should have done so before he left Phil's. Rob's staying at the King Eider Inn, and he thought it was a straight shot from Phil's front door, but now he's not sure. He works for the oil company, and this is only his third trip to Barrow. His boots squeak on the snow. He can hear the dogs barking, roaming, a pack of near-feral sled dogs. He figures he'd better head back to Phil's before they all pass out back there. He left his outer mittens on Phil's couch anyway. Which way to Phil's? Is he walking in the right direction, even? Blowing snow blinds him. The dogs' barking is closer now and coming from all directions. Rob's bladder is about to explode. What happens next? And after that? Ultimately?

2. Let's turn the heat on. She's seventy-eight and widowed. After her dear Amos died, she left Massachusetts and retired to South Florida where the winters wouldn't be so harsh. She finally finds the shopping list and her keys. She scratches her cat Felix behind the ears and heads off walking to Publix. It's July, hot and steamy. After a few blocks, she's feeling light-headed and stops to rest. There's no shade. Who ever called the useless palms "trees"? At Sheridan and Federal she waits through three lights to cross. There's always some lane of cars going left or right and never enough time. When she does manage, the impatient drivers all blast their horns at her, and that makes her heart speed up, and now she's dizzy and exhausted. Her feet are swollen; her housedress is drenched. She must look stupid sitting on the sidewalk, but what else can

> "A good writer chooses the setting which makes character and situation clear."
> —JOHN GARDNER

she do? In a minute she'll get up. She's looking forward to the air-conditioning in Publix. She'll call a cab to get home. She closes her eyes. The sun is relentless.

She wonders why she's lying on the ground. Because I'm sleepy, and it's okay if it looks funny. It's okay, Mr. Wheeler says. Mr. Wheeler from Commonwealth Gas. He asks after Amos, says they missed him at bowling Friday night. She realizes she must be dreaming and

> "The novel that fails is a novel in which there is no sense of place, and in which feeling is, by that much, diminished. Its action occurs in an abstract setting that could be anywhere or nowhere. This reduces its dimensions drastically and cuts down on those tensions that keep fiction from being facile and slick."
> —FLANNERY O'CONNOR

opens her eyes and sees that she is in an ambulance and a man is speaking to her, but it's like all underwater. Where's her purse? She can't remember her name right now, but that's unimportant. And then what?

3. You're walking through a city park by a local lake—something you enjoy doing in the early evenings. It's a time for you to think, to relax, and to unwind. You hear what seems to be a woman's scream You stop. Now she's crying. You follow a footpath around a row of lilac bushes and see a young woman being slapped by a guy. You keep your distance, but ask her if she's okay.

He says, She's my wife.
You say, I'm not talking to you.
She says, I'm fine.
You say, You don't look fine.
He says, Fuck off.
You say, I'm calling the cops.
She says, Just leave.
The guy walks toward you.
What do you do or say?

SETTING THE STAGE. There's the place and the time where the characters live and breathe and work and love and dream. There are the more specific places in the story, the places within place, where the characters get to do those things. Set your scenes, we like to say. So let's take a look at possible settings.

1. My friend Joe Young in Fort Worth just sent me an e-mail reminiscence of his grandmother's house: "I can remember they had a bathroom sink just beside their kitchen table and it had a rubber stopper that had a chain on it at one time. The chain was just a stub with 3 or 4 round nubs, no longer being attached at the other end, and us kids always liked plugging and unplugging it. There was always a thick square of Ivory soap in the depression beside the hot side handle." Now, those are vivid and significant details; those are details that open the imaginative possibilities of the place, that unlock memory and stories. So I want you to remember your childhood bedroom. Start with the color of the walls and the floor. The windows or lack of them. The bed or beds. The toys. Get more and more specific. The stains on the ceiling, the broken knob on the dresser, the wardrobe, the bureau, the chest of drawers, whatever you called that place you kept your clothes. (I filled the entire bottom drawer of my bureau with baseball cards.) In fact, open the drawers and go through the contents. Clothes, cards, jackknives, what else? Now open the closet door and look inside. What did you used to hide in there, and who were you hiding it from? Look under the bed. So that's where the alarm clock went to? What about the smell, the view? What did you tack to the walls? Your heroes, no

> "An autumnal setting can add a sense of ending to a story about doomed love, just as a spring setting can add a sense of anticipation to a story about adolescence."
> —JOHN LEGGETT

doubt. Still your heroes? Any pets in there with you? Any siblings? It's a rainy cold afternoon and you're stuck inside. You're in your room alone. What are you doing?

2. Write about the sacred places of your childhood. Your hangout, your hideout, your first sweetheart's house, the church you went to, the first-grade classroom, the schoolyard, the movie theater, the amusement park—well, you know the places that were important to you. Write in as much detail as you can. The places will come with stories—take the time to write about the events and the people you encounter. Not just the Loew's Poli Theater but the Poli on the day you went with Bobby Carrigan to see *Old Yeller*. And what the two of you talked about on the way home: What kind of sick mind would make kids watch while some kid like you shoots his dog? Remember you're bringing the news of your fictive world to our world. And we love the exotic, by the way. The more unlike our own place, the better. We love to learn about a place we've never been to, and we also love to see a part of a familiar world that we may have missed somehow—because it's so familiar, maybe. Use the strangeness of your setting as a strength. Let it work for you. And your character may have grown up in one place and been dropped down in another. A stranger in a strange land. Not always a bad thing, of course. He is a stand-in for the reader in that case. It's all new and wonderful and perhaps frightening to us.

> *"If you live in a place—any place, city or country—long enough and deeply enough you can learn anything, the dynamics and interconnections that exist in every community, be it plant, human, or animal—you can learn what a writer needs to know."*
> —GRETEL EHRLICH

I was a stranger here myself. When I first moved to South Florida in 1989 from a lovely little city in Georgia, I didn't much like it. I hated the traffic, the unbearable summer heat and humidity (which no longer bother me). I even criticized the trees (like our widow in the exercise above)—the palms that seemed as phony as the high-rises along the beach. I couldn't write about it—not for ten years or so. I couldn't understand the place. It's Latin, it's Haitian, it's Caribbean, it's a hodgepodge of cultures. Then I finally realized that I did understand my neighborhood. I knew it quite well. And I liked it. So I started writing about Dania Beach (Frank Conroy wrote about what was then called Dania in his brilliant memoir *Stop-Time*, which I read in college in a contemporary novel course, of all things, with Emmet Grandone, a brilliant, articulate, and inspiring teacher. Conroy: "We ambled along the littered promenade in the general direction of the parking field, checking the sandy ground for dropped coins. Tobey bent over and picked up a small felt pennant on a stick. DANIA-FLA. on a background of orange blossoms. 'For the tree house.'") This is my little niche in South Florida.

Noveldom

The novel is the highest example of subtle
interrelatedness that man has yet discovered.
—*D. H. Lawrence*

How do we make sense of the world? We connect. We connect the past with the present, for example. We say, The last time I backed out of the driveway I hit the mailbox, so I'll wear my glasses today. In an early draft of my novel *Deep in the Shade of Paradise*, Adlai Birdsong connected his breakfast bacon to the guy at the market and to the guy's girlfriend (Adlai's ex) and to the idea of marriage and family and domestic bliss, and connected him to "the teamster who delivered the meat to market and to the butcher who killed the hog and carved its carcass; to the architect of the slaughterhouse even, and his family; to the hog farmer in Ottumwa, and to the man the farmer buys his feed from, and to the John Deere salesman there in town, who maybe just now found out his brother-in-law Walter lost his arm in a combine accident last night—stuck his hand under the auger to catch a handful of grain. Connected him, Adlai knew, to this particular hog himself, and to his brief, purposeful, but confusing life." We connect the stars to the atoms, the rose to our love, a plasma of flame to our desires. We connect, and sometimes our connections, our metaphors, seem so breathtaking that they open our eyes to a different world, as Shakespeare does here: *That time of year thou mayst in me behold / When yellow leaves, or none, or few, do hang / Upon those boughs which shake against the cold, / Bare ruined choirs, where late the sweet birds sang.*

How do we make sense of our lives? We tell stories. Stories order the chaos of life. One of the methods of telling a story we call a novel. But what is a novel? Here's what *The American Heritage Dictionary* has to say: A novel is (1) a prose narrative—but let's stop right there for a second. *Prose: writing without metrical structure.* What then does that say about Pushkin's *Eugene Onegin*, Emily Brontë's *Gondal's Queen*, Vikram Seth's *The Golden Gate*, Anne Carson's *Autobiography of Red*, and Brad Leithauser's *Darlington's Fall*, all subtitled *A Novel in Verse*? What's a *narrative*, then? *A story told in speech or writing.* ("I am bored by narrative," Virginia Woolf wrote in her diary in 1929.)

Back to the dictionary: (1) a prose narrative of considerable length (we might wonder just what constitutes "considerable length," but let's not, because then we are into the crepuscular world of the novelette [a short novel], the novella [a short prose tale often characterized by moral teaching or satire or a short novel], the novelet [a little new book or pamphlet], or the long story, and our concerns here must be with the novelesque, not the novelettish), typically having a plot that is unfolded by the actions, speech, and thoughts of the characters. *Characters*—so it's about people, then! We've established that much. Haven't we? The word *novel* comes from the Italian *novella*, "little new thing," piece of news, chitchat, tale, from the Latin *novus*, "new." The word ultimately stems from the Indo-European root *newo-* and is related to *novice, innovate, novelty, neon, nova* (a "new" star), and *novercal*, meaning "characteristic of a step-mother" (she who is new). Perhaps we can agree, then, that in his novel, the novelist (or novelant or novelwright) tells us something we don't know, something new.

The *OED* says a novel is "a fictitious prose narrative or tale of considerable length (now usually one long enough to fill one or more volumes), in which characters and actions representative of the real life of past or present times are portrayed in a plot of more or less complexity." Let's start with that word *fictitious*. I'm all for it. I think it's all fiction. It's all made up. I think, as I've said, that memory is a fiction, is invented, and all memoir suspect as fact. Truman Capote's *In Cold Blood* has been called, by the author himself, I believe, a nonfiction novel (which still sounds oxymoronic to me). I wonder if nonfiction novelists mean to suggest that they are using the traditional techniques of the novel to tell a factual story. (We might say, Who doesn't?) And what about W. G. Sebald's work? Travelogue? Memoir? Fiction? At least one of his books is peddled as a novel. Are, then, novels self-determined?

"The real life of past and present times . . ." We know that real life doesn't have to be depicted realistically, of course.* But what about the future time? Does this dictionary definition relegate all sci fi and speculative fiction to some other non-novelistic literary kingdom? Perhaps, but should it? Let's continue to look for a practical and inclusive definition of the novel. (Henry James: "The house of fiction has in short not one window, but a million.") As to that other part of the definition, the plot, the certain complexity, we'll come back to that later.

First, let's hear from some writers on the subject. Randall Jarrell said that a novel was an extended piece of prose fiction that has something wrong with it. And that may remind us of Milan Kundera's remark: "All great works (precisely because they are great)

---

*Pablo Picasso walks into a bistro. He orders a pastis, overhears a man grumbling about how modern art does not represent reality. Picasso demands to know from him what modern art is. The gentleman smiles, opens his wallet, takes out a photo of his wife, and says, This is reality. Picasso studies the photo, looks at it upside down and sideways, hands it back to the gent, and says, "Your wife, she's awfully small and flat."

contain something unachieved." Here's Henry James again: "The only obligation to which in advance we may hold a novel, without incurring the accusation of being arbitrary, is that it be interesting . . . [And here's what we're really concerned with:] A novel is in its broadest sense a personal, a direct impression of life." Personal and direct. Maybe we can agree then that so far a novel is *long* and it's *personal* and it tells us something *new* and it's about *people*. That's a start.

In his book *A Primer of the Novel*, novelist David Madden offers this definition: "A prose fiction narrative . . . longer than a short story . . . that usually subjects the reader to an experience in more detail and depicts a greater variety of characters who are involved in a plot constituted of a multiplicity of episodes, with greater scope in time and space; and that is concerned with real people in a 'stable society' (Northrop Frye) in the real world . . ." The novel is *long*, is *personal*, tells us something *new* and deals with *people* in the *real world*.

> "But we, on the contrary, who are accused of being theoreticians, we do not know what a novel, a true novel should be; we know only that the novel today will be what we make it, today, and that it is not our job to cultivate a resemblance to what it was yesterday, but to advance beyond."
> —ALAIN ROBBE-GRILLET

Stendhal famously said: *Un roman est un miroir se promene se long de la rue.* A novel is a mirror walking along the highway. (He also said, "One can acquire everything in solitude except character." Man is a social animal, and in the real world he must interact with others to be himself, to grow. Maybe this is also part of the definition of a novel. Maybe Arthur Miller's comment on the theater goes as well for novels: there are no characters, only relationships.) The novel reflects what it sees in the world around it. And Frank O'Connor, who took Stendhal's definition as the title of his book on the novel, *The Mirror in the Roadway*, wrote this: "To me a novel is something that's built around the character of time, the nature of time, and the effects that time has on events and characters. When I see a novel that's supposed to take place in twenty-four hours, I just wonder why the man padded out the short story." Could he be talking about *Ulysses?* A 783 page short story! What does that do to our nascent definition?

Well, with time in mind, let's go back and see where the novel came from. The novel emerged from and distinguished itself from the medieval European tradition of the romance. (Europeans still use the term *roman* to describe what we call a novel. *Romance* from the Vulgar Latin *romanice*, to write.) Like the epic and the saga from which it derived, the romance featured heroic and royal characters, exalted language, events remote in time, and was given to supernatural events and divine interventions.* The epic, the saga, and the romance depicted a nation's past, a nation's culture.

The novel had to await the invention of movable type (1436) and the invention of the bourgeoisie. The reading of a novel is a solitary experience. The correspondence is always one-to-one, writer to reader (Should this, in fact, be a part of our definition-in-progress? I think it should. The novel, then, is a *long, personal narrative that tells us something new, deals with people in the real world, and is intended for the single reader.* We'll get to revise the definition before we're done. But for now, 'twill serve.) In order for this intimate discourse to take place, the erstwhile novelist needed

*It has just occurred to us that fantasy and horror literature might fit the definition of a romance. But is that a distinction that we—as writers—need or want to make? In *The Art of Fiction*, John Gardner makes a distinction between the realistic story and the fable or tale. The realistic story convinces through verisimilitude, the tale (*romance* here) through the quality of voice and "various devices that distract the critical intelligence." The world of the tale is a moral world where what ought to happen does happen, a notion that may strike us desirable, but hardly realistic.

an educated reader with discretionary income and leisure time—a citizen of the new Renaissance Europe.

New citizen—new literature. Telling a story became the job of one person, not the culture.* Whereas the romance was national, the novel was local, was right here, right now, not long ago and far away. A novel always deals with the contemporaneous, even if it is set in the distant past (*The French Lieutenant's Woman*) or the future (*Brave New World*). The novel is based on facts, not faith, on the natural, not the supernatural, on human foibles, not superhuman heroics, on the probable, not the improbable. And the novel brought a certain freedom from chivalric stereotypes of plot and character as well. Where the romance and its precursors were conservative, customary, haughty, unambitious and representative, the novel, with other roots in folk tales, fabliaux, and ballads, was subversive, unfamiliar, humble, ambitious, and individualistic. The novel's reader said, Tell me about me; not, Tell me about my culture. The status of the individual, the common man, if you will, had been elevated with the novel. Elevated and celebrated. The hero was no longer above society, but a part of it. Romance was their story. The novel is ours! Not *man*, but *a man* or *a woman*.

Milan Kundera wrote, "All novels, of every age, are concerned with the enigma of the self." "Who am I?" is one of the fundamental questions on which the novel is based. (Not "Who are we?") "Why

---

*In the central Asian republic of Kyrgyzstan, the culture is still telling the story. The Kyrgyz epic poem *Manas* is being memorized by citizens today. And it is the longest epic poem in literature. At a half million lines, it is twenty times longer than the *Odyssey*. The poem—it *is* metrical—celebrates Manas's defeat of the Uigurs in AD 840 and the subsequent unification of the forty or so Kyrgyz tribes, who at the time inhabited Siberia. The Kyrgyz, a Turkic, nomadic people, are without a strong religious or political tradition and have been governed, if not conquered, by neighbors for centuries, most recently by the Soviets. Their nation is less than two decades old, and Manas has become the country's symbol of unity and pride.

am I?" is another. And, "Who are these other people?" Perhaps this means that there is a psychological element to all novels, as opposed to the mythological element to the epic. So let's amend our definition. *A novel is a long, personal narrative that tells us something new, that deals with people in the real world, with the problems of the individual in society, and is intended for the single reader.*

Here's what else the novel introduced to narrative literature, and it's a significant contribution: laughter. That funny, uncontrollable noise we make when we are surprised, taken off guard, when we are not being pretentious. The novel did not invent the comic story— Aristophanes may have— but the comic story had

> "The novel remains for me one of the few forms where we can record man's complexity and the strength and decency of his longings. Where we can describe, step by step, minute by minute, our not altogether unpleasant struggle to put ourselves into a viable and devout relationship to our beloved and mistaken world."
> —JOHN CHEEVER

been the province of dramatic art, folk tales, and song. Mikhail Bakhtin, the literary theorist, wrote that "laughter destroyed epic distance," brought us closer to the characters and to their world, which was our world.

There's a Yiddish expression, *"Mann tracht, Gott lought."* Man plans, God laughs. (Thomas à Kempis provides a Catholic version, "Man proposes, but God disposes.") The aphorism exemplifies the humor, such as it was, of the epic, the derisive laughter of the gods as they gaze down from Olympus on hapless man. ("As flies to wanton boys, are we to the gods.") Alexandre Dumas gazed back and said, "If God were suddenly condemned to live the life which He has inflicted on us, He would kill Himself." Not very funny, perhaps, but to the point of the hubristic and humanistic novel—man is more noble and heroic than the untroubled immortals.

Religion is the gods' story. Fiction is ours. And, alas, our story ends sadly—oblivion awaits. (Yes, we've had it before, Philip Larkin reminded us, but then it was going to end.) At the heart of humor, as at the heart of all art, as at the heart of truth and beauty, is suffering. We die. The joke's on us. All we can do, it seems, is laugh. Or rage. (And our rage only tickles the gods.) When we laugh, we take ourselves seriously. We admit to our flaws, foibles, and limits, just as we reject pretension, decorum, and the flattering fabrication that we were made in His image. We understand that He was made in ours. Laughter strips us bare, reveals the naked truth.

Laughter is an involuntary behavior that changes the way we feel for the better. We love to laugh. Humor, then, is a bond between the writer and the reader and can be a door to a character's heart, can endear a character to us. If Lafayette Proulx (in *Love Warps the Mind a Little*) had not been funny and self-deprecating, we might not have stayed around to find out what happened to him. Laughter forgives many sins. Laughter suggests that the character has some distance from himself, is aware of himself and the world on more than one level. This is the laughter that charms.

There is also the laughter that stings. Satire.* Satire is topical and aggressive. It is humor with an attitude. It attacks its target with ridicule, burlesque, and parody. Satire's malicious intent and

---

*Speaking of satire, here's Mark Twain on man and his God. "O Lord our God, help us tear their soldiers to bloody shreds with our shells; help us to cover their smiling fields with the pale forms of their patriot dead; help us to drown the thunder of the guns with the shrieks of their wounded, writhing in pain; help us to lay waste their humble homes with a hurricane of fire; help us to wring the hearts of their unoffending widows with unavailing grief; help us to turn them out roofless with their little children to wander unfriended the wastes of their desolated land in rags and hunger and thirst, sports of the sun flames of summer and the icy winds of winter, broken in spirit, worn with travail, imploring Thee for the refuge of the grave and denied it." Reminds us of Pascal's observation: "Men never do evil so completely and cheerfully as when they do it from religious conviction."

its stance of moral superiority can be dangerous to the fiction writer. This isn't something a writer in search of the truth can withstand for too long. You need to love the truth more than you hate the wrong. A novel ought not to preach. Leave that to the apologists for the divine.

That said, the novel gets its start with satire, with Rabelais and Cervantes. Rabelais' outrageous tales of the giants Gargantua and his son Pantagruel (1532–1562) were bold, coarse, and strident attacks on Scholasticism and the Church (Rabelais was a Benedictine priest) and were quickly banned by Rome and just as quickly devoured by the public. Cervantes' tale of the hidalgo Don Quixote (1605–1615) was a satire of the romances then in vogue in Spain and tells the story of what happens when a rather ordinary, if idealistic, fellow declares himself a knight-errant and sets off to perform chivalric tasks.

How does humor fit into our evolving definition of the novel? Do we have to laugh in every novel? No, though that might be nice. What became important with the advent of laughter had to do with the human condition, the all-too-human hero, the bond between writer and reader, and the promise of the story itself. So let's revise that definition-in-progress. *A novel is a long personal narrative that tells us something new, that deals with real people in the real world (at least one of whom the reader can identify with), and with the problems of the individual in society, and is intended to entertain a single reader and explore the truth of the human condition.* Whew!

All right, the novel is long. But length isn't everything. Does the novel have a shape?

Almost from its inception, the novel has pretended to be something else: a compilation of letters (*Clarissa*), a travelogue (*Gulliver's Travels*), a diary (*Robinson Crusoe*), journalism (*A Journal of the Plague Year*), and so on. The disguises, intentionally or not, emphasized the realness of the world of the story, the genuineness of its characters. Here we are in a specific time and place. The novel began in innovation, and the innovation continues (though some would argue that the novel is becoming more conventional as it ages due to the pressures of the marketplace). A novel can pretend to be a memoir (*The Catcher in the Rye*), or a biography (*The Moon and Sixpence*), an autobiography (*In Search of Lost Time*), a history (*War and Peace*), literary research (*Pale Fire*), and so on.

Like Proteus, a novel can take many shapes and can be nearly impossible to get a handle on. There are picaresque novels, confessional novels, novels of character, novels of manner, gothic novels, fantasy novels, religious novels, western novels, spy novels, love novels, romance novels, science-fiction novels, philosophical novels, novels of manners, and so on and on. The novel is the most plastic of literary arts. It has no form, but many forms. In fact, this chapter could be the start of a novel, couldn't it? The novel has no limits save that of language. Henry James said, "I should remind [the novelist] of the magnificence of the form that is open to him, which offers to sight so few restrictions and such innumerable opportunities. The other arts, in comparison, appear confined and hampered."

In your own novel you might incorporate poems, dreams, songs, plays, philosophical discussions, slapstick, answering machine messages, billboards, e-mails, movie scripts, memos, radio broadcasts, recipes. A dog might talk or think (Tolstoy's *Anna Karenina*), a dead girl might tell her story (Alice Sebold's *The Lovely Bones*), an angel might sleep in the shower (Anne Enright's *The Wig My Father Wore*). You might, in an otherwise English-language novel, have a chapter on love in French (Thomas Mann's *The Magic Mountain*). You might have a narrator who seems to be God, or at

> "The novel moves like all the arts. It's transforming itself all the time."
> —NATHALIE SARRAUTE

least a godlike editor, who intrudes on his story and speaks to the reader directly (Henry Fielding's *Tom Jones*) or a narrator who may not know what the truth is (Mark Twain's *Huckleberry Finn*). You might let several people relate the same story (William Faulkner's *The Sound and the Fury*). There's no telling what you might do. "All novels are experimental," Anthony Burgess said.

So now we know (or think we know) that a novel is limited only by the limits of language (and we

> "The novel is always pop art, and the novel is always dying. That's the only way it stays alive."
> —LESLIE FIEDLER

recall Wittgenstein's suggestion that the limits of *our* language are the limits of *our* world), and we know that the novel can be fashioned into a seemingly infinite variety of forms. All this freedom, we realize, can be daunting. If you can do anything, where do you start? Anywhere? How do you get from A to Z? Nothing hobbles the creative mind more than too much freedom. Every work of art has a structure. Structure (limits) ignites creativity. A touch of arbitrary form can be introduced to keep a narrator from wandering off course for too long, for example. Say, I'll start every chapter by bringing the narrator back to the present action, whatever that is. Limits (structure) yield intensity. That's why poets write sonnets. The composer Igor Stravinsky said, "The more constraints are imposed, the more one frees oneself of the chains that shackle the spirit . . . and the arbitrariness serves only to obtain precision of execution." The immature fictioneer holds dear the naive notion that the artist is an untrammeled spirit. The mature novelist knows that freedom's just another word for confinement and circumscription.

Tobias Smollett loosely defined the novel this way: "A novel is a large diffused picture, comprehending the characters of life disposed in different groups, and exhibited in various attitudes, for the purposes of an [sic] uniform plan, and general occurrence, to which every individual figure is subservient. But this plan cannot be executed with propriety, probability, or success, without a principal personage to attract the attention, unite the incidents, unwind the clue of the labyrinth, and at last close the scene by virtue of his own importance."

What Smollett means by "uniform plan" is plot. A plot is the architecture of action. Action, we know, can be internal or external. Action begins when the "principal personage" wants or needs something so intensely that he is motivated to act, to go after it, to struggle against obstacles to get it. The plot proceeds through this character's protracted struggle and ends when the "principal personage" gets what he wants (through his own efforts, no deus ex machina allowed) or fails. End of story. It's this plot that is the guiding design of the novel, that provides coherence and authenticity to the often sprawling world of the novel, to its many thematic concerns, and to the troubled lives of the characters. When we think of the form, the shape of a novel, we're thinking of the plot.

One last go at our definition:

A novel is a long personal narrative that tells us something new, that deals with real people in the real world (at least one of whom the reader can identify with), and deals with the problems of the individual in society through a causal sequence of events of a certain complexity, and is intended to entertain a single reader and explore the truth of the human condition.

———

LET'S AGREE TO that for now. It may turn out that you'll write a novel so revolutionary that we'll have to revise our definition. (But you will do so only if you try not to. There's a Zen to fiction writing.) So now that we know what a novel is, or at least we think we do for today, let's consider what it ought not to be. An honest novel is like an iceberg, in that only a small part of it exists above the surface, its overwhelming mass invisible. Every novel must ask the question *why*. Wright Morris said, "*What* happened and *where* is history—*how* and *why* it happened is fiction." The purpose of fiction is to say to us: This is what it's like to be a human being, and this is how it feels. *What* happens in a novel—the plot or superficial action, that which breaks the surface—is not as important as *why* it happens. If we don't get below the surface, we'll never understand the values and motivation of the characters, never experience the emotional bulk of the novel. We'll never come to know what it feels like to murder, to be falsely imprisoned, to be abandoned by your parents, to lose a child, and so on.

> "One writes the novel in order to know why one writes it. It is the same with life—you live not for some end, but in order to know why you live."
> —ALBERTO MORAVIA

There are novels that confront the human condition, that ask the questions *Why?* and *How?*, that get below the surface, as I said, and there are novels that attempt to escape that confrontation and its ramifications, and in doing so, remain superficial. This is the difference between what we might call "well-drawn" or "literary" novels and, for want of a better word, "escapist" novels. The difference between John Updike and Danielle Steele. Does the writer's reach exceed his grasp, or is he satisfied to plunge his hand into his worn top hat and pull out the same scruffy rabbits? How complex are the problems that the author confronts? Are they philosophical, emotional, and technical? Or are they simply mechanical—fitting new pegs into old holes? The kind of novel that confronts the human condition—let's agree to call it "responsible" fiction rather than "well-drawn." Fiction that understands that its job is to tell us who we are and what we're doing and doesn't shirk its duty.

The responsible novel is moral by its nature because it is a forthright and rigorous search for the truth of a character's life. It doesn't preach. It explores, it clarifies. It is not a summary or an argument. Like Zen, it doesn't explain, it indicates. It doesn't tell, it asks. Responsible fiction is subversive in that it asks us to question our lives and the status quo, and it doesn't let us get away with glib answers because it is relentless in trying to understand a truth. Escapist novels, on the other hand, reinforce our contentment, reassure us, and uphold received values.

You ought to be writing responsible novels. Don't waste your time with anything less. Understand that genre novels can be responsible novels. Commercial novels can be responsible novels. Literary novels generally are responsible novels, but they might not be. Just because a novel deals with a fundamental concern of life doesn't make it wonderful art. It may only be pretentious or didactic. Responsible fiction that is well crafted enables the reader to see herself and society in a new and clarifying light. The escapist novel, on the other hand, recycles thoughts, feelings, and behaviors. It is dishonest and derivative.

> "I've had to do a lot of potboiling in my career. Let me say this: if one stays absolutely sincere and honest towards a form—even when I'm writing this Antrobus nonsense, I'm writing it with a reverence to P. G. Wodehouse. I mean every form thoroughly exploited and honestly dealt with is not shameful. . . . I mean I put as much hard work into an Antrobus story, which may or may not come off, as I put into the next chapter of the book I have to get on with."
> —LAWRENCE DURRELL

Pascal said that the problem with humanity is that no one can sit alone in a quiet room. He was talking about distraction. He was talking about one's refusal or inability to deal with the self, with one's thoughts, emotions, and confusion. We'd rather someone, anyone, took our mind off all this anxiety and uncertainty. So we fill the quiet room with radios and stereos and TVs and DVDs that obliterate the silence. Or we chatter to our friends or family, or we pick up the telephone, or we access the Internet, and we fill up the empty, silent space. All of this keeps us from examining our lives, keeps us bewildered. And so does the escapist novel, which amounts to just one more distraction

And don't write formula novels. You can read a dozen pop novels, for example, and distill the ingredients, and pour the results into your literary kettle, and cook up a tasty, if unwholesome, novel, perhaps. But remember that if you follow a formula, you are closing yourself and your characters and your readers off from surprise, for one thing, from that wonderful moment of discovery, from insight and epiphany. You are probably not going to learn anything new about yourself or the world, and neither will the characters or the reader. A formula novel may fill you up, but it will not nourish.

And yes, you're right. Many readers are not interested in learning anything new. They want their worldviews confirmed. They want to be reassured, even if they are lied to. They want to forget that they are sealed in the cabin of a 767 at thirty-nine thousand feet. They want to be soothed. But is that your job? Don't we have ministers and therapists and pills to do that? You write to see what it is you have to say, not to repeat what you or someone else has already said. We're not here to do what's already been done. Or as Anaïs Nin put it: "The role of the writer is not to say what we can all say, but what we are unable to say."

So your novel is not escapist, not formulaic. What else should it not be? In *The Art of Fiction* John Gardner identifies what he calls three "faults of the soul," and I'll call them the three cardinal sins of fiction: sentimentality, frigidity, and mannerism. Let's take them one at a time.

The dictionary tells us that sentimentality is an "exaggerated insistence upon the claims of sentiment." It can also be an excess of emotion or an overindulgence in the "sweet and tender" emotions. Sentiment is *honest* emotion or feeling and is essential to fiction. (We want our readers to feel as well as to think—but we don't want to *tell* them how to feel or what to think.) Sentimentality, Gardner says, is "emotion or feeling that rings false" because it is achieved "by some form of cheating or exaggeration." The sentimental writer then tries to get some effect without due cause, to achieve emotion without having earned it. The writer wants us to cry, for example, about a character we don't know well enough to care about, or he appeals to stock responses or tries to make us cry with cheap melodrama. He writes, "Large, sorrowful tears poured down her pallid cheeks" instead of "She cried." His diction is fustian, blustery, bombastic, and intimidating. Sentimentality relies on the reader's emotional experience rather than on the experience the writer creates in the narrative.

> "You can be a weeper in your life, you can cry at the movies as it were, but you can't cry in your work because none of that is anything but destructive to fiction, which has got to be extremely cold."
> —GILBERT SORRENTINO

The writer's job is not to tell us how a character feels, but to enable us and to allow us to feel. Sentimental writing is intrusive, and that includes the unnecessary adverb, the gratuitous exclamation point, and what Gardner calls the "superdramatic" one-sentence paragraph. Sentimental writing is mawkish, maudlin, bathetic, mushy, schmaltzy, slushy, sloppy, drippy, insipid, corny, hokey, and affected. And while it may not be the death of a greeting card, it is the death of fiction. Life is complicated; sentimentality tries to simplify it. Emotions are ambivalent; sentimentality tries to impose certainty.

And, yes, you are right again: there are readers who crave sentimentality. They are people who do not embrace the complexity and seeming incomprehensibility of life, but flee from it. They want comfort and answers. They want what sentimentality offers: the simulacrum of sentiment without the mess of visceral emotion; the commendatory pat on the head, not the cathartic punch to the gut. They don't want to change or grow. They like the way they are.

Chekhov wrote this piece of advice: "When you depict sad or unlucky people, and want to touch the reader's heart, try to be colder—it gives their grief, as it were, a background, against which it stands out in greater relief." What Chekhov is urging is narrative restraint. Fiction is the art of abbreviation, suggestion, and connotation. Less is more. Do we ever need a description of violence like the one in the following? "Haversham squealed as the bullet split his doughy skin, punctured his chest, shattered a rib, burst his lung like an over-cooked sausage, and carried visceral cartilage and connective tissue with it as it exploded out his back. The bullet ricocheted off the radiator and lodged in the crucifix over the bedroom door. The organic soup that had been Haversham's guts puddled on the linoleum. Haversham dropped to the floor, and a fountain of blood gurgled and pulsed from his back, sending blood over his son's toy soldiers and his daughter's stick-figure drawing of the family." And so on. Manipulation of the character, the bullet, the reader. To what end? While I may have been trying for pathos, I achieved bathos.

Frigidity. Gardner writes, "The fault Longinus identified as 'fri-

> "Sentimental art, for instance, attempts to force preexistent emotions upon us. Instead of creating characters and events which will elicit special feelings unique to the text, sentimental art merely gestures toward stock characters and events whose accompanying emotions come on top. . . . An honest work generates its own power; a dishonest work tries to rob power from the cataracts of the given."
> —ANNIE DILLARD

gidity' occurs in fiction whenever the author reveals by some slip or self-regarding intrusion that he is less concerned about his characters than he ought to be—less concerned, that is, than any decent human being observing the situation would naturally be." Frigidity may be said to be a lack of imagination, a deficiency of nerve or spirit. The writer who will not take the time to revise, to find the precise verb as opposed to the serviceable verb, is frigid. When a responsible writer settles for writing a potboiling piece of novelese, he is frigid.

Frigidity characterizes the writer who presents serious material and then fails to carry through with it, to give it the attention it demands and deserves. If you are going to tell the story of a difficult divorce, then you are going to have to deal with all of the confusing and painful emotions that your characters will experience. You cannot change the story in midstream, as it were—the abandoned wife falls in love with the pool boy and lives happily ever after. You have a contract with the reader, and you ought not to violate it.

Mannerism is excessive or affected addiction to a distinctive manner of treatment, characterized by stylistic exaggeration. The mannered writer pays more attention to his own presence in the story than to that of the characters or the plot. His self-congratulatory stylistics detract from the story. This is the writer who says, watch what I can do. This is a writer with a thirst for originality, who has no idea what originality is. Being different is not being original. Originality is not affectation.

Not escapist, formulaic, sentimental, frigid, or mannered. What else? Well, we don't write novels to preach. We write novels humbly, knowing that we don't have the answer, will never have the answer, because, despite what some would have us believe, there are no answers. So the reason to examine our deeply felt moral beliefs is not so we can expound on them in our writing, but so we can explore them on the page, so that this exploration can increase our commitment to the work and can add texture to the world we are making up. The world of the novel must be as complicated, as chaotic, as compelling, as frustrating as the world we live in. We must have a faithfulness, John Berger says, to the ambiguity of life. The characters must live in that world and must interact with it if we are to believe in their humanity. Remember, fiction is not an escape from reality, but a plunge into it.

Don't write a novel thinking that ideas are more important than people, don't write a novel thinking you have knowledge that we benighted souls aren't privy to, and don't write a novel to grind a political axe. This is not to say that your novel cannot be political. In fact, it ought to be informed by political awareness, the awareness that people are dying every day as a consequence of politics. But it ought not represent the platform of a political party. If you have an urge to write for any of the above reasons, write an essay, a letter to the editor, a sermon, a TV script. Get yourself a blog and do your ranting there. But don't write a novel. You don't write novels knowing answers. You write novels to pose questions correctly and muddle your way toward meaning, knowing that you won't get it right this time, but you might learn a thing or two from your characters about yourself and about your place in the world.

Week 6:

What *About* What It's About?

In demanding from an artist a conscious attitude toward his
work you are right, but you are confusing two concepts:
the solution of a problem and the *correct posing of a question.*
Only the second is obligatory for an artist.
—Anton Chekhov

MOST DEFINITIONS OF *theme* that I've come across seem
unnecessarily reductive. Here's how Wikipedia begins its
entry: "In literature, a theme is a broad idea in a story, or a message
or a lesson conveyed by a work." I don't think so. While that sort of
generalization may be beneficial for a student or teacher or critic,
it's not very useful for a writer. A theme is not an idea or a message
or a sermon or a lesson or a moral or a hidden meaning. It's not a
motif, per se, not a topic, a plot, or a subject. *Subject* is what the
story is about. *Theme* is what about what the story's about. It's the
abstraction made flesh. The idea treated by action or by discourse
or by both. Not loneliness, in other words, but what you have to
say about that loneliness. *Theme* is where the writing meets the
world.

Academic discussions of novels are sometimes premised on the notion that a novelist has a statement of purpose and that that purpose results in the theme of the novel, as if the author has something to prove about the good and evil in life. In fact, a fiction writer has *nothing* to prove. A novel is not an argumentative essay. Folks thinking this way might say to a writer, "What's your novel about?" and the writer will want to say something like, "It's about ninety thousand words," but he doesn't because he wants to be sweet and does not want to be dismissed as an effete snob or a smartass.

Here's John Gardner on theme: "Theme is not imposed on the story but evoked from within it—initially an intuitive but finally an intellectual act on the part of the writer." I rather like the *OED*'s definition of *theme* as it pertains to music: "any one of the principal melodies or motives on a sonata, symphony, etc." and "a simple tune on which variations are constructed." What goes for music goes for narrative. Think of your themes—a novel has many—as the melodies you return to in the symphony that is your novel. You return to them and listen to how they play on the various instruments that are your characters and in various settings under diverse circumstances. You fiddle with them, alter the pitch and tone, see how they resonate.

The themes arise from your own values and concerns. In fact, let's stop right here a moment and explore what your values really are.

WORDS TO LIVE BY. You have to have vision of the world to write a novel, and you have to be in touch with that vision. You always want to write from a moral position, which is not a message, by the way, but a passionate caring inside of you. One moral position you must have as a fiction writer is that honesty is everything! Only the truth matters, even if it is a truth you're uncomfortable with. (And of course we should say "a truth" and not "the truth" because, as Blaise Pascal said, "There are truths on this side of the Pyrenees, which are falsehoods on the other." He also said, "We know the truth, not only by reason, but also by the heart.") So write about your moral beliefs. Start with what you think makes the world a better place or would make it so. What makes it a difficult place, if not for you, then for others? Is there evil in the world? Can you identify it? Give it a "local habitation and a name"? What can be done about it? By you? By all of us? Why does it exist? What are your prejudices? Don't defend them, don't deny them, just list them. You're not a bad person for having them—you're normal. Where do your prejudices come from? What keeps you up at night? Or should?

————

YOU DISCOVER YOUR themes as you write, and in doing so, you might not even be immediately aware of what you have set in motion. For instance, by simply opening your novel in a cemetery, you have introduced the themes of death, loss, grief, anguish, and what else? Mutability, certainly. You may not be interested in dealing with all of the above, but you now have the opportunity to do so. You have the thematic ore that you can mine. Your scene is set in a church? God and man, faith, spirituality. You open with a husband and wife out for a stroll—well, one of your themes is marriage. Your central character is sitting at her kitchen table drinking her morning coffee. You know what's coming, but she doesn't. Upstairs her husband is dressing for work and steeling himself for what he's about to do—he's going to tell the wife that he's leaving her. He rehearses in the mirror—that mirror says something, doesn't it? You wonder what the wife is doing in the calm before the storm. You look at her and see she's reading the paper. You look over her shoulder—the movie page. You like movies, too. You like her better already. You wonder if her favorite directors are yours. And you realize you have a theme—illusion and reality. You can work with that. So the story is bigger than you thought it was going to be and you only just started. Fabulous! And yes, he was upstairs *rehearsing* his farewell speech! An actor prepares. What is real and what is false? Are we always on stage? Are we always playing a role? Good stuff. Your character shuffles a deck of cards: fortune, luck, fate. He's on the open road: romance, adventure, a chance to start over somewhere. And so it goes.

I was 150 pages into my first novel, *Louisiana Power & Light*, and I realized that my central character, Billy Wayne Fontana, needed a job. He was no longer the orphan being raised by nuns. He was a married man, and he had responsibilities. My father worked at Massachusetts Electric back in Worcester, had ever since I can remember. If I had a question about the job, I could call Lefty. So Billy Wayne was hired at the local utility company, which I was stunned to remember was called Louisiana Power & Light! I put down my pen and pushed back from the table. What had I wrought? Power! Light! The metaphorical possibilities seemed endless. Just think about *light*. There are the electromagnetic waves that enable us to see; there's daylight, public attention, a way of considering a matter, a person who inspires, a distinguished person, a source of fire, one's opinions and choices, an expression of the eyes, a guiding spirit, something that provides information and clarification. I stopped writing and spent two weeks just researching all the possible connotations and denotations of the words *power* and *light*. Dictionaries, encyclopedias, field guides, books of quotations. (Albert Camus: "The truth, as the light, makes blind.") I had a rich controlling metaphor for the novel that fit the spiritual undertones of Billy Wayne's benighted life. His job was to bring the power and light to the citizens of Ouachita Parish—but does he? And is he plugged into the grid himself? Let's think about work a minute. Let's write.

> "Love, like death, is congenial to a novelist because it ends a book conveniently."
> —E. M. FORSTER

A JOB OF WORK. The Department of Labor's *Occupational Outlook Handbook* lists thousands of jobs, from A & P mechanics, folks who work on airplanes and avionics, to zoologists. Chances are that your central character will have one of them. And she might have chosen a career in, say, social work, because of her compassion for people living on the margins of society and because she wants to feel that she is making a real difference in people's lives. We see that we have a character to whom the themes of poverty, injustice, and fairness are crucial. She wants to empower the people she works with. We don't all get to do what we want to do, of course. Some of us take the jobs we can find because we have families to support and bills to pay. A job we're not happy with will also affect the way we see the world. A law enforcement officer might sour on the human condition after seeing the worst that life has to offer day after day. He may grow cynical, and maybe that cynicism extends to his personal relationships. And maybe he begins to behave in ways that he considers reprehensible but inevitable. We're looking for themes and how they might develop from occupations. Let's consider a professional job and see what we come up with. You can do this, of course, with any job.

A chiropractor. He has a holistic take on health and an open mind when it comes to alternative therapies. His idea is to prevent illness, make the patient aware of her body, so she can take charge of her own health. (He's an optimist, then, isn't he? A person who believes we can take charge of our lives. We don't need to depend on experts to tell us what to do. There's thematic material.) He makes a good living according to the *OOH* and is respected by his patients, but not by everyone. Plenty of people in the medical community and in general think

> *"Pick a theme and work it to exhaustion . . . the subject must be something you truly love or truly hate."*
> —DOROTHEA LANGE

that chiropractic is an unethical sham. He's hurt by this, of course, even though his patients swear by his work. What do I have to do to prove myself? That's it! In everything he does in life, our chiropractor is looking for approval, for respect. It's not enough to be successful and to do his job well; he also would like recognition for it— from other, more traditional medical professionals. His self-esteem is at stake. But

> "To produce a mighty book, you must choose a mighty theme. No great and enduring volume can ever be written on the flea, though many there be that have tried it."
> —HERMAN MELVILLE

why this need for approval from the very people who are most likely to deny it? He knows it goes back to his relationship with his father; nothing he did was ever quite good enough for his father the surgeon. Is he still fighting with his father, the father who died ten years ago? We found something, didn't we? And we've gotten to know our character, too.

So now take some jobs—maybe ones that you've performed— and write about the people who do those jobs and look for possible thematic material. Our jobs define us to ourselves and to the world. Our self-esteem depends on our work status, if not our performance. Unemployment is devastating. In urban America we tend to ask people we've just met what they do. And we don't mean when they get up in the morning or when they're alone at night. We mean job. And that's what we expect to hear. So let's see your character at work, talking about work. And see how that changes the story. Remember that our figures of speech, our metaphors, our way of looking at the world all come to some degree from our jobs. What a farmer thinks of the landscape may be different from what a miner thinks, a developer, or a factory worker.

THEME IS PART of what attracts you to your material, assuming that you're writing about what's important to you and what you don't understand. Theme is why the story is worth telling. It's why you care, and why your readers will. It may even be why you started writing the story in the first place, although I would advise against beginning with theme alone. It's still an idea until it's explored, and ideas, like all abstractions, are hard to hold on to. Theme may be the element that separates what we've agreed to call responsible fiction from pulp fiction. This is what I mean. A man murders a woman, say a pawnbroker, and maybe then kills her sister who wanders onto the scene of the crime. The man steals some money and jewelry and escapes. The bodies are found, and our serial character, Detective Emlen Hutson, is given the case to crack. He realizes this was no ordinary robbery because the most valuable items were left behind. He gathers up some few clues that lead him to an unemployed and shiftless fellow who seems to be hiding something. Hutson knows the man has motive and opportunity, but he has yet to discover the means. The women were killed with an axe, but no weapon has been found. Hutson sticks to this "person of interest" and eventually, through remarkable insight, good fortune, shrewd detection, and maybe a little rough stuff, he gets his man. You can write that story and keep us in suspense, but not too much suspense, since we know that in these sorts of mysteries or thrillers the bad guy must be punished and the serial hero must triumph. You can solve the crime and punish the wicked, but is that enough? You could, on the other hand, write *Crime and Punishment* as Dostoyevsky did, and in writing the novel just described, he explored

> "They say great themes make great novels . . . but what these young writers don't understand is that there is no greater theme than men and women."
> —JOHN O'HARA

the themes of nihilism, the Übermensch, urban poverty, alienation, and guilt, among others.

Theme emanates from character, not from plot. As I said, a novel may have multiple plots, but the central plot, the pivotal idea that the novel is exploring, may be identified by asking, What is the central character's problem? What does she want? What is she striving to attain or to avoid? Let's work with this notion.

FAIR AND BALANCED. I suppose only a news organization that is patently unfair and unbalanced would need to exclaim how fair and balanced it is. But let us use the phrase without the network's irony. Let's actually try to be impartial and equitable. In fiction your job is to be honest—what is the point in being otherwise? I've said this elsewhere, and I'll say it again: Perhaps the most cynical thing a fiction writer can do is to make a character a mouthpiece for his own political or philosophical ideas. (Save your diatribes for your blog!) If we, as readers, suspect that the character is just regurgitating the notions of the author, that a character is being manipulated to suit the plot or the dialectic, then we put down the book. A novel is not a polemic. It's not a lecture. Writing a novel without presenting a meaningful opposing force to the central character is propaganda. And it ought not to be propaganda. You are not smarter

> "If there were only one truth, you couldn't paint a hundred canvases on the same theme."
> —PABLO PICASSO

than your reader, after all. You have nothing to preach, but a world to explore. Right now write about something you are passionate about: a woman's right to choose, let's say, or the depravity of capital punishment or the need for universal health care or the injustice of the criminal justice system or the arrogance of power or corruption in government or whatever fuels your fire. Write about it in as much detail as you can and with as much intelligence and ardor as you can muster in just a short time. When you're finished, take the opposite position and argue just as intelligently and ardently as you first did—this might take you longer, of course. You've never considered that you could be wrong. But you are. When you've finished these two little rants, we should be able to read them and not be able to tell which side of the issue you are on—and that's what you want to do in your novel. (On this point, playwright Jonathan Tolins says, "Always write the character you disagree with stronger than the ones you agree with.") Subplots are good places to write about your concerns, and your character might, say, be outraged about untrammeled development of the land. And that character might labor, legally or illegally, to stop the development and the destruction of the environment. Well, someone in that novel probably ought to step up and confront our environmental activist with a reasonable and coherent argument in favor of development. The reader can and will decide where he stands—you don't need to tell him. Besides, the counterargument will make your character (and you) think harder about the issue. Fiction is a humbling business. We're not as smart as we thought we were, nor as we want to be. We do not stand on moral high ground. We're in the weeds like everyone else. We're not in the novel business to lecture or preach. We're in it to tell stories. Try giving your own political agenda to a nasty character and giving an opposing view to the real sweetheart in the drama.

LOCKED AWAY. What secret are you keeping from the world? What is it that you have done that you have told no one about? Why haven't you? Afraid? Ashamed? Write about it. This won't be easy. Explore the secret that you have locked away. It's buried treasure. Let it frighten you, hurt you, and make you squirm. Don't stop. When you've written all you can, read what you've written. You'll realize you're still not finished—write some more. Burn the pages if you need to.

A ROCK AND A HARD PLACE. Three more chances to consider your values and discover some themes.

1. E. M. Forster said, "If I had to choose between my country or my friend, I hope I would have the courage to choose my friend." Agree or disagree? Why?

2. All of us who grew up in a church were told what to believe. And if you went to a church-affiliated school as I did, you were told what to believe six days a week. Are there any things that you were told to believe by the church when you were a kid that you no longer believe in? What are they? Why don't you believe? What is belief? You who were raised as atheists and secular humanists may no longer hold with the tenets of those beliefs as well.

3. Here's a problem that's getting some attention in the news and in literary circles as I write. Thirty-one years ago, novelist Vladimir Nabokov died. Before he died he asked his son Dmitri to burn the manuscript of his last and incomplete novel, *The Original of Laura*. Dmitri put the manuscript in a bank vault as he struggled with what to do. Author John Banville evoked the name of Kafka, who asked his friend Max Brod to burn his manuscripts. Brod did no such thing and so saved some of the masterworks of the twentieth century. Publish the manuscript, Banville argues. Tom Stoppard, on the other hand, says that Nabokov wanted them burned, so burn them. What would you do? And why? If friends had listened to Virgil, we would not have the *Aeneid*, and that seems inconceivable.

Week 7:

What's That Voice I Hear?

Style is the perfection of point of view.
—*Richard Eberhart*

Y OU WRITE THE novel, but a narrator, whom you also create, tells the story. Your decision of who will tell the story is made early on in the novel-writing process, but not necessarily without trial and error. (My friend Lynne Kiele Bonasia wrote her first novel *Some Assembly Required* with two point-of-view characters, using first-person narration for one and third-person for the other. Not until she was finished, not until after the novel was accepted for publication, did she rethink her decision. The two points of view together now seemed a bit unsettling. She went back and changed the first-person narration to third and rewrote half the novel to make it work.)

Week seven would be a good time to consider the point-of-view decision, if you haven't already. You have all those characters in your notebook and all that potential trouble—now you need to know who will tell the reader what happened or what is happening. (And, yes, the narrator can be what scholar Wayne Booth calls an "implied author," the author's second self, as it were. This second self telling the story, Booth explains, "is usually a highly refined and selected version, wiser, more sensitive, more perceptive than any real man can be.") Selecting the narrator and establishing his or her voice is a critical decision that will affect every other element in the novel. Who is telling the story and at what distance from the characters and the action? Think of point of view as the vantage point where the reader stands to watch the story unfold. Is he right there on the battlefield or up yonder on the bluff looking safely down on the combatants? He can see a lot more from up there, but what can he feel? No point of view is better than another. They're just different, as we'll see.

You can have a character tell a story or you can have a storyteller who does not appear in the action, but who may, perhaps, intrude and editorialize, as does Henry Fielding's omniscient narrator in *Tom Jones*, who steps in to talk to his dear readers, to reassure us, to philosophize, and to expound on his story and his characters. Points of view have traditionally been categorized by person. We have *first-person* narrators, who *are* characters in the novel, and so have a stake in the outcome and in our understanding of the nature of the events. First-person narrators use the pronoun *I* when referring to themselves. Like this: "After my father died when I was twelve, my mother married Harvey Fahl-strom." *Second-person* narrators employ the pronoun *you* in telling the story, but not the "dear reader" *you* employed occasionally by an omniscient third-person narrator. This *you* is a character in the story or this *you* is a substitute for *I*. ("After your father died, etc.") We'll get back to this in a moment. *Third-person* narrators use the pronouns *he* and *she* when talking about their characters. You can think of them as characters who tell the story but aren't in it. "Clovis Coy can barely keep his

> "Every man mistakes the limits of his vision for the limits of the world."
> —ARTHUR SCHOPENHAUER

eyes open, and yet here he is driving his pickup on an empty two-lane desert highway in the dead of night."

SCARED STIFF. Before we go on, let's do a little writing exercise that'll address point of view and explicate at least one of the benefits to you as a writer of considering alternative viewpoints. First, make a list of ten people in your life who have frightened you. If you can't think of any, then you aren't thinking hard enough. Most of us could make a much longer list once we got started. Ready? Did you put yourself on that list? Dad? Mom? A teacher? A priest who called you a viper in the confessional when you told him you stole money from your mother's wallet? (Oh, wait! That was me.) Boss? Boyfriend or girlfriend? Babysitter? Now choose one of those people to write about. The further back into childhood you go, the better this might work. Maybe write about the person and event you feel the most energy around right now. The memory still scares you, perhaps. Now begin to tell the story of the time that person scared you. We want the event and the behaviors. Not a character sketch. We want scene. Show, don't tell. Use present tense. Use the vocabulary of the younger person you were. You understand only what that child would understand, and so on. Write that now. Be detailed. Get into your younger mind. One memory leads to the next. When you've finished that, begin to tell the story once again, this time from the point of view of the other character, the person who frightened you. Let that person tell his or her own side of the story. Use his diction, his patterns of speech, his thoughts, his feelings, and so on. Be honest. Put yourself in his shoes. Try to imagine what was going through his mind. What was his motivation? What was he feeling? When you've finished, consider the differences in the points of view. What did it feel like to write from the viewpoint of this frightening person? Every story is many stories. You learned something about this person you hadn't known. When you write your novel, and you're stuck because you don't know the character well enough, let her talk to you in first person in your notebook. You may be writing the novel in third person, but every character can speak to you in your notebook if you'll give him his voice and tell him you'll listen.

———

THIRD-PERSON NARRATORS are identified by the degree and manner of access the reader is afforded to the hearts and minds of the characters. (It's not necessary to remember the names of the various viewpoints, just so you understand what tools are available to you.) You could decide, for example, that your narrator will not get into the consciousnesses of any of the characters. (You'd be giving up the chance to do one of the things that fiction does best— entering the heads and souls of the characters, seeing through their eyes, detailing their rich interior lives. But it's your choice.) That's called *third-person objective* or dramatic point of view or the fly-on-the-wall point of view or the camera-lens point of view. It is fiction that approaches theater. (Maybe I should write a play! you think.) The narrator reports what the camera would report in a rather distant and impersonal way without comment or interpretation. (Of course, the very choice of what to report can be thought of as a subjective editorial decision.) What you see and hear is what you get.

Or you might decide that your narrator will get into the mind of the central character only. This is called *third-person limited*. We get the thoughts and feelings of the central character, but no one else's. Or you might shift points of view from character to character in what's called *multiple selective omniscience*. Or go all the way and use an *omniscient* narrator who knows all, but can't tell all. In fact there is not really any completely omniscient narrator—her story might never end.

IN OTHER WORDS . . . Take the opening paragraph of several stories or novels that you like and rewrite them from different points of view. It's somewhat easy to shift from first person or second to third-person limited, or vice versa, you'll see, but more difficult to shift from first or second to third-person objective. As you rewrite, consider what is gained, what is surrendered with each version. Before you start, here's an example using Flannery O'Connor's "A Good Man Is Hard to Find."

> The grandmother didn't want to go to Florida. She wanted to visit some of her connections in east Tennessee and she was seizing every chance to change Bailey's mind. Bailey was the son she lived with, her only boy. He was sitting on the edge of his chair at the table bent over the orange sports section of the *Journal*. "Now look here, Bailey," she said, "see here, read this," and she stood with one hand on her thin hip and the other rattling the newspaper at his bald head.

That's Miss O'Connor's opening. Third person, limited to the grandmother's mind. Here's a version in second person: *You didn't want to go to Florida. You wanted to visit some of your connections in east Tennessee, and you were seizing every chance to change Bailey's mind. Bailey was the son you lived with, your only boy,* and so on. Change the *you* to *I* here and you have first-person.

Now third-person objective: *The grandmother stood in the middle of the kitchen with one hand on her thin hip and the other rattling the newspaper at Bailey's bald head. Bailey was sitting at the edge of his chair at the table bent over the orange sports section of the* Journal. *"Now look here, Bailey," she said, "see here, read this."*

"Momma, we're not going to Tennessee. We're going to Florida."

And now third-person multiple selective omniscience: *The grandmother didn't want to go to Florida. She wanted to visit some of her connections in east Tennessee and she was seizing every chance to change Bailey's mind. Bailey was the son she lived with, her only boy. He was sitting at the edge of his chair at the table bent over the orange sports section of the* Journal *trying to tune his momma out. He was sick to death of all this talk of her Tennessee kin that he knew had all long since died.* Now it's your turn. Just take an opening of any story you admire and play with point of view. When you've finished, consider why it was that the author made the point-of-view decision that she did.

THERE ARE AT least a couple of ways to write a story in first person. There is the narrator who seems to create a story as it is happening (let's call him the informant), and there is the reminiscent narrator. The former has a single *I*. ("In walks these three girls in nothing but bathing suits. I'm in the third checkout slot, with my back to the door, so I don't see them until they're over by the bread.")* The latter has two *I*'s, the kid in the checkout slot, in this case, and the kid grown up remembering the afternoon he would lose his first job. ("It all started when I was sixteen and got my first summer job working the register at the A & P. I'm in the third checkout slot with my back to door, so I don't see them at first, when in walks . . .") First-person narrators have the benefit of being eyewitnesses to the events. They were there and know what happened. So we should trust them, right? Well, maybe not. Perhaps you've heard the Russian saying, "He lies like an eyewitness." They are actors in the drama and may be trustworthy or may be unreliable through mendacity, naïveté, or insanity. Since she is a character, we don't have to believe everything she tells us. Is she being honest? Does she have an axe to grind? Does she understand

*This from John Updike's "A & P."

what happened to her? How unreliable is she? Why is she telling us the story? To gain sympathy for herself? Would that be honest? (We don't ask these questions of a third-person narrator.) If you want your narrator to not be completely trustworthy, you must let the reader know early on. How do you know or even suspect (which will have the same effect here) that someone is lying to you? The story sounds rehearsed, maybe. She's exaggerating. She says one thing, but we see another. (If someone just said this to you, "Granted: I am an inmate of a mental hospital; my keeper is watching me, he never lets me out of his sight; there's a peephole in the door, and my keeper's eye is the shade of brown that can never see through a blue-eyed type like me,"* would you trust the story he was about to tell? You might admire the inmate's full disclosure but wonder about his social skills, perhaps. Let's try out these viewpoints.

First-person informant: "Julian's not sure what he's looking for, but he says he'll know it when he feels it. Julian's my father and we've been living here in Cabin 7 at the Harbor Lights Motor Inn since early May. These three months in Provincetown are the longest time we've stayed in one place in quite a while. We came here after a rainy month at the Silver Horseshoe Motel in Memphis, Tennessee. Before that Julian was a sign painter in Eureka, Kansas. We lived at Falconetti's Motor Lodge until a twister lifted off the building's corrugated roof. Julian and I have traveled through forty-five states and have lived in seventeen in just the last four years."† The narrator is a twelve-year-old girl named Chloe, we'll find out, and she's about had it with the nomadic life. She's pleading her case to us, we'll see, perhaps as rehearsal to pleading with her dad. Chloe, our informant, has a single *I*. This is who I am, and this is what's going on in my life.

---

*And this from Günter Grass's *The Tin Drum*.

†From my story "People That Dream, Whales That Dance."

First-person reminiscent: The next way to tell a first-person story is with a reflective narrator, and this narrator has two *I*'s, the person, in this case the young girl, who experienced the event and the older, wiser, we assume, person who tells the story. Here's how the adult Chloe might begin her story: "Many years ago when I was twelve I lived from place to place with my father Julian, who had lost his wife, my mother, and who was not sure just what he was looking for, but he said he'd know it when he felt it." And so on. Chloe now shares some of the advantages of the omniscient narrator in that she knows how the story will turn out before she begins. She knows the narrative future, as it were, knows what is significant and what is not.

First-person unreliable: Probably this shouldn't be a separate category at all. The reliability of every first-person narrator is in question, and the narrator has to earn our trust. We talked about this a few moments ago. Here's how another, less forthright, Chloe might begin her story: "You would not believe the hell my maniac father put me through when I was a kid. Mom left us because he was a total loser, and then he decides we'll be gypsies. Because why? Hell if I know." And if she began like this we might say, Hold on! Why is she beating up her dad like that? That attitude does not sound like honesty. Is she trying to hurt her dad or excuse her own sorry present circumstances, whatever they may be? We will read on suspending our credulity, and we might learn that Chloe is in pain and is lashing out at Dad because she doesn't know what else to do, and when she gets to be straightforward enough to realize this, we'll start to believe what she's saying.

Second-person point of view: In this case *you*, as I said, is not the reader addressed. *You* is a character in the drama, making the viewpoint a lot like first person. There are a couple of ways second person works, which I'll call *The I-Substitute* and *The Reader as Character* (nice trick if you can pull it off).

The I-Substitute: "Julian's not sure what he's looking for, but he says he'll know it when he feels it. Julian's your father and both of you have been living here in Cabin 7 at the Harbor Lights Motor Inn since early May. These three months in Provincetown are the longest time you've stayed in one place in quite a while. You came here after a rainy month at the Silver Horseshoe Motel in Memphis, Tennessee. Before that Julian was a sign painter in Eureka, Kansas. You lived at Falconetti's Motor Lodge until a twister lifted off the building's corrugated roof. Julian and you have traveled through forty-five states and have lived in seventeen in just the last four years." This is a not very subtly disguised first-person point of view. It's Chloe we're hearing. She's distancing herself from herself and from the reader, moving her ego offstage, asking us to imagine what it might be like to be in her situation. Perhaps the emotions involved in telling us the story are too raw, the events she'll relate too painful to admit in first-person. She would not be able to confess, as it were, if she thought we recognized who she was.

> "The whole intricate question of method in the craft of fiction, I take to be governed by the question of point of view—the question of the relation in which the narrator stands to the story."
> —PERCY LUBBOCK

The Reader as Character: "Let's imagine that your wife has just left you and run off with some cowboy singer, and you have a daughter, call her Chloe, and you are so distraught and unbalanced that you don't know what you'll do, but you pack the car, lock up the apartment, and hit the road. When Chloe asks you where you're headed, you tell her you don't know, but you'll know it when you feel it." Here the reader is asked to imagine himself a character in the story. This can draw the reader into the story if you do it right or put him off if you don't. This story deals in speculation, with what might be but is not, and since it's rooted in our common desire to start over, to get a second chance, to find redemption, you hope the reader will enjoy the opportunity to pretend to be this guy whose wife ran off, the guy who takes his daughter and looks for a new life.

Whichever way you do it, second-person point of view is always unconventional and always catches the reader's attention, and that's what you want, isn't it? But it can also seem gimmicky or distracting after a while and works best, I think, for shorter stretches, but Tom Robbins's *Half Asleep in Frog Pajamas* and Jay McInerney's *Bright Lights, Big City* are successful second-person novels. And both are written in present tense, which seems to work naturally with the viewpoint. On to third-person.

Third-person limited (sometimes called selective omniscience or third-person attached): Here we'll get Chloe's thoughts and feelings, but not Julian's and not anyone else's. If one of the benefits of first-person narration is intimacy and immediacy, we get that as well in third-person limited. "Chloe's father Julian tells her he's not sure what he's looking for, but says he'll know it when he feels it. Chloe, who's twelve and has her mother's light blue eyes and her father's auburn hair, is thinking that she and Julian have been traveling long enough. She's tired. She wants to stay in one place for longer than three months. She wants friends she can keep." We're close to Chloe here, but the narrator can also see Chloe from the outside, can describe her looks, for example, and is not restricted to just her consciousness. We can get closer still to our character in a subdivision of third-person limited that Henry James called central intelligence.

> "I become the character I write about. When I write about a thief, I become one. . . . I become the character I write about and I bless the Latin poet Terence who said, 'Nothing human is absent to me.'"
> —CARSON McCULLERS

Central intelligence, or unified point of view: This has a lot in common with first-person and shares the same limitations. Only what the viewpoint character knows, sees, hears, feels, guesses at, and so on, can be told. So it can also be unreliable in the sense that our viewpoint character might be misinterpreting her world, let's say. We enter her mind only, and we stay there. The narrator seems to vanish. All the events of the story are filtered through her consciousness, and what's important in the story takes place in her mind. So here's Chloe again: "Chloe Marie Martel-McDermott, whose mother had abandoned her and Julian, Chloe's dad, left them for some bogus cowboy crooner, stares out the passenger window at the succession of look-alike motels along the highway. Are we still in Pennsylvania? She cracks the window. Smells like the ocean. Will this drive never end? She must have dozed off, but for how long? She isn't sure where they are or even what day it is or where Julian's driving them to or if these years on the road with her dad are a bad dream that's about to end. She puts her head against the window and feels the vibration of the car in her skull and in her teeth and she feels helpless." We get Chloe's thoughts, feelings, her confusion and her emotion. We get her diction, her adjectives. A third-person narrator might have written *ersatz* to describe the philandering cowboy, *indistinguishable* instead of *look-alike* to describe the motels.

Multiple selective omniscience: Third-person narration can and will, in this case, shift viewpoint from one character to another. If you're going to shift between or among characters, you ought to set that precedent early in your narrative. So we'll do it immediately in our example. The trick is not to confuse the reader about whose head we're in at any given moment. The narrator can also pull out of the minds of the characters and into his own consciousness to give us another take on the characters' behaviors. "The two of them, Chloe and her father Julian, stared straight ahead as Julian drove the Chevy on down Route 6A past a succession of indistinguish-able motels. Julian let the car follow his unfocused stare and tried to determine at just which moment his marriage to Chloe's mom began to fall apart, but all he kept seeing was the empty dresser drawers and the apologetic Post-it note on the bathroom mirror. Chloe tried to imagine what this motel they were headed for would look like. Harbor Lights Motor Inn. Well, you ought to be able to see the ocean from there. She saw a little kitchenette with a two-burner stove in need of a good scrubbing and one of those adorable little refrigerators. She looked at Julian, at his gloomy face, and she could almost read his addled mind."

Third-person omniscient: The narrator as pansophical God. The almighty voice of the classical epic. He can know anything about any character, can be in any place at any time in the present, the past, or the future. You get the idea. Here we go: "The two of them, Chloe and her father Julian, stared straight ahead as Julian drove the Chevy down Route 6A past a succession of indis-tinguishable motels toward Provincetown. Julian let the car follow his unfocused stare and tried to determine at just which moment his marriage to Chloe's mom

> *"The object of the novelist is to keep the reader entirely oblivious of the fact that the author exists— even of the fact that he is reading a book. This is of course not possible to the bitter end, but a reader can be rendered very engrossed, and the nearer you can come to making him entirely insensitive to his surroundings, the more you will have succeeded."*
> —FORD MADOX FORD

began to fall apart, but all he kept seeing was the empty dresser drawers and the apologetic Post-it note on the bathroom mirror. The note was a lie, but he didn't know that yet. She had never loved him is what she would have written, except that her boyfriend Elwood said that would be unduly vicious. Elwood liked to think of himself as a stand-up guy. Chloe was hoping that P-town would be their last stop. She was sick and tired of the nomadic life." A problem with the omniscient narrator is focus, as you might have guessed. He can tell all, but he shouldn't. He may tend to wander and to digress, and your job is to rein him in. Appear to digress, but don't. And as with a first-person narrator, he has a tendency to tell and not to show. He's an authority, and so he assumes our trust. We'll believe what he says. He forgets that scenes do more than earn our trust. Scenes involve us emotionally in the story. Scene is where we witness, where we empathize, where we become viscerally involved in the *action*.

Third-person objective: In this point of view we are always outside the character, remember. It's like watching a play. So: Julian said, "I don't know exactly what I'm looking for, Chloe, but I'll know it when I feel it."

"Don't I have a say in any of this?"

Julian tapped his finger on the steering wheel. He looked at his daughter. Her head rested against the window.

She said, "I hope you find it in Provincetown."

Julian squeezed her shoulder. "So do I."

"Does the Harbor Lights Motor Inn have a kitchenette?"

"It does. We have our own little cabin."

Chloe sat up. "It'll be like our house. That's sweet!"

Julian smiled and turned his attention back to the traffic.

Chloe said, "You're thinking about her again, aren't you?"

In this dramatic viewpoint you must illustrate thought and emotion through speech, through imagery, through tone, and through behavior in the way that a screenwriter must (though you don't have the blessing of music to help you insinuate tone), the way that a playwright or actor must. What does your character do when she's sad? Maybe she leans her head against a car window and seems to deflate. Maybe fog has settled on the highway, and your characters are trying to make a trip though they can only see as far ahead as the taillights of the car in front of them.

Before we leave point of view, we'll spend a minute on a couple of other techniques primarily associated with third-person narrators: interior monologue (direct and indirect) and stream of consciousness. Both are methods of getting deeper into a character's thoughts and feelings by rendering them as they pour from the mind of the character.

Interior monologue: Here we aren't told what the character thought, so much as we experience the thought itself. We are in the mind of the character.

"Chloe wondered when this was ever going to end, this dreadful moving from town to town. Why won't Julian stop? She's going to have to put her foot down, that's all, going to have to say, This is it, I'm fed up. She'll tell him tonight at the Harbor Lights, tell him she's tired, she wants some friends.

> "A novelist can shift his view point if it comes off, and it came off in Dickens and Tolstoy. Indeed this power to expand and contract perception (of which the shifting point of view is a symptom), this right to intermittent knowledge:—I find it one of the great advantages of the novel-form, and it has a parallel in our perception of life."
> —E. M. FORSTER

Dad, I need friends that I can keep. I don't always want to be the new girl in class. Do you know how hard that is? No, you don't, do you? And I'll cry if I have to, if that's what it takes to wake him up." That last sentence "And I'll cry . . ." is her actual thought. There is no intermediary processing the information for us. This is *direct* interior monologue. But earlier, in ". . . tell him she's tired, she wants some friends," she did not actually think *she*; she thought *I*: "I want some friends." This is *indirect* interior monologue, and it allows the narrator to be both inside and outside the character. We get the thoughts still, but not as unequivocally.

Stream of consciousness: Not all of our thoughts are as ordered, as well-mannered, and as understandable as they appear to be in interior monologue. Stream of consciousness tries to record the flow of the countless, incessant, meandering associations and impressions that impinge on the consciousness and rational thoughts of a character. Unlike direct interior monologue, which it resembles, stream of consciousness is not as solicitous of the reader and does not try to edit, arrange, or clarify the thoughts. Like this: "Chloe rested her head against the window. Where's my postcard collection? Must be in the trunk. Or in the backseat under the afghan. Mom's afghan, all we got left of her. Can't even remember her face. What if I left them in Pennsylvania? She looked at her father behind the wheel. Daddy, Daddy, tell me a story, a story with a happy ending. The mother comes home and hugs her daughter and they all live happily ever after. But what if she comes home and we're not there? Chloe grabs the afghan from the backseat and covers herself with it. She smells her mom. And if that mockingbird don't sing, Momma's gonna buy you a diamond ring."

FROM WHERE I'M STANDING . . . Now that we've tried it, it's your turn. Take an opening paragraph of a story or chapter of your own and try out the various points of view.

THE END OF THE AFFAIR. A marriage of long standing has just ended. Why? What happened? How did love turn to . . . indifference? Surely not hate. Let her tell the story of the breakup and the divorce. And then let him. Now let's say they have a child. Let the child tell his version of the endgame.

DO YOU SEE WHAT I SEE? Three people observe the identical landscape, let's say they're on a wooded hill and they're looking down on a meadow, a brook, a farmhouse, a barn, and a forest beyond. Let each of them describe what they see, hear, smell. The first person is dying, but don't tell us he or she is dying. The second person is pregnant, but don't tell us that. The third person is a landscape painter.

TRANSGENDER. I've heard students claim that a man can never and should never write from the point of view of a woman (and vice versa, of course). I mention Emma Bovary and Anna Karenina. I've heard them say that a white American male has no right to set a story in Haiti, let's say, or France, for that matter. We ought only be able to write about our own culture, and that culture ought to be defined as narrowly as possible. These are students, writers, who seem tragically lacking in imagination, and I guess what's going on is that they figure since they're trapped in their own small world of classrooms and parties and weekend movies that everyone else ought to be as well. *Trapped,* of course, is not the verb they'd choose, I'm sure. They are unable, unwilling, and uninterested in empathizing with others. They're ~~doomed~~ destined to write lyrical poetry and contemplative essays. Not that there's anything wrong with that. At any rate, our job as storytellers, our privilege as fiction writers, is to imagine and inhabit the lives of others. So let's do it now. Write a two-page or longer monologue by a character of the opposite gender. Last night he or she learned some terrible news. What was it? Let the character tell you.

WE GET LETTERS. Most narrators talk directly to a reader, but that doesn't have to be the case. The narrator might be talking to someone else, and we overhear it. A novel might be a series of diary entries, secrets that we become privy to. Many early novels like Samuel Richardson's *Pamela,* his *Clarissa,* and Pierre Choderlos de Laclos's *Les Liaisons Dangereuses* were written as a series of letters. More recently Steve Almond and Julianna Baggott wrote *Which*

Brings Me to You, a novel in the form of letters between erstwhile lovers. And that's what you can do now. The lovers are separated by miles and by what else? He longs to be with her and she with him. Let her write to him about the depth of her love and the pain of her loneliness. Let him answer. If you want to, let the letters be an e-mail exchange.

Weeks 8-11:
This Blessed Plot

Man is eminently a storyteller. His search for a purpose, a
cause, an ideal, a mission and the like is largely a search for a
plot and a pattern in the development of his life story—a story
that is basically without meaning or pattern.
—*Eric Hoffer*

W E'VE GOT THREE weeks to begin our work on this plot business. We don't know where we're going yet, so what's the
hurry? We talked about plot earlier and about how we might stir
a plot into motion. Just a little reiteration before we proceed. Plot
has a beginning, a middle, and an end, Aristotle told us. Setup,
buildup, payoff. Think of plot as a completed process of change.
From "General Principles of the Tragic Plot" (in *Poetics*): "We have
established, then, that tragedy is an imitation of an action which is
complete and whole and has some magnitude . . . 'Whole' is that
which has a beginning, middle, and end. 'Beginning' is that which
does not necessarily follow on something else, but after it something else naturally is or happens; 'end' the other way round, is that
which naturally follows on something else, either necessarily or
for the most part, but nothing else after it; and 'middle' that which

naturally follows on something else and something else on it. So then, well-constructed plots should neither begin nor end at any chance point but follow the guidelines just laid down." Complex plots, the best plots, he said, proceed through a series of reversals and recognitions. A reversal is a change in a situation to its opposite. (The messenger from Corinth tries to allay Oedipus's fear of marrying his mother by telling him who he really is. The message produces the opposite effect.) A recognition is a change from ignorance to knowledge. (Oedipus now understands the terrible truth that he had struggled to learn.) There's a visual depiction of Aristotle's notion of plot called *Aristotle's Incline* that I first saw in *The Weekend Novelist* by Robert J. Ray and that looks like this:

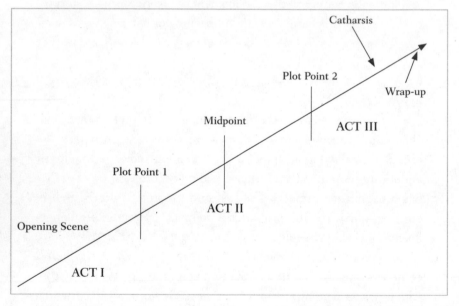

That depiction resembles the one that Syd Field developed (adapted?) for his screenplay paradigm in *Screenplay: the Foundations of Screenwriting* and *The Screenwriter's Workbook*, only Field's illustration is uninclined.

In *Aspects of the Novel*, E. M. Forster wrote: "Let us define a plot. We have defined story as a narrative of events arranged in their time-sequence. A plot is also a narrative of events, the emphasis falling on causality. 'The king died and then the queen died,' is a story. 'The king died, and then the queen died of grief,' is a plot." Plot, then, is a causal, not a chronological sequence of events. It's not just one thing after another. The reader has the comfort of knowing that there will be a resolution to the central character's problem. John le Carré would later use this example: "'The cat sat on the mat' is not a story. 'The cat sat on the dog's mat' is." Conflict! Looming trouble.

John Gardner, in *The Art of Fiction*, and I'm paraphrasing and annotating here, wrote that every plot was the same plot. A central character wants something, and wants it intensely, goes after it despite opposition (conflict), and as a result of a struggle comes to a win or a loss. You have one central character and only one. She wants something intensely, and it is this intensity that will motivate her to act. No passive central characters. She struggles to achieve her goal. (And you're seeing to it that her struggle is as difficult as possible.) Struggle implies a protracted effort. It can't be too easy for your character to get what she wants. And as a result of her struggle (and not as a result of an outside force—no deus ex machina) she gets what she wants or does not. And she is a different person now than she was at the start. Plot is what the character does to get what she wants. Let's write.

TRUE ROMANCE. Earlier this week I saw a frame from a romance comic book on the Internet. (I think it may have been from an essay on modern love in *Harper's*.) A young woman, blond and blue-eyed, stares at a photograph, also in a frame. Her fingernails, lips, and diamond-shaped earrings match the red of the drapes behind her and the red of the picture frame. Her brow is handsomely furrowed, her black eyebrows dip in dismay; the fingers of her left hand rest on her cheek. Beyond her, through the window, a driving rain suggests a storm of tears and sorrow. She stares at the picture and thinks, "So, you're *NOT* Mr. Perfect, Brad . . . but *MARRIAGE* means more to me than love *EVER* could!" We have our trouble; let's find our story.

You've got a central character, let's call her Inge, and she has trouble in her life. She doesn't love Brad. It would seem that she's about to make what we might consider a tragic mistake. What Inge wants is to be married. Write a plot summary of what might be her story. Ask yourself why she considers marriage more important than love. (Is she pregnant? Is there another man she does love? A woman?) Let her tell you why. Why does she so desperately want to be married, and why now, and why to this man she may like but not love? If what she wants is to be married, then it ought to be difficult for her to marry—she struggles with her own self-doubt and against the advice of friends who tell her she's being foolish. Brad gets cold feet.

> *"Writing a plot summary makes the writing of the actual book a needless extravagance."*
> —JORGE LUIS BORGES

But maybe you think that the real story begins after the marriage, maybe on the honeymoon, when she begins to regret her decision. If that's the case, write about the marriage in trouble. She decides, perhaps, that though she is not in love, she will stay in the marriage. It's the honorable thing to do. And in order to stay she has to struggle against her own desperate loneliness, the temptations of other men, the cruelty or indifference of her husband (but do we want to make him so villainous?), the desiccation of her dreams. And just what were those dreams?

PLOT IS NOT imposed on a novel. So you probably don't want to begin writing with a plot outline in mind. Plot emanates from the desires, values, motivations, and behaviors of the characters. Plot is characters in action. This action must be motivated, of course, must be causally sequential, must be credible, and must be compelling. In his essay "Building Without Blueprints,"* The late Tony Hillerman said that he never outlined his novels because an outline was not possible or useful to him. He trusted in his imagination to guide him. All he needed to begin were these ingredients, and I quote (without quotation marks):

- A setting with which I am intimately familiar.

- A general idea of the nature of the mystery.

- A theme.

- One or two important characters.

Let's think about what Hillerman had to say here in terms of your own material. You've been writing now for nearly two months: you've generated a lot of material, and you're beginning to make some connections and to see some possibilities in these people and their world. So now let's focus on these four areas mentioned above and write about them.

MY WORLD AND WELCOME TO IT. Hillerman said you need to know your setting intimately. You may be setting your story in the place where you live now, and that will certainly make your job a bit easier. You may be creating a town that does not exist—so you have a lot of fascinating work to do. You get to be architect, town planner, landscaper, and civil engineer. In week five you wrote about the

*In *Writing Mysteries,* edited by Sue Grafton.

place where you grew up. Do the same thing here, but about the place where (and when) your novel is set. Think about the place where the character lives, where the action unfolds, and, of course, the time in which she lives there. How is this place different than any other place? What are the local rituals that make it unique? Think about language, vocabulary, dialect, and accent. Think about foods, think about the work people do. What are the annual events that everyone looks forward to? The schools, the architecture, the folkways. The town or neighborhood legends. Walk around the town or the neighborhood and put your five senses to work. Stop and talk to the people you find there. What do they think about living here? Think about the seasons, the light, the ground, the schools, the churches, the secret places your character goes to, her sacred places. Whatever your place, now is the time to get to know it even better than you do. What are the locations where you might set your scenes? Think about the places that are beautiful, that are ugly, that might be frightening to your characters, that you might use to affect the tone of your story.

THE GENERAL IDEA. Tony Hillerman wrote mysteries, and you might be writing a mystery as well. But let's expand his second ingredient to also include nonmystery novels: you want to have a general idea about the nature of the central character's struggle, of the story you're telling. So write about what you think you're doing. What is at the heart of your story? What made you excited to write about these particular people? Write about what your central character wants. Discover motivations you hadn't considered earlier or hadn't realized were there. Can you sum up your novel in a few sentences? Try to do that, not to reduce the novel to a capsule description, but to get an idea of where it's at right now. It's going to evolve and get much more complex and intriguing.

THE PRINCIPAL MELODY. Back in week six, you had a chance to write about theme, and you wrote about many because this is a novel, not a poem. But consider the central theme as you now see it. Write down what it is. Let's say it's *humiliation*, which is the "square root of sin," Carson McCullers says. Freewrite on humiliation for five minutes. (Of course, you'll do your own theme. Not humiliation, but redemption, maybe.) Just on the theme. Forget your characters for now, forget the plot and setting. Just the word and the concept. Don't think; let the words carry you where they will—you're tapping into the unconscious, the nonverbal mind. We have responses and opinions about everything, but we may not be aware (conscious) of them. Now consider all the possible meanings, the denotations and connotations of your theme. Go to the dictionary and the thesaurus, to the encyclopedia if appropriate. How do all these meaning apply to your novel?

THE PRINCIPAL PLAYERS. Consider your central character and another important character—his nemesis, his lover, whoever it is. Now spend some time getting to know these two better than you do—and you probably know a lot about them by now. Write about what you don't know. Find out their secrets. Pry. Coax. Discover. Let them talk to you. Interview their parents, friends, enemies. Not everyone holds the same opinion of your darlings as you do. We behave differently when we're with different people. We all take on many roles. We're son, father, uncle, friend, co-worker, intimate, husband, acquaintance, boss, and so on. Your job now is to examine your characters in every role they assume. And how do they feel about each other, if they even know about each other?

I AGREE WITH Hillerman, by the way. I don't outline. Outlines preclude discovery, it seems to me. How can you presume to know what's going to happen in your novel when you've only just met your central character and don't know him well enough yet to know what he'd do in any given situation? Your knowledge of the character will grow as you write. Be patient. And you won't know him well enough to know what your novel's about until you write through that first draft. At some point he's going to do something you didn't expect—now he's alive and breathing and no longer your puppet.

There's always a story we think we're going to write and the one we do write, and they are not the same. The story you write is better, is more textured, dramatic, and compelling. The story you thought you were going to write served its purpose by triggering the story you did write. The danger in outlining is that it may legitimize the ill-conceived story

> "But there is only one plot—things are not as they seem."
> —JIM THOMPSON

that you thought you were going to write. This is the MapQuest method of composition. It's safe, dependable, quick, and efficient. You won't get lost. You type in where you want to begin and where you want to end, and you click on *Get Directions,* and MapQuest prints out the whole route for you. No more thinking to do. No more wandering, no more wonderful discoveries. You follow the directions you asked for, and you *will* get to where you're going. But you will not be surprised, and the novel will not exceed your expectations.

The first draft of the novel, what we're doing in these twenty-six weeks, is an exploration. You invent characters and you wonder what they'll do. You watch them, and they surprise you, delight you, and maybe they shock you. You gather information, do research, and generate scenes. You write it all down with a temporary disregard for logic, transitions, and grammatical conventions. In the process, you learn that the story you set out to write is not as interesting as the one that has emerged on the page. The purpose of exploration is discovery, and what you discover in writing that first draft are character, structure, plot, theme, tone, and setting. In short, you begin to discover what it is you have to say about what it is you're writing about. Trust in the writing process. It may take you on tangents, lead you astray more than once—that's its purpose. It might cost you reams of paper and days of your time, but none of it is wasted.

Having said all that, I have to admit some people like to outline. If you're one of them, if outlining makes you feel more confident, then by all means outline—with this caveat: Don't be inflexible. In other words, know that you're going to have to revise your outline the same way you revise your sentences, paragraphs, chapters, and novel. That's just the first draft of the outline you have in your hands.

BACK IN 1936, FitzRoy Somerset, the Fourth Baron Raglan (who famously said, "Culture is everything that we do that monkeys don't"),* classified the journey of the mythical hero into twenty-two archetypal incidents in his book *The Hero.* He begins with the virgin birth and the royal father and ends with a mysterious death and an unburied body.† In 1949, Joseph Campbell wrote *The Hero*

---

*And less famously, but more wittily, said, "If, instead of saying that thieves will go to prison or liars to hell, we could make people think that stealing is as bad as going to a funeral in a coloured tie, or lying as bad as frying a sausage on the parlour fire, we should achieve a colossal reformation."

†Lord Raglan's archetypal incidents: (1) The hero's mother is a royal virgin and (2) his father's a king and (3) often a near relative of the mother, but (4) the circumstances of his conception are unusual, and (5) he is also reputed to be the son of a god. (6) At birth an attempt is made, usually by his father or maternal grandfather, to kill him, but (7) he is spirited away, and (8) reared by foster parents in a far country. (9) We are told nothing of his childhood, but (10) on reaching manhood he returns or goes to his future kingdom. (11) After a victory

with a Thousand Faces, and in it reduced and significantly altered Lord Raglan's stages of the hero's journey to seventeen. Campbell's interests were more psychological than Lord Raglan's. Christopher Vogler, a Hollywood producer, took Campbell's seventeen steps and reduced it to the following paragraph in a memo called "A Practical Guide to *The Hero with a Thousand Faces* by Joseph Campbell," which he distributed to screenwriters in his company, and which you can find online. Here it is (numbers added): (1) The hero is introduced in his ordinary world, where he receives (2) a call. (3) He is reluctant at first, but (4) is encouraged by a wise old man or woman to (5) cross the first threshold, (6) where he encounters tests and helpers. (7) He reaches the innermost cave, (8) where he endures the supreme ordeal. (9) He seizes the sword or the treasure (10) and is pursued on the road back to his world. (11) He is resurrected and transformed by his experience and (12) returns to his ordinary world with a treasure, boon, or elixir to benefit his world.

THE HERO'S JOURNEY. We're going to work with Vogler's summary of Campbell's distillation of Raglan, not by way of outlining your novel (you know how I feel) but to explore the potential in your novel and to begin to think ahead, to begin to consider possibilities and potential, to begin to see a shape.

1. What is the ordinary world of your hero? What does he do for a living? What does he do for pleasure? Who are his friends? What

---

over the king and/or giant, dragon, or wild beast, (12) he married a princess, often the daughter of his predecessor, and (13) becomes king. (14) For a time he reigns uneventfully and (15) prescribes laws (16) but later loses favor with the gods and/or his people and (17) is driven from the throne and the city, after which (18) he meets with a mysterious death, (19) often at the top of a hill. (20) His children, if any, do not succeed him. (21) His body is not buried, but nevertheless (22) he has many sepulchres.

are his tastes in movies, literature, TV, music, and so on? What are his habits and rituals? Take your time and write as much as you can. This exercise is going to take all week. Don't worry. Slow down. Your hero may have to leave this world to get what he wants, and you want him to miss it so much he has to come back.

2. What form does her call take? What is it or who is it that calls your hero to her adventure, to her quest? Who or what helps her identify her goal and begin her struggle to attain it? Is there a problem? A challenge? Your hero, let's say, works in middle management for an international corporation. The vice president of Peruvian operations has been kidnapped by left-wing guerrilla forces who demand a ransom. Your gal is asked to carry the cash into the jungle and exchange the money for the executive. She asks, Why me? They asked for you specifically, she's told.

3. The reluctant hero. In the above example, she hesitates. She's never been to the jungle. She's not getting paid enough. She doesn't know this guy. She thinks the company may have been exploiting Peruvian workers, and so on. She's got a boyfriend and they're getting serious. What are all the good reasons why your character is reluctant to pursue her goal? Your hero has a mad crush on a woman and doesn't know how he can live without her. But she'd never give him a second look, and anyway she's married. To his friend.

4. Encouragement from a sage or mentor. Some trusted family member, some old professor, the widow down the hall, the boss, the priest, someone gives your character the encouragement and the confidence to go ahead. What is the advice given? Maybe write this scene. "You know what, son, if you don't go after that girl, you'll regret it for the rest of your life."

5. The first threshold. Our gal arrives in a small town in the Peruvian Andes. She's overcome with altitude sickness. Nothing is familiar. She's disoriented. She holds tightly to that precious briefcase. The hotel manager says they've been expecting her. What is the first threshold in his quest that your character crosses? What

gives him the courage to do so? How has his world changed? Where is he? If your character is an agoraphobic who wants to live a normal life, who wants out of the prison of her home and her terror, then opening her door and walking out to the front porch represents the literal first threshold. And a very courageous one, at that.

6. Tests and helpers. What are the tests your character must pass? And as he passes each one, does he grow bolder? Who comes to your hero's aid? Our gal in Peru meets a dissolute CIA agent, who's going to give her the lay of the land. He carries a flask in his pocket. He's rude, crass. Or is that an act? Our agoraphobic finds a therapist who works with her. The therapist suffered the same disorder as a young woman. Or your love-struck young man is befriended by a friend of the beloved one, a friend who tells him the husband is abusive and philandering.

7. The innermost cave. Think Dante in the ninth circle of hell, Orpheus descending, think Theseus in the Labyrinth, think peril, darkness, and despair. (Christ, it is said in the Apostles' Creed, descended into hell, but his visit there has gone undramatized in scripture. Perhaps you could write that novel.) Everything is a stake. Where is this place of peril for your character? Describe in as much detail as you can. Show how unlike it is from the world where she comes from.

8. The supreme ordeal. Your hero endures. What is this ordeal? How does he do it? He faced the possibility of death, perhaps, or the annihilation of his dreams. What is this metaphorical beast she must defeat? Her own incomprehensible fear of people, perhaps. The trigger-happy guerrillas. He goes into his beloved's house and confronts the enraged and sociopathic husband and rescues her.

9. He takes something of value. Might there be something that your hero can acquire here that would prove helpful later on? Maybe it's simply the knowledge of how easily life can end. Maybe it's the mantra her therapist taught her to say when frightened.

Maybe it's a pistol that a snoring guard left in the open. Or was that intentional?

10. The long road home. The hero has what he wants, but he's not home yet. The crazy husband is on their trail. The guerrillas have a plan to ambush the woman, the agent, and the wounded vice president. Our recovering agoraphobic sees a woman hit by a car on the street. Just when you think it's over, it's not over. What are the further complications your hero might encounter? What else can go wrong?

11. Finally the hero emerges from the world of adventure. This is akin to a rebirth. And she is transformed. She is not the person who set off on this quest. What has changed for your character, both positively and negatively? His world will never be the same again—why?

12. What has he brought back with him? A bride? A sense of personal worth? Write about your character at the end of her struggle. Let her tell you what this all meant and what it did for her.

No novel is going to contain all of these steps so neatly, if at all. That's not your purpose here. You're just exploring the world of the novel and its possibilities, seeing where it might go, and more importantly learning about your central character as you write. That, and taking a look at the long haul. A novel demands a bit of complexity, and you're beginning to address that. By the way, if we were to diagram the hero's

> "With me it's story, story, story."
> —BERNARD MALAMUD

journey as plot it might look like the capital letter V, with the start of the story at the top left of the letter and the hero's descent on the downstroke to the nadir of the letter on the baseline, followed by the ascent, the return home along the upstroke to the top at the right. Back home, but in a different place and time.

SUBPLOTS. You know what your central character wants and why—or you think you do, and that's fine for now. It will certainly change as you write. Don't fret. That's normal. You have a place to start. The central character's struggle will define the arc of the novel. When he gets what he wants or doesn't, the novel's finished. But you have all of these other important characters in the novel and each one of them has an agenda, has something she desperately wants. Every novel is many stories. You focus on one, but you can explore the many. These are your subplots. (And, in fact, your central character may be the focus of his own subplot or two.) So now make a list of all of your important characters. Give each of them a page and ask the important narrative questions of each. What does he want? Why does he want it? What's stopping him from getting it? How will he struggle? Will he get what he wants or not? How has he changed? This will help you better understand your characters and what they want in terms of your central character. Let their struggles be dramatized as well, as long as they don't pull us further away from our central concern.

> "Passions spin the plot:
> we are betrayed by
> what is false within."
> —GEORGE MEREDITH

THE PARADIGM. The conventional paradigm for a Hollywood screenplay posits a three-act Aristotelian structure. Let's think of the novel as a screenplay for a moment. Act I is the setup. It introduces your characters, establishes the problem, the issues, the need, or the goal, gives the reader (in our case) the information she needs to know before the story proceeds. Act II, the buildup, develops the plot, the relationships, sets obstacles in the central character's way, and dramatizes his struggle. Act III, the payoff, resolves the story after perhaps intensifying the conflict and raising the stakes. Look back at the diagram of Aristotle's Incline. Near the end of the first act comes plot point 1. Here something happens in the novel that shifts the focus, ratchets up the tension, makes the problem even tougher than it had seemed. The plot point might be a speech, a behavior, an image, anything that moves the story along and sends the novel off in a new direction and into the second act. Then there's the midpoint. Here all may seem hopeless and lost. This is your central character's low point. And then plot point 2 near the end of Act II twists the plot again and sets up the third act and the resolution. Let's think about this a moment, understanding that your novel is not a screenplay and that all we're doing is trying to explore the potential of our characters and our world. Imagine the following scenes—drama not summary, showing not telling. The opening scene of your novel, the plot point scene at the end of Act I, the scene at the midpoint, the plot point scene at the end of Act II, and the final scene of your novel. Now take notes about each of those scenes. Where do they take place? Which characters are in the scene? Give us the sensual details of the setting and the people. What do they say, if they say anything? Now write the scenes.

THE PLOT THICKENS. Plot is the writer's organizing and unifying principle, her magnet to which all the other narrative elements attach. The characters need something to do, and the reader needs to know that this journey is purposeful, that he is headed somewhere. Plot is not a matter of choice. So let's see how you might let the requisite plot do your thinking for you and see how this consideration of plot will lead you to matters of characterization, tone, theme, setting, drama, and so on. So this is about how you as a writer might go ahead and think about your story and begin com-

> "The beginning of a plot is the prompting of desire."
> —CHRISTOPHER LEHMANN-HAUPT

posing it. We'll try to construct a first act, at any rate. We'll work from a given situation and then you can follow the model and work with your own characters and premise.

Kurt Vonnegut said, "Every character should want something, even if it's only a glass of water." So let's get our character wanting something right away. Something simple. He wants to sleep. (Probably not enough to drive an entire novel, but who knows? At least it gets us going. And maybe we'll learn that his physical fatigue is a metaphor for his emotional lassitude, and the sleep he's after is the big sleep.) He's dead tired.

> *"Amateurs wait for inspiration; the rest of us get to work."*
> —PHILIP ROTH

Remember the example sentence from the point-of-view chapter? "Clovis Coy can barely keep his eyes open, and yet here he is driving his pickup on an empty two-lane desert highway in the dead of night." Let's overstate the case a bit and agree that everything important in your novel should happen in scene and that nothing unimportant should happen in scene. That means that our opening will be in scene, of course. Just to emphasize the fatigue, we'll start the story with a stronger statement: "He's tired as a tombstone." And then the driving. And that new line also includes an ominous image that might, and probably should, resonate later. Death is in play as a theme. So we don't tell the reader that Clovis is driving, and he's tired, we show the pickup, the highway, and dramatize his fatigue. To do that, of course, we need to know everything we can about the truck and the landscape. We look around the cab. There's a radio and it's set to an AM station. What's he listening to? There are empty coffee cups on the floor, coins in the ashtray. A bolo tie with a silver Kokopelli clasp hangs from the rearview mirror. The highway is empty. We're in the desert Southwest, and there's not a lot to see at this time of night. Just that mesmerizing white line on the highway. His coffee is cold, the window is open to let in the air.

We know what Clovis wants—to sleep—and why he wants it—he's dead on his feet. We know this is a dangerous situation as well: fall asleep while you're driving, and it's all over. So there will be obstacles in Clovis's way; we'll put them there. And every time he tries to get what he wants, tries to sleep, we'll write a scene. So all we really need to do to get our novel going is to consider what he does next to try to sleep. Well, he sees a rest area and pulls over. He rests his head on the window frame. He dreams he's asleep in a bed. But here comes a state trooper who tells him to move on and won't listen to reason. This ain't a motel, he tells Clovis. What next?

He comes to a convenience store, the only thing open in this little town. Antelope, New Mexico. He gets himself a coffee and asks the guy on duty if he can sleep in his car in the lot. No, he can't. Boss's orders. I'll lose my job. The clerk tells Clovis about a motel down the road a few miles. Cut to the motel. There's a vacancy, thank God. Well, what will we find to complicate what would seem to be a solution to the struggle? Can't let it be this easy. The motel's infested with rats, so the manager leases a cat to Clovis. Just the smell of the cat will keep the vermin away, he says. So just as he's about to nod off, Clovis finds a nest of rats in the bed. What's next? He tries to sleep on a bench outside, but is awakened by a violent fight between a man and a woman in another room. He takes the cat and gets in the truck and drives. He names the cat Django. (Because that's your cat's name, and he's sleeping on the desk as you write. Put your cats in your novels.)

He's heading for home. Hasn't seen his mom in a dog's age. Maybe she's dying, and he wants to see her before she passes. (Aha! That tombstone.) Or maybe he's dying, and he's come home to be buried with his kin. There's still a lot we don't know, and some of that knowledge will change our story when we find out. But so far, so good. He falls asleep and dreams that he's driving and wakes up as the car rides off the shoulder onto the hardpan.

Clovis is scared. He figures now he'd better get himself a coffee, and so he pulls into an all-night diner. He gets coffee for himself and milk for the cat. He chats with the waitress. And maybe this is where we learn some of Clovis's backstory and the reason for the late-night drive. Clovis meets a man who says he could use a ride up the road. Clovis says sure. You can talk and keep me awake. In the next scene they're driving. And maybe this stranger presents us with the complication that twists the novel off into a new direction. Does he have a gun? Is he a lunatic? Does he invite Clovis to his house? Does he have a story we'd like to hear? Well, we'll find out before they reach the crest of the next hill.

Do the same thing with your novel. Just begin with what your character wants (and know why he wants it) and put some obstacles in his way and let him go try to get it. Every time he does something to achieve his goal, you write that scene. Take this as far as you can. You may not follow this path later, but you'll know a lot more about your character, and you may, in fact, use some of the scenes.

Week 12:

A Work in Progress

If the work weren't difficult, I'd die of boredom.
—William Gaddis

YOU'VE ALMOST REACHED the halfway point in writing the first competent draft of your novel, the draft that will generate the many fruitful revisions to follow and result in a finished novel you will be proud of. You've been writing like crazy, so take a moment now to catch your breath, to step away from the writing before you forge ahead. Now you can take a look at what you've done and what still needs to be done. (A pause right now will be refreshing, and you'll get a day or two away from your own work, so that when you go back to it, it'll seem that much fresher.) Now you get to assess the product and the process. But before you do that, let's read.

LEARNING FROM OTHER WRITERS. Your job before you read your notes and the pages of your novel-in-progress is to reread a novel by an author you admire. Maybe it's your favorite novel. It's the novel that made you want to be a writer in the first place. Maybe it's a model for the one you are working on. Read with a pen in your hand and take notes. About scenes, characterization, language, POV, pace, digressions. Keep a list of everything this writer did that you can do in your novel. When you finish reading, write down what you learned from the novel and what you will apply to your writing.

REFLECTION. Take a look once again at what you've done so far. Read what you've written with a pen in your hand and take notes. When I'm writing a novel, I like to organize the very messy work at least a little bit. I write longhand on writing tablets, so I keep the notes in file folders. You can do something similar on the computer if that's your preference. Each character gets a folder. And descriptions of the character go there. (I know where to look if on page three hundred I can't remember what color hair I gave my hero's daughter early in the novel.) Any of the exercises that deal with the character go there. Anything he might say or wear or dream about. When you consider your characters, you might ask yourself what you think of each of them. If you have nasty thoughts about some, then you might want to find something about them to admire. If you think this person is a saint, then look for her flaws.

> "The most essential gift for a good writer is a built-in, shock-proof shit detector."
> —ERNEST HEMINGWAY

I give each theme a folder. Each setting. Plot gets a folder, and later, each chapter will get a folder. You're taking notes as you read and you're consolidating and organizing all those notes. You begin to see how the elements begin to connect

> "What about the creative state? In it a man is taken out of himself. He lets down as it were a bucket into his subconscious, and draws up something which is normally beyond his reach."
> —E. M. FORSTER

with each other. Your brain is very good at making associations. In reading all of what you've written, you come upon some notes that you had forgotten, and now they are reinforced. You think about tone, scene, theme, time, setting, point of view, the title or possible titles, the prose style, the plot, and the subplots. There might be some ideas you had early on that don't seem to be panning out. They served their purpose and got you to the ideas that are more compelling. Get rid of those ideas now. (Put them in a folder of their own if you don't want to toss them. I call that folder "Extras.") Now that you see what you have, write about what you still need to do. Be as specific as you can be. You are outlining your tasks for the next fourteen weeks and for all the months of revision that will follow. You know

> "It's like making a movie: All sorts of accidental things will happen after you've set up the cameras. So you get lucky. Something will happen at the edge of the set and perhaps you start to go with that; you get some footage of that. You come into it accidentally. You set the story in motion, and as you're watching this thing begin, all these opportunities will show up."
> —KURT VONNEGUT

how long you have to complete the draft. Now you need to know what it is you must do in that time. Address all of the technical and aesthetic aspects of the novel: POV, pace, characterization, plot, description, etc. Look ahead, of course, and write down what it is you have yet to address or to accomplish. And when you think about plot, do the next exercise.

PROBLEMS, PROBLEMS. Ask yourself what else could possibly go wrong in your central character's life. Even the little things, like his car breaks down; he loses his health insurance; he has pains in his chest; his child is dealing dope; he broke his glasses, forgot his mother's birthday, any of the trouble you've had in your life or that you are afraid will happen to you or to someone you love. That's exactly what makes a plot compelling—things happen that you would not want your family to suffer through. There will be places in the novel for lots more distress. Don't forget the big problems too. Death in the family, divorce, infidelity, etc.

HANGING OUT. The idea here is just to hang out and have fun with your central character. Your relationship has been all business lately, and you're forgetting what you liked about her. So go back to your notebook and look for a situation that you haven't written about yet, a situation that you have no intention of putting in the novel, perhaps. Write the scene that doesn't belong because it has nothing to do with the story you're telling. The point is just to get reacquainted with your character(s) in a nonthreatening, nonwork setting. And then have lunch together and write about that. Talk about movies, about the other characters in the novel.

PROCESS IS OUR MOST IMPORTANT PRODUCT. In the long run, you want to be a writer more than you want to have written one book. Learning the creative process is more important than writing any single story or novel. You want to be able to do it again and again. To that end, think about what you've done in your, what, twelve weeks of work. Write a history of your novel-in-progress. When did the idea for the novel first occur to you? When did your central character appear? When did you know this was what you wanted to work on? What attracted you to the story? To the characters? How does the novel reflect your obsessions and concerns? If you don't feel totally engaged with the novel, do you know why? If you do, do you know why? Write

> *"Every thought tends to connect something with something else, to establish a relationship between things."*
> —L. S. VYGOTSKY

about your inspiration, about the novel's incubation (which may, in fact, be ongoing). What were your original ideas and how did they change? What has worked for you in the writing process and what has not? (Remember you are not only trying to write a novel; you are trying to learn *how* to write a novel, and to do that you need to pay attention to your own process. You are already working on all the novels you will ever write.) Remember when you felt stuck. How did you come unstuck? How do you feel right now about this novel? Write about that feeling.

THE SUM OF ITS PARTS: Write a one-sentence, one-paragraph synopsis of your novel as you now envision it. Cannot be more than a hundred words. This is what it's all about.

The Shape of Things to Come

Short-story writers are jewelers, sharpshooters, photographers, and jugglers. Novelists must be symphony composers, stage magicians, but above all, engineers and architects. Short-story writers can illuminate in a flash; they can hit-and-run. Novelists must create successions of mysteries and solutions, deploy chains of intrigants and cliff-hangers, develop momentum, sustain suspense, provide variation, and bring it all to a satisfying conclusion.

—*Jerome Stern*

As I begin this chapter, I know that I will have to solve the problem of how best to tell you what I want to tell you, and I'm not even sure what exactly it is I want to tell you. (Writing is solving problems, and in my case, at least, solving them slowly.) So in the course of writing the essay, I need to arrive at a clearer understanding of what it is I'm talking about when I talk about the structure of the novel. Maybe *structure* is not even the word I want. *Shape* might be better. *Fiction*, after all, comes from the Latin *fingere*, to shape. Maybe *configuration* would work—the arrangement of parts or elements in a particular form. The novel is the environment that you fashion to house and surround your characters, themes, and plot. A novel's power is its scope, and the scope needs a well-defined shape to keep it focused. Madison Smartt Bell called what I'm thinking of the *narrative design*: the structural, formal organization of all the elements present in a given narration. By *structure* (or whatever we eventually call it) I don't mean plot (which I've discussed elsewhere),* but something larger, which encompasses the plot and the point of view. Structure concerns time. Time is the dimension of change. Change is what a novel is about. And structure also concerns presentation.

We could call it the *gestalt* of the novel, I suppose. *Gestalt*—a shape or structure, which as an object of perception that forms a specific whole or unity incapable of expression simply in terms of its parts. You can't separate a melody from the notes that make it up, for example. Maybe the gestalt is what Flannery O'Connor was referring to when she said, "A story is a way to say something that can't be said in any other way, and it takes every word in the story to say what the meaning is." Remember this notion of the *gestalt*, but let's stick with the friendlier phrase *narrative structure* for now.

Let's begin thinking about structure with E. M. Forster, who, in *Aspects of the Novel*,† wrote that the basis of a novel is a story, and

*See the chapters "The Queen Died of Grief" and "Plottery" in *The Lie That Tells a Truth*.

†I bought my used copy of *Aspects of the Novel* some years ago at Robert Hittel's Bookstore in Fort Lauderdale for $2.75. Hardcover. Dust jacket a bit worn and foxed, but entire. This pocket edition was published in London in 1961 by Edward Arnold (Publishers) Limited and sold for ten shillings, sixpence. One day in December 1962, one Henry Harper Hart of Oakledge, Southbury, Connecticut, purchased the book from (and I'd like to think at) Blackwell's Bookstore in Oxford, England. Over the course of the next couple of years, beginning on December 28, 1962 (and I'd like to think still on Christmas holiday) and ending on March 25, 1964, Henry read the book a dozen times (or at least at a dozen sittings, and at each reading underlined and annotated in the book in a different color pen. (I've used a yellow highlighter for my own reading.) So that I know that this quote from the Introduction, "The pseudo-scholar often does well in examinations (real scholars are not much good) . . ." was underlined on

a *story* is a "narrative of events arranged in their time sequence"—
dinner after breakfast, decay after death, and so on. No novel can
be written without an allegiance to time. You have to come up with
a chronological sequence for your actions, a time frame for your
novel, even if you choose not to tell the story chronologically. Plot,
Forster wrote, is an organism of a higher type, and it is also a narration of events, the emphasis this time falling on causality. In a story,
we ask, "And then what?" In a plot, we ask, "Why?" So maybe we
can say this: The plot is the form that the causal sequence of events
assumes, and the narrative structure is the shape of the entire
utterance, the whole novel. Plot is the force that drives through
the novel. (Mother Ann Lee: "Every force evolves a form.") Narrative structure is the matrix (from the Latin for womb) in which the
plot is nurtured and developed. (And this idea of a matrix suggests
geology to me—the matrix being the rock mass in which fossils and
gems are embedded, and this in turn reminds me of Michelangelo's
famous explanation of his sculpting process: "I saw the angel in the
stone, and I carved to set it free.") Plot is the causal shape of the
novel; structure is the chronological and the architectural.

We'll deal with time first, and then with presentation. Every
novel is a clock and a calendar. A time machine. And time travels
in diverse paces, we know. A decade might pass in a clause: "When
he got released from prison ten years later . . ." Seconds might last
for pages: "Many years later, as he faced the firing squad, Colonel

---

the very first reading. (I like to think that Henry walked from Blackwell's over
to the Turf Tavern [mentioned in *Jude the Obscure*] and sat by a fire with a mug
of warm scrumpy cider and read that line and felt vindicated by it.) And I know
that Henry left the following marginalia on February 22, 1964, at the end of
chapter three in his tiny, embellished script: "Many persons find the characters
in novels more real to them than the persons they meet in real life because the
latter do not reveal themselves then [sic] the good novel is a sort of revelation,
and the novelist can reveal himself better in the novel than in normal life."

Aureliano Buendia was to remember that distant afternoon when his father took him to discover ice" (from García Márquez's *One Hundred Years of Solitude*). Hans Castorp's first day on the Magic Mountain lasts most of the first hundred pages of the novel. Nicholson Baker's novel *The Mezzanine* takes place during the central character's lunch hour and almost entirely during his ride on an escalator. Seven years. One hour. What is the time period of your novel?

Time is a continuum in which events occur in an apparently irreversible succession from past to present to future. The plot of your novel exists on that continuum. Your plot begins at Point A and ends at Point B, but it can, and most probably will, incorporate events that occurred before Point A (in flashback, perhaps, or in a character's memory or by reference in a conversation)* and events that occur or will occur after Point B (in the denouement, maybe, or in an epilogue).

That path from Point A to Point B, by the way, is not a straight line, but an arc. *Arc*, from the Latin *arcum* (*arcus*, nominative) for bow, arch, curve. With bow in mind, let's consider archery for a moment. You've got many factors to consider when launching an arrow on its flight to the target. There are the weather and gravity, just for starters. What else? The force of the bow, the efficiency of the bow, the mass of the arrow, the length and the weight of the arrow, the length and height of the fletching, the length of the pull back, the angle of release. Once you've made all of the calculations

---

*Aristotle said that every *now* necessarily had a *before*, and, therefore, time could have no beginning. And now it appears that he may have been correct. Cosmologist Paul Steinhardt, in the journal *Science*, wrote, "What we're proposing in the new picture is that the Big Bang is not a beginning of time but really just the latest in an infinite series of cycles, in which the Universe has gone through periods of heating, expanding, cooling, stagnating, emptying, and re-expanding again."

and decisions, once you aim and release, physics takes over. There is now only one place where that arrow can possibly land—at the target, you hope.

Every novel needs a trajectory, a path for you to follow as you write and for the reader to follow as he reads. Trajectory is the arc described by the novel in its passage through time and space. Trajectory is the character's arduous journey, the plot. Like the archer, you have many decisions to make: point of view, voice, characterization, place, time, want, need, motivation, and so on. Once you've made these decisions and launched your novel, the result is inevitable (though it needs to be surprising to you as you write and to the reader as he reads). If the archer misses her shot, she gets to take another, to readjust, to recalculate, and to re-envision. And so do you. And in revision, your aim is true.

You can tell your story chronologically, beginning with Point A, as William Trevor did in *The Story of Lucy Gault*: "Captain Everard Gault wounded the boy in the right shoulder on the night of June the twenty-first, nineteen twenty-one." You can begin at Point B and tell your story backward, as Martin Amis did in *Time's Arrow*: "I moved forward, out of the blackest sleep, to find myself surrounded by *doctors* . . . American doctors . . ." You can frame your story the way Joseph Conrad often did. The narrator recalls a still afternoon on the deck of a ship when he and his colleagues listened to Marlowe tell them the story of his trip upriver, into the heart of darkness,

> *"The most important thing in a work of art is that it should have a kind of focus, i.e. there should be some place where all the rays meet or from which they issue. And this focus must not be able to be completely explained in words. This indeed is one of the significant facts about a true work of art—that its content in its entirety can be expressed only by itself."*
> —LEO TOLSTOY

to find Mr. Kurtz. You can jump back and forth in time as I did in *Louisiana Power & Light*, from the present time of the story to the distant past to the recent past to the future, even, and then back to the present. No matter how you choose to tell your story, however, you must compress time. Do not confuse time, in other words, with duration—the continuance, the persistence of time. Not every moment in time is as significant as every other moment.

E. M. Forster wrote about the novelist's two allegiances—to "life by the clock" and to "life by values." This dual allegiance is

> *"All human happiness and misery take the form of action."*
> —ARISTOTLE

succinctly illustrated in Thomas Ford's lines "I did but see her passing by, / And yet I love her till I die." A single moment. A lifetime. The novelist must cling to time, but in so doing, must embrace the significant moments in time and disregard the trivial. Yes, you will need a timeline for your novel; you will have to provide an accurate chronological sequence of events in your novel; you will need to know the dates of major and minor occurrences. But remember that we don't need all of those nights of going to sleep, all of those mornings of waking up. We don't need to witness the weeks and months of boredom and routine prior to the next crisis or complication. Time is measured in minutes, hours, months, and years. Values are measured in intensity. And intensity takes time and space.

Which brings us to presentation, to chronography. How do you turn time into space? How do you construct your temporal architecture? You can write in chapters or not. Your chapters can be long or short. You can do as Faulkner did and tell your story in fifty-nine first-person segments or tell the same story four times. And you don't have to begin at the beginning as folk tales often do. Literary stories tend to begin *in medias res* or even *ad finem res*. The *Iliad* begins in the ninth year of a ten-year battle. John Cheever begins his story "O Youth and Beauty!" at the end of the party with this brilliant sentence: "At the tag end of nearly every long, large Saturday-night party in the suburb of Shady Hill, when almost everybody who was going to play golf or tennis in the morning had gone home hours ago and the ten or twelve people remaining seemed powerless to bring the evening to an end although the gin and whiskey were running low, and here and there a woman who was sitting out her husband would have begun to drink milk; when everybody had lost track of time, and the baby-sitters who were waiting at home for these diehards would have long since stretched out on the sofa and fallen into a deep sleep, to dream about cooking-contest prizes, ocean voyages, and romance; when the bellicose drunk, the crapshooter, the pianist, and the woman faced with the expiration of her hopes had all expressed themselves; when every proposal—to go to the Farquarson's for breakfast, to go swimming, to go and wake up the Townsends, to go here and go there—died as soon as it was made, then Trace Bearden would begin to chide Cash Bentley about his age and thinning hair." The dramaturgical beginning need not be the chronological beginning.

> "Writing a story or a novel is one way of discovering sequence in experience, of stumbling upon cause and effect in the happenings of a writer's own life."
> —EUDORA WELTY

You need a shape for your novel, but you need to discover it as you write. Flannery O'Connor wrote: "The more you write, the more you will realize that the form is organic, that it is something that grows out of your material, that the form of each story is unique." Strunk and White also speak to the issue of shape: "The more clearly the writer perceives the shape, the better are the chances of success." And it's important to understand the shape of your novel as early on in the writing process as you can. And this is why:

Every novel, like all closed systems, tends toward disorganization, entropy. This tendency to dissipate is the order of the artistic as well as the physical universe. Left alone, your novel will revert to the chaos from which it arose. Impose your will with shape, with structure.

Years ago writer, critic, editor Clifton Fadiman (*Lifetime Reading Plan*) addressed the issue of novel structure by suggesting three basic shapes. The *horizontal novel* follows events chronologically, Point A to Point B, and so, he said, is best suited to the plot-driven novel. The horizontal novel may, of course, include flashbacks, which will briefly and occasionally interrupt the story's forward movement. The *converging novel* follows a number of separate characters with their separate subplots and sequences of action until the events and characters meet at a single culminating time and place. As the *vertical novel* proceeds chronologically, it sends down shafts into consciousness in order to mine the memory of the central character, and this is based on some order other than the chronological. As the recollections accumulate we come to some understanding about the character's total experience.

YOU CAN USE a time frame to shape your novel, or you can look for a metaphor and apply it. James Joyce found his inspiration in the *Odyssey*. W. G. Sebald used a walking tour along the coast of southeast England as the shape for *The Rings of Saturn*. In both of these cases the metaphor is life as a journey—perhaps our oldest metaphor. A journey of ten years or twenty-four hours or a hundred miles. A journey to the moon or back into time. Donald Hays's wonderful baseball novel, *The Dixie Association*, begins on the Arkansas Reds' opening day game and ends with the league championship. Shape is aesthetic order. Shape gives your novel proportion, harmony, unity, and coherence.

Let's say your novel is about a classically trained musician—an oboist in a prominent symphony orchestra. In fact, he specializes in the oboe d'amore—which has a sweeter sound, both as a name and as an instrument. Let's give him a sweet name, too. Valentine D'Amato. He is in love with the first violinist, Martine Juneau, but he's never told her so. He's never even spoken with her. He stares at her through every performance. Already, whatever else your novel is about, it's about romantic love and sublime music. Well, it may occur to you to use a musical form as the shape of your novel. The sonata might work—you remember that Tolstoy wrote a novella called *The Kreutzer Sonata*. You might title the novel, *Moonlight Sonata* or *The Long Sonata of the Dead* or *Autumn Sonata* or something more clever than that. Or maybe you're feeling expansive and decide to try a symphony, a sonata for orchestra. This gives you more flexibility. Already you see the book divided into five sections, movements, which you'll name *Allegro, Scherzo, Andante, Presto,* and *Coda*.

So, now with a shape, you take notes about what might happen in the respective movements. The opening movement is in sonata form, meaning in three parts: exposition, development, and recapitulation. As the exposition opens we meet your principal subject, Valentine. A principal theme is established, say his passion for music. This passion may serve as the bridge to carry us to principal subject two, Martine, and theme two, Valentine's unrequited love (obsession, perhaps) for her. At the end of the exposition, their eyes meet for the first time. They exchange smiles, and this sends Valentine off into flights of fancy and fantasy. Here is the development wherein Valentine plots how he'll win the hand of Martine. He composes music for her, waits for her outside Symphony Hall (looks to me like we're in Boston), asks her to lunch.

Martine is pleasant but otherwise unresponsive. Has Valentine made his intentions clear to her? And so begins the recapitulation.

We're alone with Valentine, somewhat despondent, still admiring Martine, but now, feeling rebuffed, he is more cautious. There's a Christmas party for the orchestra which will serve as the bridge back to Martine. We see her, as Valentine does, laughing and smiling with the percussionists. (And everyone knows what they're after.) And then, following a particularly grueling rehearsal, Valentine once more catches Martine's eye. She smiles to him, nods her head. Yes, she'd love to go to lunch. Valentine soars. You understand that you still need to work in the contrast of keys, as it were. A characteristic of the sonata form is the movement away from and back to the principal key, Valentine let's say. Perhaps you'll contrast the personalities of Valentine and Martine, or better yet contrast his passion for music with his love for her. And maybe at some point, you realize, he'll have to choose between them.

You've switched around the traditional order of the second and third movements for dramatic purposes. Your second movement is the scherzo, Italian for joke. The movement is fast and lively. This is the blossoming of the romance and the love between Valentine and Martine. You write this section in the scherzo's usual ternary form: ABA. So you open with the two of them at the aforementioned lunch, both shy, unsure of themselves, having a good time, but not sure where this is all going. Valentine's certain of what he wants. Martine isn't sure she's ready for any kind of commitment. But then in the middle section we see them cheering at a Red Sox game, eating oysters at Legal Sea Foods,

> "You can't write unless you're willing to subordinate the creative impulse to the constriction of a form."
> —ANTHONY BURGESS

walking hand in hand through the Public Garden, her head on his shoulder as they ride a swan boat. We hear them talk about music and about their futures. We see them make love as the "Ode to Joy" plays on the stereo. (Or maybe you're more subtle than that.)

The third section (A) returns us to the first. They are at lunch and once again are ill at ease. They both realize that the relationship has gone to a deeper level and that they now have to decide if they can commit to each other. Valentine wishes the circumstances would not change and is surprised at himself. He has become addicted to

> "Art is limitation; the essence of every picture is the frame."
> —G. K. CHESTERTON

the high intensity of their courtship and fears that settling in together might—no *might* about it—*would* dull the passion. He thinks he's crazy for thinking like this. Martine has noticed that her playing has been less than sharp lately. And Heinrich, the conductor, has also noticed. She needs to buckle down, or she'll lose her chair. You can't practice the obligatory eight hours a day when you're cavorting around town till God knows when.

And now the story slows down for the next act, the andante. You might consider writing this movement in the sonata form later on, but for now you'll settle for the more manageable ABA or song form, as in the scherzo, with a main section, a contrasting middle section, and a return to the original section. Martine has called off the romance. She can't go on deceiving Valentine, deceiving herself. Music is more important in her life than romance is. And in this section your writing becomes more lyrical and reflective. Martine throws herself back into her art, and her playing gets better and better. Meanwhile, Valentine finds little solace in music. He dates a brass player. He eventually decides he can't torment himself any longer, can't bear to watch Martine every day and not have her, and he gives his notice to the symphony. He's quitting. And now we're back to the original section. Martine comes to Valentine's apartment in the North End, and tells him she's calling off their separation. Music means nothing to her if she can't share it with him. Valentine tells her he's engaged to be married to the French horn player.

And so begins the presto movement, the finale. The action is fast and furious. As Valentine's wedding—a very big deal, the French horn player comes from a prominent and, needless to say, wealthy Brahmin family—approaches, he and Martine can't stay away from each other. They are both dolorously miserable and deliriously happy. You wonder what they'll do, and in wondering, you'll learn what they do, and you'll write it down. And you know you have one more section, the coda. The story is essentially over, the climax reached, but you want to offer the reader a peek into Valentine's future.

You see Valentine and Martine playing in the symphony. Valentine smiles broadly as he watches his pregnant wife play a solo. Or they're in their apartment teaching their three-year-old boy to play anything but the French horn. Or Valentine and Martine huddle in the corner at Locke-Ober at one of their clandestine trysts. Valentine's wife is skiing in Switzerland with her family.

Week 13:

Picture This

You make a scene when you want attention.
—*Jerome Stern*

WE'LL SPEND THESE next three weeks thinking about, drafting, and revising scenes. So we ought to be clear on what we mean by scene. You've got two narrative strategies to use when you're writing a story: scene and summary. Showing and telling. Both are necessary in your novel. Summary, for example, accelerates the narrative tempo and hurries us through events that, while necessary to know about, are not necessary to have witnessed in scene. In *Techniques of Fiction Writing: Measure and Madness*, Leon Surmelian defined a scene in this way: "The scene is a specific act, a single event that occurs at a certain place and lasts as long as there is no change of place and no break in the continuity of time. It is an incident acted out by the characters, a single episode or situation, vivid and immediate." Maybe a slight amendment is in order here. The place of the scene can change if the action being depicted is uninterrupted—the characters can step out of the car, for example, and continue their argument in the parking lot and then in the restaurant. And here's John Gardner:

"By scene we mean here all that is included in an unbroken flow from one incident in time to another . . . unbroken in the sense that it does not include a major time lapse or a leap from one setting to another. . . ." A scene may include brief authorial intrusions for background explanations or flashback—the character's mind, in other words, may drift. I think that tells us what we need to know Scene is where the novel breathes. Scene is what is remembered. Scene is where emotion lies. Scene is characters in action, and action causes reaction, and action (as Shakespeare reminded us) is eloquence.

Here's a list of some differences between the two narrative methods. Of course, it's oversimplified but, I hope, illustrative:

SCENE	SUMMARY
Shows	Tells
Drama	Explanation
Particular	General
Is happening	Has happened
Spontaneous	Qualified
Emotional	Intellectual
Approximates real time	Accelerates time
Foreground	Background
Focused	Panoramic
Individual	Society
Intimate	Distant
Dynamic	Static

A newspaper report of an event tells us what happened. The fictional report of that same event lets us witness what happens by showing as well as telling. Here's an actual headline from this morning's newspaper. "Nude man found swimming with alligators

. . . again!" The report mentions an abandoned pickup that led police to the man in Saddle Creek Park up in Polk County, Florida, who'd stripped and gotten in the water. They arrested him. End of story. The short story we write, however, might begin inside that pickup. Radio's on, one of those late-night right-wing call-in shows. Someone from Georgia's ranting about our loss of precious civil liberties. Our hero has driven to the edge of the lake and shone the pickup's headlights at the water. When he catches the glow of the gator's eyes, he takes the last swallow of Bud Light and turns off the radio. He rubs the stump of what had been his left arm. We'll show our Ahab taking off his clothes, dipping his toe in the warm water. He shines the flashlight ahead, chums the water with marshmallows, holds the knife between his teeth, and wades in when he sees the widening V-shaped ripples coming toward him.

A scene is the creation, you hope, of a memorable (because it's emotionally engaging) moment, and moments are what we read for. Scene brings action and dialogue to the reader who watches what goes on. A scene slows time. What takes seconds to happen may take paragraphs to relate. When you write a scene, you render sensations fully so that we feel the sting of the insult, the thrill of victory, the agony of defeat, as the old TV sports promo had it. In writing scene you will use direct dialogue, physical reactions, gestures, smells, sounds, tastes, textures, and thoughts. When you were a child and wanted attention from your mom, you may have "made a scene," as your mother labeled the behavior, and it worked. Not always to your advantage, regrettably.

Summary (or panorama or exposition) explains, interprets, or *tells* what happened. It condenses actions into their largest movements. It is necessary, usually serving as a bridge between scenes, preparing the reader to accept the illusion of the coming scene. It brings in the large and complex world and makes for greater realism. It adds density to the slighter world of a particular character. But exposition is static. It stands for the general. The events, psychologically, have occurred in the past even if the exposition is written in present tense. Like this: "He opens the door to Room 11 and finds the place a mess, the squalor overwhelming." There is no emotional engagement there and no attempt to earn it.

A scene is the opposite of telling. It *shows* what happened. Scene brings action and dialogue to the reader with a fullness comparable to what a witness might observe. This is where fiction does its work of engaging the imagination of the reader. A scene is psychologically in the present even if written in the past tense. We can open up the expository sentence about Clovis (who was dead tired in Week 7, if you remember) above with scene. "Clovis opened the door to Room 11 and stood in the doorway, looked around, listened. He put the pet carrier down, stepped into the room, snapped on the light. Cockroaches scooted along the paneled walls. He kicked the bed, the desk. He opened the bathroom door and stepped back. He put the pet carrier on the bed, saw that the red message button on the phone was flashing. He

"Drama is action, sir, and not confounded philosophy."
—LUIGI PIRANDELLO

picked up the phone, punched a button, and listened to a man say, 'Words cannot describe the pain, Rhonda. Words only come when the pain is over. When everything is over. *Comprende?* Everything.' Clovis turned on the TV. The screen was snowy, the sound staticky. He tried a few channels, turned it off. There was a linen postcard on the TV of a desert sunrise: ocotillo and sage, and in the distance a yellow sun peaked over purple mountains, brightening the indigo sky to silvery blue. He turned the card over and read. 'Life is a journey, my ass. We're never going anywhere. We'll never get out of here. Rhonda.' Clovis lay on top of the bed, covered his eyes with his hat."

Scene stands for the particular. Novelists look at the world one person, one neighborhood, one town at a time. When you tell something, you distance the reader somewhat, hold him away from the action. When you show, the reader looks on, participates, and emotes. Knowing what scenes are required in a novel is at the heart of the fictional art. The author has to write the obligatory scenes so that nothing of importance happens offstage. She must write the pivotal scenes and make the quick expository moves from scene to scene. We cannot have three paragraphs to get the character from the front porch to the backseat. And no small talk. Nothing trivial, nothing of minor importance can happen in a scene. That's what narrators are for. Here's the opening of Hemingway's "A Clean, Well-Lighted Place":

> It was very late and everyone had left the café except an old man who sat in the shadow the leaves of the tree made against the electric light. In the day time the street was dusty, but at night the dew settled the dust and the old man liked to sit late because he was deaf and now at night it was quiet and he felt the difference. The two waiters inside the café knew that the old man was a little drunk, and while he was a good client they knew that if he became too drunk he would leave without paying, so they kept watch on him.

That's exposition, telling, summary. And these lines follow:

> "Last week he tried to commit suicide," one waiter said.
> "Why?"
> "He was in despair."
> "What about?"
> "Nothing."
> "How do you know it was nothing?"
> "He has plenty of money."

We're not told the men talked; we listen to them talk. That's scene.

WE ALL NEED to be touched, even if metaphorically. We are not, despite the enduring American myth, rugged individuals Most of us aren't, anyway. We are social animals. (Rugged individuals wouldn't be caught dead writing or reading fiction is my guess.) We need people near us. Without intimacy, we fall apart or break down. And for too many of us intimacy can be hard to come by. Our knowledge of others, of ourselves, is often superficial. It's easier to hustle through the daily grind that way, focused on the task, our minds uncluttered with concerns for our colleagues. Fiction offers

> "In the world of fiction, nothing is so strange as the commonplace."
> —WRIGHT MORRIS

us the opportunity for intimacy, intimacy that is as decided as it is profound and lasting. We can, in a very short time, get to know the hearts and minds of people we only just met. We can know these fictional people better than we know ourselves, better than we can know anyone else. We can know them completely. And their lives will touch us. This is what Aristotle meant when he said the purpose of tragedy was to touch our hearts to move us emotionally. Catharsis. The business of moving the reader emotionally is achieved primarily in scene.

Everything of importance in a novel ought to be dramatized in a scene. (Overstated, yes, but let it stand for now.) In other words, every time your central character tries to get what he wants, tries to achieve his goal, we get a scene. Don't tell us he held up a 7-Eleven. Put him (and us) in that 7-Eleven, and have him pull out the starter's pistol and hand the clerk a note. Have him say, "I'm sorry to do this, but I've got a sick baby at home who needs formula." And nothing unimportant ought to happen in scene, no small talk. And don't interrupt the scene, or you'll be telling us it's really not that significant, this business we're watching. Save the background information for later. Don't distract or intrude. Don't undermine the tension and drama.

Chekhov's story "Misery" opens with a bit of exposition to set the scene in a very painterly way:

> The twilight of evening. Big flakes of wet snow are whirling lazily about the street lamps, which have just been lighted, and lying in a thin soft layer on roofs, horses' backs, shoulders, caps. Iona Potapov, the sledge-driver, is all white like a ghost. He sits on the box without stirring, bent as double as the living body can be bent. If a regular snowdrift fell on him it seems as though even then he would not think it necessary to shake it off. . . . His little mare is white and motionless too. Her stillness, the angularity of her lines, and the stick-like straightness of her legs make her look like a half-penny gingerbread horse. She is probably lost in thought. Anyone who has been torn away from the plough, from the familiar gray landscapes, and cast into this slough, full of monstrous lights, of unceasing uproar and hurrying people, is bound to think.

What does the sentence about the horse tell us? "She is probably lost in thought." The voice of the narrator is established, and we see that he is concerned about this horse, and considers the horse capable of thought. Endearing, I suppose. And he doesn't know everything—he's not omniscient, not here, at any rate. He tells us what he doesn't know and speculates on what the thoughts might be and invites us to do so as well. Iona's son has died, such a tragic and unnatural event. Iona needs to tell someone about the death and about his son. That's the simple plot of "Misery." And every time he tries to tell the story, we get scene. The next lines of the story give us scene:

"Sledge to Vyborgskaya!" Iona hears. "Sledge!"

Iona starts, and through his snow-plastered eyelashes sees an officer in a military overcoat with a hood over his head.

"To Vyborgskaya," repeats the officer. "Are you asleep? To Vyborgskaya!"

In token of assent Iona gives a tug at the reins which sends cakes of snow flying from the horse's back and shoulders. The officer gets into the sledge. The sledge-driver clicks to the horse, cranes his neck like a swan, rises in his seat, and more from habit than necessity brandishes his whip. The mare cranes her neck, too, crooks her stick-like legs, and hesitatingly sets off.

Scene is not only reserved for these large moments, these plot points. (Think of these as the obligatory scenes that we'll talk about in the next two weeks.) There is room for small incidents, for bits of conversation, for minor but significant events. You might want a scene to illustrate a character trait or to set a tone or to foreshadow. You might want to introduce a detail that will resonate later. But when you write the plot-driven scenes, think of them as small stories themselves with beginnings, middles, and ends, with characters in conflict, and with change. Each of these scenes is a microcosm of the whole

> "Always get to the dialogue as soon as possible. I always feel the thing to go for is speed. Nothing puts the reader off more than a great slab of prose at the start."
> —P. G. WODEHOUSE

novel, in a sense. And they do at least two of the following: advance the plot, reveal character, and express theme. And maybe they also establish a particular tone or amplify earlier images.

In some ways the most important sentence in your novel is the first sentence because that's the sentence that breaks the silence that carries us out of our world and drops us into the world of your story. We'll all read the first line of anything. Your first sentence has to make us want to read the second. And by extension your first scene has to be compelling enough that we'll want to stick around for the next. Your first chapter has to hook us so that we can't put the book down. We just need to know what's going to happen to these intriguing characters. What we'll be working on is the first scene, which might not be the very opening of the book and may end up not being in the book at all. But it is a place where you think right now that your story begins. In your opening scenes and your opening summary, you're setting the tone of your novel, and you're teaching the reader how to approach this book. You're making a first impression, and so are your characters.

WHEN WILLS COLLIDE. You may not know it, but you're ready to begin writing that first scene. You know your central character will be in the scene. Who else will be? Consider the possibilities from your list of characters. Interview your other characters, audition them for the costarring role. Your choice does not have to be the antagonist in the whole novel; he needs to be the antagonist pro tem. For each character in your opening scene decide on the following: What does he or she want in this scene? Why does he want it? (Your central character should want whatever it is intensely enough to do something to get it.) Motivations in collision create conflict. That's another definition of plot. So your central character wants something from the other character in the scene, who does not want to give it to him. It might be information; it might be a kiss; it might be five bucks to go to the movies; it might be respect. That's all we need to get us going.

THE LAY OF THE LAND. Before you can write the scene, of course, you need to know where it takes place. So think about the setting. Picture it. Where and when? Interior or exterior? Day or night? Write the details of the room, the field, the office, the car, wherever. What's the date? Weather? Time? What are the sounds, the smells, the textures, the tastes, if any? See the place clearly so that your reader will be able to see the place and the characters clearly. We can't attend to the characters until we know where they are, until we can see them in a physical context.

VOICE LESSONS. Dialogue is often an integral element in scene. You need to know how people speak. Listen to people talk, and listen with your notebook on your knee and a pen in your hand. Sit yourself in a crowded restaurant or bar or other convenient venue for eavesdropping. Note the idiosyncrasies of individual speech you hear around you. They may become your characters' idiosyncrasies. I have a friend who pronounces *different* as *diffent,* and to my ear he uses the word remarkably often, but it just might be that I am conscious each time he does. Speakers may have pet words or phrases that they overuse. *You know what I'm saying?* What are they? Other folks might speak in fragments or might omit the subjects of their sentences. *Going to the store. Be back later.* We've all heard people who refer to themselves in third person and others who ask and answer their own questions. *Am I happy I failed the geometry quiz? No, I'm decidedly not happy. What do I plan to do about it? I plan to buckle down and hit the books.* How do various speakers build their sentences? Listen to the music of speech. And watch people as they speak and make note of that as well. What are her eyes saying as she talks? Her body? How do you speak differently than anyone else? Your characters' speech may also reflect the place they're from. A New Englander's speech will likely sound different than a South Carolinian's. And their vocabularies and idioms will differ.

> "What I really work hard on is the beginning. Where do you begin? In what tone do you begin? I almost have to have a scene in my mind."
> —DAVID McCULLOUGH

CURTAINS UP! I. So now you know what your character wants and you know why she wants it. You know she wants it intensely enough to do something about it. You know what stands in her way, and you know there'll be more obstacles later on. You know where and when the opening *scene* of the book (which is not the same thing as the opening of the book, necessarily) will take place, and you're ready to write it. You may suspect when you write the scene that it will almost certainly not be the opening scene of the final product, as I suggested earlier. But you know now that you're going to surprise your character with trouble. You also know that nothing gets written easily and mechanically and that you have work to do before you can bring those characters to life. Just as it takes time for a scene to unfold, so it takes a lot of time to write the scene. So today do the following: Read some opening scenes from books that you admire and try to figure out what is working there. The heart of every scene is conflict, so consider what the conflict will be here at the start. What is your character thinking about? How does she feel? Mood? Who are the people in the scene? Describe them and their attire (this so you can see them clearly, not so a lot of extraneous details will appear in the scene). What is your character doing? Describe in detail. Do the same for any other character. What might the point of view in the scene be? Who is the narrator? What is the climax that the scene will build to? What might the last line of the scene be? The first line? Will characters talk? How does each person speak in terms of tone, diction, figures of speech, dialect, whatever. You're not looking for answers here; you're looking to open up the scene, to offer yourself possibilities, and to gather potential material.

CURTAINS UP! II. Write the opening scene. Get black on white. As John Gardner put it: See your characters clearly, wonder what they'll do next, see what they do, write down what they do in the best, most accurate words you can, knowing that you'll be changing the words later and that the subsequent vision will be sharper than your current vision. Don't worry about logic or grammar or transitions. Write it fast. Make it one long sentence if you want. I'll sometimes just write the dialogue first if conversation is at the heart of the scene. I listen to the characters and write down what they say as fast as I can. I don't try to censor them, question them, or edit them. I just listen and write. And then I'll go back and begin to cut and reword and revise, and I'll begin to paint in what they do while they speak. And I'll lay in

> "The first scene will contain the moment in the 'time' of your fiction in which the happening, the action, becomes sufficiently inevitable to put the writing into motion and aim it down the right path. The right path is the path into what happens and how what happens ends."
> —WILLIAM SLOANE

relevant details of the place. And then I'll tighten the dialogue again. And if I note a place where a character is being vague or reluctant, I may tell him to be honest and think harder. And by now I'm in revision mode.

CURTAINS UP! III. Revise the scene. Consider rewriting first of all without even looking at what you wrote yesterday. Tighten the dialogue. Focus on details and images. Dramatize the conflict. Strengthen the verbs, lose the qualifiers. We ought to know what the trouble is, what our central character wants and why, and we should have an indication of what his struggle will be. And we should have a reason for caring about him. You have to make us want to read the next chapter, the next scene. And now we're off and running. Like the novel as a whole, the scene has a plot, a beginning, a middle, and an end. The scene is a brief story in that way. The central character in the scene wants something and goes after it despite obstacles, and so on. When she gets what she wants or fails to get it, the scene is finished.

FAMILY REUNION. Here's a consideration for an opening scene. Why not try it? Family rituals are wonderful to write about. So get all the members of a nuclear or extended (even better) family together at a wedding, funeral, Thanksgiving dinner, Christmas, the Independence Day Reunion, or what have you, and something dramatic, troubling, and maybe, if you're lucky, catastrophic is bound to happen. (You may remember some unpleasant moments from your own life that you can draw from.) Plus the events themselves and the holidays have built-in symbolism and traditions. So get all of your central character's family (or her husband's) together. You might even make the seating arrangements at the dinner table with potential trouble in mind. Sit Uncle Jimmy the drinker next to Aunt Marie the Mother Superior. You sent out invitations, but maybe someone hasn't come. The others talk about why that might be and how they feel about the absence. What is it that goes unspoken at this gathering? What is talked about? Sit them all down, have someone say grace or welcome the guests or whatever opening ritual the family prefers. Just sit back and write down what everyone says. And what they do. Try to listen to all of the conversations. Who's that raising his voice? Who just tossed his napkin to the table? Who's back at the bar? The patriarch is telling the same story he tells every time the family gets together. Let's hear it. And so on. Just keep going—you're learning a lot about the characters and the relationships even if much of the material won't make the page of the novel in black and white—it'll be there still. Now write the whole scene again, this time from the point of view of your central character. He can't hear everything, can he? So you'll need to select the richest and most provocative material. What's this central character talking about when he speaks and to whom does he speak? Whom does he ignore? Remember he has an agenda—maybe it's just to survive the ordeal—but then it must be difficult for him to do so. What's he thinking at various moments? What's he feeling? Even if you don't open with this scene, you may find a place for it later. By then you'll know the characters even better than you do now. You'll be privy to secrets and lies that you know nothing about now. And that information might further enliven an already volatile scene.

Weeks 14-15:

Behind the Scenes

All fiction writers work by indirection; to show, not to tell; not
to make a statement about a character, but to demonstrate it in
his actions or his conversation or by suggesting his thoughts, so
that the reader understands for himself.
—*Eudora Welty*

L ET'S TALK ABOUT dialogue. First of all, it's not the way we
speak. It's not natural, that is to say, but it must suggest natural-
ness. Fiction is art, not life, and while life may be extemporaneous,
at least for those of us without a Day Planner or BlackBerry, art is
not. Dialogue is not spontaneous, while conversation generally is.
Dialogue, then, is speech condensed, refined, and distilled. If a
phone were to ring in your life right now, you might hear the person
in the next room say something like this:

"Hello? Fine, thanks. And you? That's terrific. What was that? Is
this a joke? What do you mean, there's been an accident?"

If that call happened in your story, you might cut out the first six
sentences. Realistic is not the same as *real*. Dialogue is the essence
of conversation. It's what you remember from the conversation you
had a month or a decade or a lifetime ago. It's what you tell others

that you said that night you left your husband. Dialogue leaves out what is unnecessary: the repetitions, the ums and ahs, the ritual lines of greeting and parting, the small talk, the false starts, the meanderings, and so on.

Every verbal exchange tells us something new about the story and reveals something new about the speakers. Every conversation should also dramatize the relationship among the speakers. Each bit of dialogue should advance the novel's plot as well, and perhaps express one of its themes. What is not said can be as important as what is said. Body language can be as important as verbal language. What dialogue is not about is information. Narrators can give us any information we need. Dialogue is too important to be simply a vehicle for facts.

There are a multitude of reasons to want to talk to someone. We talk with each other for various reasons: to inform, to compare, to seduce, to clarify, to cloud, to charm, to deceive, to alarm, to evade, to demur, to bedevil, to reassure, to offend, to warn, to befuddle, to flatter, to belittle, to thank, to bluster, to rattle, to arouse, to soothe, to illuminate, to apologize, to inquire, to amuse, to brag, to inspire, to order, to explain, to encourage, to dissuade, to convert, to argue, to process, to instruct, to vent, to accost, to excuse, to call attention to ourselves, to hear the sound of our own voices, to be polite, to pass the time. And if a conversation is about evasion, then tension will mount, and pressure will build. We'll wonder what on earth is going to happen next—and that's what every writer wants to hear. Let's try an exercise.

> "Scenes of high drama—suicide, rape, murder, incest—or scenes of great beauty are difficult to do in fiction because we already have strong feelings about these things, and literature does not operate on borrowed feelings."
> —ANNIE DILLARD

CROSS-PURPOSES. One character (use the characters from your novel if you can) wants to come clean about a secret. The character he's talking to can't or won't hear it. Put your character in bed or in another intimate place with her spouse or with another significant character, and let them talk for *several pages* about important matters. Here's the catch. No speech of one character can ever answer or even address the speech that goes before it. The characters speak at cross-purposes. They have their own mutually exclusive agendas. Remember that in conversation, characters do things as well as say things. A student of mine, Christopher Kelly,* did this exercise during the writing of a novel called *There Are Many Paths to God.* In the cross-purposes scene, his central character Carlos comes home from spending his Mardi Gras carousing with friends and with the intention of finally telling his wife Veronica, whom he loves, that he's gay. She's waiting up for him, reading in bed. "I'm so sorry," he begins. She refuses to hear him, however, and as he tries to confess, she talks about the family, the holiday barbecue that he failed to attend, their dog, and so on. The result is a heartbreaking scene, and it opened, I'm sure, avenues into his characters' lives that Chris had never wandered down before.

ALWAYS THINK DIALOGUE, not monologue. Don't let your characters deliver speeches. Speeches are all about information and explanation. We want drama and tension. If your character wants to make a speech, have another character interrupt him. And remember that characters don't all speak alike and probably only one of them speaks like you do. Use the verb *said* to attribute dialogue almost exclusively. What's important in dialogue is what's

*An extract of the novel, which culminates with the start of the scene mentioned, appeared in *Gulf Stream* magazine #17.

inside the quotation marks. The attribution is only there to let us know who's speaking. If you don't need the attribution, don't use it. If you do attribute, don't qualify the verb with an intrusive adverb, as in *he said, anxiously.* Show the anxiety in what was spoken. Show the dialogue, No talking heads. Keep us seeing, as well as hearing, the characters. And in long dialogue you can break up the direct discourse with indirect discourse, which reports what was said. Like this: *"Where do you think you're going?" my mother said. I told her I was going to church. "Wait, I'll go with you," she said.* The narrator's answer was reported, not spoken directly. Let's try another scene centered on dialogue.

SECRET SHARERS. Write a conversation between a pair of lovers in which every single thing they say to each other is the revelation of another secret. See how far you can take it. Perhaps they come to realize in the end that they don't know each other at all. It might begin something like this:

"I never told you I had polio as a child? I thought I had."
"I haven't told you everything, either."
"I hate it when you're like this, when you feel like you have to top everything I say."
"My ex-wife wants a second chance."
"I know. She told me."
"She called you a jezebel."
"And she told me something disturbing about you."

THE LOBBY. This one should have dialogue but not necessarily lots of it. A man and a woman sit on a couch in the lobby of a posh hotel. They're waiting for someone or something. They've ordered drinks. They are dressed formally. He has on some kind of lapel pin, and she's wearing heirloom jewelry. Give these two names and write their scene using the words *dismal, charm, deliverance, mercy,* and *sin.* The waiter who brings their drinks has something surprising to tell them.

A SCENIC PARADIGM. This is an exercise I adapted from an exercise called "Emergency Fiction" that I learned from my friend Steve Barthelme, the author of *And He Tells the Little Horse the Whole Story* and, with his brother Frederick, *Double Down.* Steve teaches creative writing at the University of Southern Mississippi in Hattiesburg.

1. A scene follows an *active character* through *emotionally charged* experiences which *change* him or her.

2. Put things you like in your scenes. (If you like baseball, put Babe Ruth in a scene. If you like single-malt scotch, we're in an upscale bar.)

3. Put things which make you nervous in the scene. (Afraid of Republicans? There's a coven of them living next door. Afraid of spiders? An orb spider the size of your fist is spinning a web across your front porch. Acrophobic? You're trapped on a ledge in the Grand Canyon and no one knows you're there. Only the heel of your right foot has purchase, and that on gravel. The foot already hurts, and your hands are pressed above your head against the sandstone but have nothing to grab on to. This threatens, however, to be a very brief scene. [I had that dream last night.])

4. Here is how you create a character:

Dion

5. Here is how you create a setting:

lifted the Sanalin sheet from the cadaver's face, said, "Good morning, Lindle." He folded the sheet in thirds, in thirds again, and placed it on the floor by the aerosol cans of Restor Skin.

6. Here's how you set the tone:

His cat, Grasshopper, slept curled in the stainless steel sink. Dion patted her head, scratched behind her ear. She purred, stretched, put her foreleg over her eyes, and settled back into sleep. Dion turned on the cassette player. Bill Monroe. He lowered the volume a bit. He sprayed the body with disinfectant, washed it down.

7. Here is how you create a situation with a second character. New paragraph:

Dion's boy Delaney entered the prep room and squeezed past his daddy. He knocked a wax spatula off a tray, which startled the dozing cat, who leaped up and knocked her head on the faucet. Of course, she pretended she meant to do it. Delaney tossed a trocar button to the middle of the room, and Grasshopper went after it.

8. Here's how to emotionally charge the situation. New paragraph:

Delaney said, "I'm quittin' Paradise, Daddy. I'm done with being a mortician."

9. Here is how to emotionally charge the situation again. New paragraph:

Dion looked at the red and black spider's-web tattoo on his boy's forearm and shook his head. "I wish you wouldn't. This funeral home is your future."

10. Here's how you add a small surprise to make the world of the story as rich as the world the reader lives in, while at the same time developing character and suggesting his mental state:

He held up a pink and white birthday candle, and Delaney lit it with his Bic lighter. Dion burned the hairs from Lindle's ears, made a wish, and blew out the candle.

11. Here is how you add emphasis to what has just happened:

He looked up and met Delaney's eyes. He held back his tears. "How will I live without you?"

12. Here is how you intensify the situation. New paragraph:

"Don't do this, Daddy. It's all settled," Delaney said. "I've got a job in New Orleans. Starts Monday." Delaney turned. "It's my own life." He walked to the door and opened it. "Are you going to wish me luck, bon voyage, or something?"

13. Here is how you further intensify the situation and bring it to resolution. New paragraph:

Dion got out the bruise bleach, the cavity fluid, the suction pump, and the trocar. Delaney closed the door behind him. Dion wiped down the trocar with a prep towel. He said, "This is going to hurt me more than it hurts you," and then apologized for the gallows humor. Bill Monroe sang, *And we shiver when the cold wind blows*. Dion placed the trocar point three inches above the navel. Grasshopper lay on her side on the cool tile floor, put her feet against the wall, and walked her horizontal self across the room. Dion punched the trocar through the skin.

Here it is, not a bad beginning:

Dion lifted the Sanalin sheet from the cadaver's face, said, "Good morning, Lindle." He folded the sheet in thirds, in thirds again, and placed it on the floor by the aerosol cans of Restor Skin. His cat, Grasshopper, slept curled in the stainless steel sink. Dion patted her head, scratched behind her ear. She purred, stretched, put her foreleg over her eyes, and settled back into sleep. Dion turned on the cassette player. Bill Monroe. He lowered the volume a bit. He sprayed the body with disinfectant, washed it down.

Dion's boy Delaney entered the prep room and squeezed past his daddy. He knocked a wax spatula off a tray, which startled the dozing cat, who leaped up and knocked her head on the faucet. Of course, she pretended she meant to do it. Delaney tossed a trocar button to the middle of the room, and Grasshopper went after it.

Delaney said, "I'm quittin' Paradise, Daddy. I'm done with being a mortician."

Dion looked at the red and black spider's-web tattoo on his boy's forearm and shook his head. "I wish you wouldn't. This funeral home is your future." He held up a pink and white birthday candle, and Delaney lit it with his Bic lighter. Dion burned the hairs from Lindle's ears, made a wish, and blew out the candle. He looked up and met Delaney's eyes. He held back his tears. "How will I live without you?"

"Don't do this, Daddy. It's all settled," Delaney said. "I've got a job in New Orleans. Starts Monday." Delaney turned. "It's my own life." He walked to the door and opened it. "Are you going to wish me luck, bon voyage, or something?"

Dion got out the bruise bleach, the cavity fluid, the suction pump, and the trocar. Delaney closed the door behind him. Dion wiped down the trocar with a prep towel. He said, "This is going to hurt me more than it hurts you," and then apologized for the gallows humor. Bill Monroe sang, *And we shiver when the cold wind blows.* Dion placed the trocar point three inches above the navel. Grasshopper lay on her side on the cool tile floor, put her feet against the wall, and walked her horizontal self across the room. Dion punched the trocar through the skin.

Now try writing a scene with your own character following these steps.

FIT TO BE SCENE. There are scenic moments in a novel, call them half-scenes, which are not meant to advance the plot or to present some kind of dramatic resolution, but are meant instead to offer a glimpse of the character being himself or to focus our attention on an image or to establish a certain tone or to illustrate what the narrator is saying. But the scenes we're concerned with here are the ones that advance our plot. You know that everything important in your novel ought to be shown and not told, ought to occur in scene and not summary. So look at your three and a half months of notes, especially your notes on plot. When you have had time to refresh your mind, do the following. (1) Jot down a brief description of fifteen to twenty scenes that you have already thought about for your novel. Or scenes that you know you'll have to think about at some point. You were hoping to cross those bridges when you came to them—and you still can. We're just trying right now to see where those bridges might be and how they might be constructed. You can do this on index cards if you like. (2) Now add details to each scene: time, place, temperature, season, lighting, characters, purpose, and if it pops into your head, jot down some dialogue. You're not writing the scenes, but you're preparing yourself to. Some of these scenes will make the final cut; some will not.

> "The thing to do is to say to yourself 'Which are my big scenes?' and then get every drop of juice out of them."
> —P. G. WODEHOUSE

SHOW AND TELL. Take a paragraph of exposition, yours or anyone else's, and turn that summary into scene by putting characters into motion so that the reader has to see them and hear them, witness what they do, so that the reader participates in the creation of the novel. Here's an example of a summary:

> Brandi met this Bulgarian guy at the diner, this guy Rado who was trying to convince her to marry him. He told her how it's a win-win situation. She gets $2,000, and he gets to stay in the country, and after two years, they walk away and both are better off. She tried to tell him how important marriage is to a woman.

An intriguing situation, but we don't know who these people are yet, and we don't get to eavesdrop on the conversation. Here's a bit of a possible scene:

> Brandi thanked the waitress for the refill. She told Rado, You can understand, can't you, how this is a significant disappointment?
> You'd be helping me out, Brandi.
> A wedding is supposed to be one of the highlights of a woman's life.
> Helping yourself out.
> It's not supposed to be a good deed, a casual business proposition.
> It's not the wedding that matters, Brandi. It's the marriage.
> And what kind of marriage will this be?
> One without deception. Better than most.
> Marriage should be the start of a new life.
> We have a saying in my country: Marriage teaches you how to live alone.

And so on. Now try yours.

SCENE AT ALL THE RIGHT PLACES. It's probably a good idea to think of your novel as a series of scenes. Robert Olen Butler told me once that he outlines all of his scenes on index cards and then spreads them out on the floor and rearranges them when the time comes. And then he connects the scenes with the appropriate exposition. Go back to Weeks 8–11, which were all about plot, and take a look again at Aristotle's Incline and then at the exercise under the heading "the Paradigm." Let's think of the scenes that we might have at the start of the novel, at the appropriate plot points, and at the end of the novel. We're not outlining, so much as exploring and considering. Every scene in the novel is a plot point in the sense that each is unprecedented, and in each the central character is somehow changed, even if very subtly. You already have the **opening scene** fleshed out, if not polished. Now think of the scene you need at what we called **plot point 1**, where there will be a twist that sends the novel off in a new direction and into the start of Act II, where the setup becomes the complication. Now a scene at the **midpoint** of your novel. This might be the lowest point in your character's struggle, when all seems lost. Then the scene at **plot point 2**. Then the **climactic** scene. The hero gets what he wants or doesn't. The **final** scene. Write an outline for each scene as you envision them now (they will change). Think of characters, setting, dialogue, details, etc.

> "I write my big scenes first, that is, the scenes that carry the meaning of the book, the emotional experience."
> —JOYCE CAROL OATES

Don't write the scenes yet. Write the scenario: an account or synopsis of a possible course of action.

ADDING TEXTURE. Now look at each of the six scenes you described and consider for each: (1) its function—what is it doing and what else is it doing?; (2) the event or events depicted; (3) the controlling emotion; (4) the structure—how do I put this together?; (5) the setting—note all the significant details; (6) the moment of highest tension. Write down your thoughts.

ROOM IN NEW YORK, 1932. We've been writing about scenes, and now we'll practice writing a scene again. What you do in scene, remember, is show characters in action. And that action is going to be compelling and important, and so you want to avoid interrupting the action with explanation or with extended flashback—save that stuff for later when the scene is done. Otherwise, we'll think the scene is merely a pretense to get some information across to the reader. Don't distract or intrude. Don't undermine the tension of

> "Don't tell us the old lady screamed. Bring her on stage and let her scream."
> —MARK TWAIN

the important dramatic business taking place. So I'll present you with a still life, and you animate the characters. A man and a woman are in a room in New York in 1932. It's evening, but the room is splashed with light. High ceilings. Three framed prints hang on the yellow walls. There is a large paneled door beyond the couple. He's wearing a vest and white shirt and a tie. She's in a red sleeveless dress. He sits forward in his red overstuffed chair, elbows on his knees, reading a newspaper. She sits sideways at an upright piano, her left elbow resting on the side of the keyboard as she stares at the keyboard and plays notes with her right hand. There they are; now put them in motion. You might consider what exactly he's reading about and what tune she's pecking out. Remember the place; remember the year.*

DREAM A LITTLE DREAM. Dreams are our daily/nightly fiction. The unconscious mind is trying to make sense of the scramble of details and events in our daily lives. Or maybe it's just playing around. At any rate, what we think is important may not be what the

---

*The tableau is from an Edward Hopper painting called *Room in New York, 1932*, if you haven't already guessed that. You might take a look at the painting before you write.

sleeping brain thinks is important. Dreams are lyrical, visceral, and narrative. Dreams, like fiction, exist in images. So write about one of your dreams, but write about it in realistic fashion, as if nothing at all is out of the ordinary. Read some Kafka if you want an idea of how this might be done. You wake up, you're a beetle, and you're on your back in bed. You can't turn over. It hurts. Must have slept on your elytron again. You'll be late for work. I recently dreamed that I stopped on my walk to be neighborly, to chat for a moment, with a couple I don't know. We go to my house and talk. (Nothing happens, so I don't need that in my scene.) Maybe it hasn't started yet. Maybe it starts when they take me (make that "my central character") to their house and introduce him to their kids, one of whom, a little girl, has an excess of fingers, all with long curved fingernails. Our hero shakes her hand. An Italian greyhound wearing an aluminum face mask and an aluminum cape walks into the room, rather proud of his costume. Our hero suddenly realizes that he's come to tell the couple that the neighborhood is not zoned for a mill, and their constant and clamorous grinding is keeping the neighbors awake, and the neighbors are threatening legal action. The couple wants to know how they'll feed their brood without the mill.

> "I tell students they will know they are getting somewhere when a scene is so painful they can just barely bring themselves to write about it. A writer has to draw blood."
> —ROBERT MORGAN

CRIME OF THE SCENE. If one of your characters is going to commit a crime in the novel, now is the time to write a draft of the scene. If no one's going to engage in criminal activity, then imagine a character who does. Or imagine a time in one of your characters' past when she did commit a crime. Write a scene, which does not need to include dialogue, in which your character commits a crime.

A crime of violence or a white-collar crime. It probably ought not to be an unintentional crime, however. We want him to know what he's doing. And let us see the act in detail, in slow motion, as it were. If it's a crime of desperation, don't tell us that your character is at the end of her rope; show her at the end of her rope, and the reader, without being told, will think, Jesus, here is one desperate woman. Desperate women take desperate measures. Maybe we ought to feel the tension and the danger, whatever's going on. Your city buildings' supervisor accepts a bribe from a developer to expedite the demolition of a trailer park. Maybe the developer is wired. Your grandmother shoplifts cat food. Your high school student sets fire to a local church.

Week 16:

This and That

The ugly fact is books are made out of books.
The novel depends for its life on the
novels that have been written.
—*Cormac McCarthy*

Y OU'VE GOT SCENES to work on, characters to develop, places
to describe, themes to explore, and a world to get to know, so
keep on writing this week, and while you do, I'll talk about some
other writerly considerations.

AUTHORITY. When I was writing *Louisiana Power & Light*, I needed
a boy to kill himself accidentally, so I had him take the twelve-volt
car battery off his brother's wheelchair and touch the wrong termi-
nal to metal and electrocute himself—I'm sure it was more complicated than that, but I forget now how I did it. At any rate, I got
a note back from the copy editor, who said a jolt from a twelve-volt
battery wouldn't kill the boy. So I called my brother-in-law, who
does avionics, and Conrad told me the copy editor was right. And
he told me how the death could happen (puddle/electric drill with
metal housing). Had the original scene gone to print, my narrator

would have lost the reader's trust, and the novel would have been ruined. How can you have faith in someone who doesn't take the time and effort to check his facts? The narrator needs to gain the trust of the reader at the start and to hold on to it. He does so by being accurate and attentive in his depiction of the fictional world. If you're writing about a particular period, you'd better get it right. No anachronistic details or language. There are catchphrases that we use now that were not used "back in the day." There's one. I don't recall anyone in 1999, say, using that phrase. So it better not slip into your fin de siècle novel. Here are some others: "Not so much"; "Too much information"; "It's all good"; "It is what it is." Maybe we shouldn't use those anyway, since they've become clichés. (See the discussion on clichés below.)

CHAPTERS. You can, of course, and you might, write your novel without chapters, but most of us break the novel down into discrete units that have beginnings, middles, and ends. Chapters can be long or short, can be numbered or not. I practice what I myself consider an outmoded, and never very popular, custom of titling my chapters. It's one more chance to say something about my darlings, and I can't resist the poetic impulse. I also frequently begin each chapter with an epigraph that usually relates to a theme in the chapter. When you end a chapter, you're saying I'm going to shift direction now. I'm going to pick up on another theme, or we're going to visit a different group of people, or we're going back in time or forward in time or to a new setting. Or I think you and I need an emotional break right here. There's a logic that you'll discover as you write, and every novel will have its own periodic rhythm. Short chapters might suggest the hectic, discontinuous, and unsettled world your characters are living in. Longer chapters offer the opportunity for discourse and digression.

CLICHÉS. We think of a cliché as an overused word or phrase that has lost its freshness and often its meaning. "Hot as a pistol." There are also hackneyed characters and situations that fit the definition. The hooker with the heart of gold, the hard-boiled detective, and so on. Clichés are a sign of lazy thinking in a writer, a narrator, and a character. But you can take a cliché and transform it into something new. You might, for example, say that writing fiction is a love of labor; or this: to err is human, to revise divine. Or write what might sound like a cliché, but isn't: as hot as a cat on a skillet. Or take a clichéd character, a sleazy used-car salesman, and make him into a three-dimensional person whom we can understand and sympathize with if not admire. If you are honest with your characters, they will not be stereotypes or clichés. So as you revise, be alert to every cliché or hackneyed word or phrase, every overused or unnecessary modifier. If you've heard it often, don't use it.

DETAILS. "Caress the detail, the divine detail," Nabokov tells us. "God is in the details," Mies van der Rohe tells us. And Hemingway writes, "Every man's life ends the same way. It is only the details of how he lived and how he died that distinguish one man from another." Details are the individual and easily overlooked parts, the particulars that constitute the whole. What I'm thinking about here are the sensual details. When I was learning how to write fiction, my first teacher, Bill Harrison, told me I could write, but I didn't know what a story was. I asked him to tell me, and he told me about plot. I went out and constructed my first plot. Then he said, Nice story, but you don't have enough detail. So I went down to George's Majestic Lounge on Dickson Street (this in Fayetteville, Arkansas) and started writing a story that would end up being called "Addie" and which got published and won me a couple of awards that year. Bill walked in and asked me what I was doing. I said, I'm writing a story with more detail than I need. He said, You can't put in too much detail. The story opens in a lunch counter, what we called a spa in New England, and I remember seeing my hero and his uncle Addie seated at the counter. And then, because of what Bill told me, I thought, I'd better take a closer look at those stools they're sitting on: "ten red vinyl porcelain-based stools." And then I looked at what I now saw was a tintype ceiling and saw the two oak paddle fans. The counter itself was a "polished length of striated white Vermont marble." Then I looked behind the counter at the Hotpoint Rocket 12 griddle, and then at the people in the spa, and so on.

> "It is well to remember
> that grammar is common
> speech formulated."
> —W. SOMERSET MAUGHAM

What had happened, I realized, was that the advice got me to pay attention to this world, to apply my senses, and not to hurry along with my preconceived notions of what the story would be. And each detail told me something about place and characters that I didn't know before, and so changed and deepened the vision of the story.

Fiction writers learn to look at the world an inch at a time. So when you're writing, look close and think hard. Details focus the reader's attention and engage his senses and his imagination and his memory, all of which he needs in order to complete the act of creation that you began. Details also earn the reader's trust—he knows that you're paying attention. The first act of writing is noticing. W. H. Auden said that. And one precise, vivid, and significant detail can furnish a room or outfit a character—the tear in the plaid sofa that's been mended with duct tape; the brown shoes with chunky heels and frayed laces.

DIALECT. A dialect is a regional or social variety of a language distinguished by pronunciation, grammar, or vocabulary, especially a variety of speech differing from the standard literary language or speech pattern of the culture in which it exists. That from *The American Heritage Dictionary of American English*. There are well over a hundred dialects of English. Cockney is a dialect, Nuyorican English is a dialect, Jamaican English is a dialect, and so on. We're not talking simply about accent here, but grammar and vocabulary, as the dictionary said, as well as usage, syntax, and cadence. If you are not intimately familiar with a dialect, don't even attempt it in your fiction—you'll get it wrong. If you do need dialect, then try to achieve it with the rhythm of the prose, with the peculiar syntax, the unique diction, the regional idioms and figures of speech, with the vocabulary indigenous to the locale and not with what is called eye dialect, which *The Columbia Guide to Standard American English* defines as "created by deliberately misspelling words to suggest in writing a Nonstandard or dialectical pronunciation: *wimmin* for women and *gonna* for going to. . . . Both these spellings reflect the actual sounds of Standard speech, *gonna* of course rather literally transcribing speech at a lower level, whereas *wimmin* suggests by its spelling that the speaker is too uncultivated to be able to spell it correctly anyway." Dialect can be difficult and distracting to read. Use it sparingly if you use it. And it may be regarded as pejorative. You want the character to seem regional, but he seems stupid instead. Uneducated. And anyway, trick spellings and lexical gimmicks are the easy way out.

ENDINGS. Margaret Atwood's brilliant comic short story "Happy Endings" resolves the variations on John's and Mary's lives with this: "The only authentic ending is the one provided here: *John and Mary die. John and Mary die. John and Mary die.*" In fiction we can never write, "They all lived happily ever after" because they didn't. No one achieves the "ever after" part, and so there goes the "happy" part.

Every ending is a beginning. The end of every sentence should compel the reader to begin the next sentence. The end of a chapter should compel the reader to begin the next chapter. The end of the novel should compel the reader to begin thinking about what has just happened to her in this world, with these people. But how to end and make that happen. This is the ending I want to talk briefly about here, the one on the last pages of the book.

Endings shouldn't drift or dissolve. They should make a statement. They can be dramatic or muted. The novel has already made its point or it has failed. The ending cannot bail the novel out, in other words, cannot impose a meaning that wasn't already evident. A good ending must, of course, resolve what has gone before it, and must somehow rise above the novel, must stand as an emblem of the novel. If the novel is unresolved, then the novel isn't finished. This is the third part of the structure, remember: beginning, middle, and end. We need all three. What needs to be resolved is the central character's problem. You start your ending when you write the first line of the story. The ending should be inherent in the opening. It ought to seem inevitable once we get there. We don't need to know what else has happened in characters' lives— the end is not a time to introduce new information. We don't need a moral or a message. We need the problem resolved and perhaps a bit more. You have had a cast of characters who have come and gone. We would like to know what happened to them, as well, if only briefly or in passing, especially to those whom you made us care about so deeply. To this idea, Chekhov wrote in a letter to Louis Friedland, "My instinct tells me that at the ends of a novel or a story I must artfully concentrate for the reader an impression of the entire work, and therefore must casually mention something about those whom I have already presented."

Don't end the novel, if you can help it, with a thought, an idea, or a spoken word. Leave the reader with a compelling sensual image of the central character, if that's appropriate, or of the setting, one that is so resonant and arresting that it stays with us when we close the book. This is what I meant earlier about the end being the beginning of a reader's consideration of what he has just experienced. James Joyce leaves us looking at Gabriel Conroy, who stares out the hotel window in Dublin in "The Dead": "His soul swooned slowly as he heard the snow falling faintly through the universe and faintly falling, like the descent of their last end, upon all the living and the dead." Here Cormac McCarthy ends *Blood Meridian* with a visual image: "He never sleeps, the judge. He is dancing, dancing. He says that he will never die." Here a chilling aural image suggests a visual image in Richard Wright's *Native Son*: "He heard the ring of steel against steel as a far door clanged shut." And here aural and olfactory images combine in Kate Chopin's *The Awakening*: "There was the hum of bees, and the musky odor of pinks filled the air." Joseph Conrad leaves us with a stunning and eloquent land-and-skyscape at the end of *Heart of Darkness*: "The offing was barred by a black bank of clouds, and the tranquil waterway leading to the uttermost ends of the earth flowed sombre under an overcast sky—seemed to lead into the heart of an immense darkness." At the end of the book you want to elevate the reader but not leave him in the air. Resolve the plot. And no surprise endings or melodramatic flourishes. Your job here is to stop gracefully, meaningfully, and expressively.

> "Style is everything and nothing. It is not that, as is commonly supposed, you get your content and soup it up with style; style is absolutely embedded in the way you perceive."
> —MARTIN AMIS

FLASHBACKS. Backstory is everything that has happened before the situation that opens your novel, which happens in what we'll call the novelistic present, in which your plot unfolds. We may

need to know some of what happened in the past in order to understand what is happening now. Backstory can come in a prologue
or in a character's memory or can be presented by the narrator in
summary. (You have accumulated
plenty of backstory already, just
in doing the exercises. You have
all those notes on your characters. You know their childhood
traumas, dreams, and disappoint-

> *"I see but one rule: to be clear.
> If I am not clear, all my world
> crumbles to nothing."*
> —STENDHAL

ments. Not all of the backstory will make it, or need make it, into
the novel, not in black and white, at any rate. But it's all been crucial in your getting to know the character and the place.) Another
way to get deeply into the past is with flashback. I think of flashback as the past rendered in scene and not filtered through the lens
of the novelistic present. We are not looking back at an event; we
are back at the event. Flashback is a very natural structural element
and is as old as the *Odyssey*, which begins ten years after the fall
of Troy. We get most of the action, all that happened to Odysseus
during those ten years, in flashback as Odysseus tells the story of
his wanderings to his Phaeacian hosts. In the novelistic present of
the epic, Odysseus is trying to get home to his wife and son.

If you find yourself continually flashing back, ask yourself if you
have started your story too late. If the real trouble is in the past,
maybe the past needs to be the new novelistic present. Sometimes, in the process of writing, we think we're writing one story,
but that story leads to a more powerful story, and if that happens,
abandon the triggering story and go with the one generated. One
more caveat: The premature flashback—the one that comes in the
first chapter of your novel—induces the reader's lethargy. You can't
expect a reader to be interested in a character's background before
he's interested in the character's foreground.

GRAMMAR AND MECHANICS. Yes, spelling is important and so are grammar and punctuation. You're a writer, so for you these considerations should be sacred. (But not in the first draft, necessarily.) Here's Noah Lukeman from his book *A Dash of Style*: "As a literary agent I've read tens of thousands of manuscripts, and I've come to learn that punctuation, more than anything, belies clarity—or chaos—of thought. Flaws in the writing can be spotted most quickly by the punctuation, while strengths extolled by the same medium. Punctuation reveals the writer." Let your attention to grammar and mechanics reveal you to be a writer who cares about his prose and about his reader. Punctuation is all about clarity. Written language stands alone—there are no facial and bodily gestures to help with meaning, no imposed pauses, no changes in the tone of voice—so it has to rely on punctuation to make some of its meaning. Here's a group of words that without punctuation seem to make no sense: <<*that that is is that that is not is not is not that it it is*>> What on earth? Here it is with punctuation: *That that is, is. That that is not, is not. Is not that it? It is.* Try this one. <<*Jones where Smith had had had had had had had had had had the examiner's approval*>> Yikes! Eleven straight *had*s! Here it is making sense somehow: *Jones, where Smith had had "had," had had "had had." "Had had" had had the examiner's approval.* (I found these confounding examples among my notes, and have no idea where I discovered them originally, but I notice them now at various Web sites.) Correct punctuation is organic and not arbitrary. It ought to be an essential element of the meaning.

You owe it to your characters to make sure that no editor has a chance to say no to their story because of something you did or didn't do. You didn't take the time to get the words and the punctuation and the syntax right. You didn't line-edit thoroughly; you didn't proofread and then proofread again. If an editor sees that you didn't care enough to put in the time, then the editor will put the book aside.

There are conventions of grammar and mechanics that we have all agreed to. (Not always with consensus.) Learn the conventions. There is room for experimenting, for differences of mechanical opinion. "Usage is the only test. I prefer a phrase that is easy and unaffected to a phrase that is grammatical," W. Somerset Maugham wrote. But heed T. S. Eliot's advice: "It's not right to violate the rules until you know how to observe them." Knowledge is freedom.

Your knowledge of grammar and punctuation will help you as a writer. If you do not know at least the basics of grammar, how can you possibly write a story that builds on that foundation? If you don't know how to punctuate a complex-compound sentence correctly, you're likely to opt for a simple sentence. I'm not saying that any of this is easy. (As proof of that, I have here at my desk *The Copyeditor's Handbook*. Copy editors are the geniuses of grammar and mechanics. They are the people who will save you from embarrassment when your book is in galleys. And this handbook, put together by the best of the best, contained twenty-six errors in its first printing, by its own admission.) But I am saying you ought to have the tools you need near your desk. Like the above-mentioned *Handbook* and *The Chicago Manual of Style*, like any of dozens of other books dedicated to English usage and grammar. You don't have to have anything memorized. You just need to know where to find the answers.

Your knowledge of grammar and mechanics will also help your reader understand what you're saying, will keep her involved in the story. In *The Art of Fiction*, John Gardner compared fiction writing to creating a dream in the reader's mind. In order for the dream to work, it has to be vivid and continuous. It can't be interrupted. But it will be interrupted by bad technique, by mechanical and usage errors, by faulty punctuation. How do you stay in the dream when you read, "She heard the whaling from the room from under the door"?

LANGUAGE. "Words are all we have," Samuel Beckett reminded us. Every character we animate, every room we construct, every town we build, all of it we do with words. With words we cast our spells. In a letter to Balzac, Stendhal wrote, "Often I ponder a quarter of an hour whether to place an adjective before or after its noun. [He was writing in French, of course.] I seek (1) to be truthful, (2) clear in my accounts of what happens in a human heart." That's how important language is, or ought to be, to a novelist. Flaubert's protégé Maupassant wrote, "Whatever you want to say, there is only one word to express it, one verb to set it in motion, and only one adjective to describe it." Susan Bell, in her marvelous book *The Artful Edit*, contends that "language determines that transcendent aspect of the writer's work: her unique style, her voice." She has a checklist of editing suggestions: keep language fresh; keep it precise and concise; keep it active; and keep it real. In a letter to Joseph Conrad, Ford Madox Ford addressed language: "We used to say that a passage of good style began with a fresh, usual word, and continued with fresh, usual words to the end: there was nothing more to it." The fresh, usual word. Not the esoteric word; not the lexiphanic word (like that one), but the word you've heard before but never in quite this way or in this position in the sentence. Hart Day Leavitt explained: "It is not unusual words that count but unusual combinations of usual words." You can never know enough about the English language. Every entry in the *OED* is a poem. Just consider Wittgenstein's remark: "The limits of my language mean the limits of my world." Stretch your limits.

NAMES. Stanley Elkin said that great characters demand great names. *Sherlock Holmes, Humbert Humbert, Ahab, Aureliano Buendía, Binx Bolling, Hazel Motes.* Names can tell us so much. They may tell us about parental aspirations, tell us how much a family is governed by its past or by its politics or by its aspirations and avocations. A name can tell us about ethnic background, social standing. Names are important. They are never neutral. They always signify, even if it is only ordinariness. *Joe Buck, Charlie Marlow*. If you have a child, remember how much energy and time went into naming that baby. Take some of that care with your characters. Use a phone book to hunt up good names. Visit a cemetery in your town or on the Internet. If you're writing about Minnesota, get a phone book from there—the library will have them, or try online. Baby name books are good for first names. When I see a name I like, I write it down on a slip of paper and put it in a story file. Just pulled these two out of a file for the novel I'm contemplating while I'm writing this book: *Fussell Stumpo* and *Venise Withstanley*. I found Fussell in the obits, and I can't remember where I found Venise. And Fussell's last name was a typo in the headline. In the body of the obit, it was *Stampo*. I like *Stumpo* better. Venise and Fussell are both likely to show up in the novel, once I discover who they are.

> ***"The language must be careful and must appear effortless. It must not sweat. It must suggest and be provocative at the same time."***
> **—TONI MORRISON**

READING. There are two ways to learn how to write fiction: by reading it and by writing it. We're doing the latter right now. Writing every day is crucial to your development. After your first novel comes out, take a day off. (You probably won't be able to.) And so is reading every day. (I mentioned this early on, but it bears repeating.) The best teachers of fiction are the great works of fiction. You can learn more about the structure of a short story by reading Chekhov's "The Lady with the Dog" than you can in a semester of Creative Writing 101. You can, that is, if you read like a writer, which means you have to read everything twice. When you read a story or a novel the first time, just let it happen. Enjoy the journey. When you've finished, you know where the story took you, and now you can go back and reread, and this time notice how the writer reached that destination. (You may only want to do this with books you admire, novels that carry you out of your world and set you down in the world of the story. We have no time for mediocrity, according to that splendid curmudgeon, Harold Bloom. We're all reading against the clock. Although there is something to be said for rereading a book that went wrong—wrong from your standpoint—and finding out where it failed.) Notice the choices the writer made at each chapter, each sentence, and each word. (Every word is a choice.) See now how the transitions work, how a character gets across a room. All this time you're learning. You loved the central character in the novel, and now you can see how the writer presented the character and rendered her worthy of your love and attention. The first reading is creative—you collaborate with the writer in making the story. The second reading is critical.

If you want to write novels, you have to read novels. You have to read the classics, and you know what they are. The ones your teachers foisted on you year after year. And you have to read your contemporaries. And as a fiction writer you need to read everything else, from Wittgenstein's *Blue and Brown Books* to the backs of cereal boxes. The writer's problem, and her opportunity, is knowing the world. That's why we can never have enough reference books. Reference books supply the facts we need, and then, as Kenneth Clark put it, "Facts become art through love, which unifies them and lifts them to a higher plane of reality."

READER. In a letter to Maxim Gorky, Chekhov offered this bit of advice: "When you read proof, take out adjectives and adverbs wherever you can. You use so many of them that the reader finds it hard to concentrate and he gets tired. You understand what I mean when I say, 'The man is on the grass.' You understand because the sentence is clear and there is nothing to distract your attention. Conversely, the brain has trouble understanding me if I say, 'A tall, narrow-chested man of medium height with a red beard sat on green grass trampled by passersby, sat mutely, looking about timidly and fearfully.' This doesn't get its meaning through to the brain immediately, which is what good writing must do, and fast." Chekhov is speaking to the same point made by Umberto Eco: "Every text is a lazy machine asking the reader to do some of its work." The making of a story is partly the achievement of the reader. And the reader needs to feel she is contributing to the creation of the narrative. A novel allows the reader to participate creatively with the writer.

You get the reader to participate, says John Gardner, by engaging his imagination and by making him care about made-up people. Stories are not primarily a way to communicate information—that's what an essayist does or a science writer or a reporter. The aim of fiction is to affect the reader both intellectually and emotionally. You get the reader to participate by doing what Chekhov said to do. If you overspecify, as in his second example, the reader has nothing to do, and you're saying that the information is what's important, not the character. Details make the novel tellable, but using extraneous details means you're telling a news story. Give the reader the clues and let the reader finish the work. You put your character neck-deep in the river and the reader sees the arrow of ripples around her body, sees the gunmetal gray of the water. You want the reader active, but not overactive, and that's a balance you'll have to determine for each novel you write.

You have a reader, not an audience. Your publisher may have an audience in mind, but you have one person at a time holding your book in her hands. When you think "audience," you're taking your attention away from the important problems of the story at hand and shifting it to the problems of the marketplace and to a hypothetical mass. You're telling a story. Someone is listening. And you have to learn to impersonate the reader of your novel as you're writing the novel. You have to be able to anticipate the questions she has as she's reading, and you have to address them in the text.

Don't play with the reader's goodwill. Be honest and respectful. That means no tricks, no gimmicks, no sentimental intrusions. Trust your reader's intelligence and sensitivity. You want from your reader what you want from a friend: generosity, intensity, loyalty, and you want her to stick around till the end. So treat her like a friend. Be considerate of her needs.

SOCIOLOGY. Every novelist is a sociologist. One of the things you're doing when you write a novel is you're bringing the news of this brave new world to the reader's world. You're saying this is the way we live now, even if *now* is a thousand years in the future or in the past. Your focus is on the drama of the individual, your hero, but that hero's struggle takes place in a social matrix. That's the sense in which I mean that as a fiction writer you are a sociologist. Not in the survey-taking, scientific way in which that subject is sometimes taught. You're not trying to draw broad conclusion about your society, you're just writing down what you see there. You don't need to comment—although you will if you're writing satire—but you will want to show us what this world is like. And we all love to learn about a new place, so bringing in the world is to your advantage. Is life like this? we ask. Yes, it is.

STYLE. This is not something you worry about in your first draft. Style is hard to define, but it's what is between you and the reader. It's not a technique itself, but is the result of techniques. It's how you tell the story, how you express yourself on the page. It's the words you use, the phrases and sentences, the syntax, and the paragraphs. It's the rhythm of your prose; it's your transitions. It's everything there on the page and everything not there. You'll find yours, and your novel and its needs will help you do that. Style responds to subject. You won't be employing inflated rhetoric if your characters are trying to survive life on the mean urban streets. To some degree, your style is who you are; it's how you live and how you think, and it's what you notice and how you sound. It can't be bought or borrowed. It's you, but as Henry Green put it, "[the writer's] style is himself and we are all of us changing every day—developing, we hope." The style of your novel is what remains after you've written and rewritten and rewritten. We're all attracted to certain writers, and some of the attraction is to the writer's characteristic style. We begin by imitating the style. And then another writer's style. We're learning how to sing and trying different voices, and then one day we realize that we're hearing our own voice. And it's an exhilarating moment. Everything that was false has dropped away. If you want a brief and practical treatise on style, read Chapter V of Strunk and White's *The Elements of Style*, which includes advice like "write in a way that comes naturally," "write with nouns and verbs," "be clear," and eighteen other reminders.

> "An essential element for good
> writing is a good ear:
> One must listen to
> the sound of one's prose."
> —BARBARA TUCHMAN

TENSE. The conventional and familiar way to tell a story is in the past tense. All fairy tales are in the past tense. It's the tense we use when we talk about the dramatic moments in our own lives. "Last night I was sitting at the bar when in walked this guy, tattooed from forehead to ankles, with a python draped around his neck." Because past tense is so natural and conventional, it's your first choice when writing your novel. If you don't use past tense, you ought to have a good reason for not doing so. It's your first choice, but not your only choice. You may decide to write your novel in present tense. Rather than saying my hero did this, that, and the other, which means the drama is complete, you might say my hero does this, that, and the other, which means that the story is still unsettled and in the making. And you might want that, and it would probably work especially well in a mystery novel. (William Gass wrote, "The present tense is a parched and barren country. In the past, writers rarely went there.") I think the present tense works most gracefully with a first-person narrator. Don't pick the present tense because you think it adds a sense of immediacy. Don't confuse *tentative* with *immediate*. Immediacy comes more definitely from scene and from the truthful rendering of the emotions of the moment than it does from tense, from the fact that it claims to be happening in the past or in the present. Remember, we have your novel in our hands—the action of the novel is over, the story has already happened—it is de facto, in the past.

The past tense is flexible and comforting. You can use it with any point of view. The reader knows that someone has thought about and shaped the story, has left out what is not important and focused on what we need to know. The writer runs less risk of distracting the reader from the fictive dream because the past tense is what we're used to seeing and hearing.

You can switch the tense of the novel just as you can shift points of view. You might decide to write about the past in the present tense and the present in the past tense because it would be fun. You'll find out if it works soon enough. If you do shift, just be sure the shift makes sense. If you're writing about the novelistic present in the past tense and you flash back, you'll need to signal us with the past perfect tense. "Before I left the scene of the crime, I had made note of the curious scratches on the bedside table." And then drop into simple past. Past perfect tense is used to indicate a time before a time in the past. And one more thing, be aware that if you do write in present tense, you are likely to slip back into the more natural past tense. Be sure to check your verbs in revision. And if you make that slip too often, maybe your story is trying to tell you something.

TITLE. We might wonder if *Let Us Now Praise Famous Men* would have fared as well under its original title *Three Tenant Farmers* or if Steinbeck's *East of Eden* would have made the splash it did as *The Salinas Valley*. How about *Trimalchio in West Egg*? That was Fitzgerald's earlier title for *The Great Gatsby*. The title is important. It's the first thing the editor sees, and the first thing the reader sees. It's right there in large letters on the book jacket screaming for attention. It's part of the novel. Naming your book is like naming the new baby. Take your time with it. Call it whatever you want as you're writing it, but stay alert to titles that may turn up. Edward Albee found the title *Who's Afraid of Virginia Woolf?* written on a barroom mirror in soap. If I can see that the writing of the novel is coming to a close (in six months or a year) and I don't have a title, I start reading all the poetry I can and rifling through Shakespeare and the Bible, looking for a title.

TONE. J. A. Cuddon's *A Dictionary of Literary Terms* defines *tone* as "the reflection of a writer's attitude (especially toward his readers), manner, mood and moral outlook in his work; even, perhaps, the way his personality pervades the work." We often speak of a person's tone of voice as conveying meaning above and beyond what he is actually saying. The tone of a speaker's voice may reveal unspoken information about his thoughts and feelings. Tone might be comic, belligerent, facetious, haughty, philosophical, somber, joyous, or anything from admiring to zealous. We don't have the benefit of audible tone in fiction, but we still want to be able to let the reader know our attitude toward the work, our feelings for the events and people in the novel. Tone suggests musical qualities like pitch and timbre, and tone is the quality of writing that approaches music. And, in fact, we do partially control tone with sound, rhythm, cadence, stress, and so on, and also with diction, syntax, and imagery. Here are tonal variations on a theme:

- After my father died when I was twelve, my mother married Harvey Fahlstrom.

- After my poor father died when I was twelve, my mother ran out and married Harvey Fahlstrom before she planted flowers on Dad's grave.

- After the cancer took my dad when I was like twelve or so, the old lady settled for that lard-ass Harvey Fahlstrom.

- I'm twelve; Dad dies; Mom remarries; life goes on.

Same information presented with different attitudes. I could write a love story many ways. Here are a couple of them. A young man of little means falls head over heels for a debutante from the prosperous side of the tracks. She's dating a wealthy fellow whose family controls a Wall Street investment firm, and she barely notices the young man. He determines to make his millions, and in that way he will first attract her attention and then win her heart. Meanwhile, she marries the arrogant and shiftless heir, who, it turns out, ignores her. Our young man returns—he has made millions and given millions away to the world's poor—wins her heart with his love and his generosity, and he saves her from a bleak and harrowing marriage. That's one way to tell the story. A bright and optimistic way. Another: A young man of little means falls head over heels for a debutante from the other side of the tracks. She loves another man, as above, whom she marries. The young man takes a job with his rival's Wall Street investment firm and quickly works his way to the executive boardroom. He's had to step on certain toes along the way; he's admired for his take-no-prisoners attitude. He begins his campaign to win the woman's heart, and indeed, though she loves her hapless husband, she's not *in love* with him, and she begins her affair with the young man, who now understands that, in fact, he doesn't need to marry her; he only needs to keep her. The heartbroken and humiliated husband is driven to drink. The young woman hates what she has done, what she has become. Our young man marries his rival's sister and now stands in line to inherit her share of the firm. And that's a more cynical take on our love story, I suppose.

VULNERABILITY. The way to protect yourself from praise and from derision in a writing workshop discussion or in a *New York Times* review is to simply write the next novel. Busy yourself with creation and not with criticism. You may soothe your wounded pride after a harsh review by reminding yourself that writers are people of talent trying to prove it to people who have none. But that would be spiteful. Still, Kenneth Tynan characterized the critic as a man who knows the way, but can't drive the bus. You put yourself out there in the marketplace. You're vulnerable. Some people take shots at easy targets. The more risks you take with your work, the more ammunition they use. Console yourself, if you need consolation,

> "You must be aware that the reader is at least as bright as you are."
> —WILLIAM MAXWELL, JR.

with the bad reviews that Faulkner and Joyce and every other brilliant writer has received. *Kirkus Reviews* said this about John Barth's *The End of the Road*: "This is for those schooled in the waste matter of the body and the mind; for others a real recoil." Clifton Fadiman famously wrote of Faulkner's *Absalom, Absalom!* in *The New Yorker*:

"The final blowup of what was once a remarkable, if minor, talent." Here's the opening sentence of the *New York Times* review of *Ulysses*: "A few intuitive, sensitive visionaries may understand and comprehend 'Ulysses,' James Joyce's new and mammoth volume, without going through a course of training or instruction, but the average intelligent reader will glean little or nothing from it—even

> *"You have to saturate yourself with English poetry in order to compose English prose."*
> —VLADIMIR NABOKOV

from careful perusal, one might properly say study, of it—save bewilderment and a sense of disgust." None other than the *New York Review of Books* complained that Joseph Heller's *Catch-22* "gasps for want of craft and sensibility." Enough said. (Makes you recall James Russell Lowell's remark, "He who would write and can't write, can surely review.") They don't always get it right, so not to worry.

You are just as vulnerable to praise. Your job is not to please critics, but to tell stories. The reader is your auditor. A critic is one reader who, you hope, is so engaged with your novel that he wants to respond. He thinks books are that important. Good critics make for good writers, make for a lively literary community. Let the critic do her job. You do yours. Write!

ZEN. "The truth of a thing is the feel of it, not the think of it," Stanley Kubrick said. Novels should be written with as little consternation as possible and without desire. That's what Chekhov thought. In that way each word, each sentence is a unique event and not simply a means to an end. Fiction is not ambition. It should not look beyond itself. "One must avoid ambition in order to write. Otherwise something else is the goal: some kind of power beyond the power of language. And the power of language, it seems to me, is the only kind of power a writer is entitled to," Cynthia Ozick wrote.

Fiction is a simple act—a looking into the heart of chaos. Like any simple act, fiction is difficult to perform. The more you think about it, the more complicated you make it. So maybe the idea is not to think about the novel, but to look at it. Doubt what you think, but not what you see. Look at the novel and listen to it. Don't project your notion on the story. Let the story project its notion on you. Be enlightened by your story.

Both fiction writing and Zen find the sacred in the profane, knowing that the profane is sacred. Both witness and do not judge. Both require humility and concentration. Both provide questions, not answers. Questions like, What's going on here and why is it going on? And like a provocative Zen koan, an effective novel should knock you out of your complacency. It should surprise, puzzle, and encourage you with mystery. Alan Watts said, "Zen never wastes energy in stopping to explain; it only indicates." Show, don't tell.

ALL THE NEWS THAT'S FIT TO PRINT. We're back to writing. *Novel* comes from the Italian for "the news." When you write your novel, one of your jobs, as I suggested above, is to tell us about the world of the characters through the political, social, economic, etc., events of their day. Spend some time today researching the days and weeks of the events of the novel. Read newspapers, newsmagazines, etc., for the local and world events which would have influenced your characters' thoughts, feelings, and lives. Remember in *Farewell, My Lovely* where Marlowe keeps reading the papers to see how Joe DiMaggio's hitting streak is going? If your story is contemporary, did your characters follow the presidential election campaign? How did they feel about it? Did they live through the Vietnam War? Think local, as well as national, global. Take notes. You'll find places for this information later.

MY LIFE FROM NOW ON. Look at your novel, your scene or scenes, your outlines, notes, lists, and synopses, all that you have, and then look ahead at the time you have left. Now decide on your strategy for finishing the draft of the novel. How are you going to complete this seemingly impossible task? Start with what you'll do later today when this exercise is finished and your characters wait for you. Set some goals for yourself and your novel. Think about what has been fun and exciting in the writing. Write down what that is and promise yourself to do more of it. What do you think you need to do more of? Less of? At this point, let me remind you and reassure you. The first draft is only for discovery. It will not be what you hoped it would be. Everything important happens in revision.

IN THE HEART OF THE HEART OF THE STORY. What is the controlling metaphor, the central image, the fertile symbol that directs your novel or is the source of its energy? It's in there already, or it's in your notes. It may even be your working title. In *Louisiana Power & Light* the utility company with its transcendent name served as my central metaphor. Mann and Hemingway used mountains as central images and all that their isolation, majesty, and dominance suggested. We all know about the whiteness of Melville's great whale and Harper Lee's mellisonant and tragic mockingbird. So determine your central image or metaphor. Read all about it. Use dictionaries, thesauruses, encyclopedias, field books, Web sites, books of quotations, etc. The idea is to open up that image, discover all its possible permutations, connotations, and uses. Take notes.

UNE LIGNE DONÉE. Begin a draft of a chapter, any chapter, with this gift of a first line: *She rests in the bathtub and looks ahead to tonight's party.* Let the line guide the writing. Write fast, don't worry about making connections with other material. Maybe connections aren't important. If they are, you'll see them later.

THE WORLD INTERVENES. Read your Sunday paper of choice to find material for your novel. Do this in two ways. (1) Assume your character is reading the paper, and an article affects him strongly for some reason. Write about it. Four hundred children are rescued from a polygamous compound, for example. Now find a place for him to read the paper somewhere in your novel. It could be a paragraph, a sentence, a scene, a chapter—something he reads affects him strongly and we see how and why. And it will all have something to do with the theme of your novel. (2) Look for an incident seemingly unrelated to the novel and your characters. For some reason—it's odd, intriguing, bizarre, whatever—it catches your attention. Make notes about the story or clip it out and keep it in your novel file. Begin to think about how you might use it.

Weeks 17 & 18:

All the Lonely People

The bad novelist constructs his characters; he directs them
and makes them speak. The true novelist listens to them
and watches them act; he hears their voices even
before he knows them.
—*André Gide*

C HARACTER IS WHY we read fiction, and it's what we remember
when we close the book. We want to connect with the people
we meet in novels. We want to care about them. Caring is what
makes us human. We spend too much of our lives not feeling, not
living so much as acting, going through the motions. So with this
acknowledgment that character is at the heart of your novel, let's
spend the next two weeks exploring the lives of the people you're
writing about. You're writing about these people you made up, and
you're waiting for that moment when they do something that you
didn't expect them to do or say something that surprises you. That
moment won't happen until you've gotten to know your characters well enough. And now they are people and not puppets to be
manipulated. You can trust them. Perhaps one or two of them have
already done the unforeseen. Until the central characters, at least,

do so, you don't have a novel yet. Don't worry about all of this, however. Not just yet. It may take you until the next draft before it happens. Or the third. But it will. Trust the process.

Keep in mind while you're writing these two weeks that you are trying to get to know your characters more intimately and intensely than you already do. The purpose of the exercises is not to provide you with scenes for the novel, although they might, but rather to surprise the characters in the act of being themselves and to surprise yourself with penetrating and revelatory insights into their hearts and minds. And now you'll know more clearly who they are, how they will behave, what they are likely to think and feel, fear and desire. Not all of the material will show up on the page in black and white, but its presence will be evident in the actions of your characters.

THE SECRET LIFE OF CHARACTERS. Take a minor character from your novel, a character you're not all that familiar with yet, but whom you like and admire. You've pictured his life as one of routine and order. Fulfilling, but rather unadventurous, let's say. But now you realize that this person is more than logic, politeness, good grooming, and kindness. He has an imagination that you know nothing about. Imagine his secret life, the one you were previously unaware of. Just for starters, what is it he thinks about while he's on his

> "If you are inclined to leave your character solitary for any considerable length of time, better question yourself. Fiction is association, not withdrawal."
> —A. B. GUTHRIE, JR.

lunch break? Or thinks about at night before he falls asleep? The answers should come as a surprise to you. Who are the people he knows—these people who are more important than your central character, perhaps, in his life? What is it that he wants in his life?

And why? Think about this character. Use the answers as the basis for a larger role in your novel. For example, let's say this character never traveled. Has never been out of the state, so far as you know. He is always around and available. But then one afternoon, you run into him as he sips coffee at Starbucks, and you see he's glancing through a photo album on his computer—his slides of his Antarctic vacation. He says, "For my next trip I'm going solo the length of the Amazon."

LIE. What was the last lie your central character told and to whom did he tell it? Why did he tell it? How did he feel about telling it? Would he tell it again?

TRAUMA. In this exercise you're looking for present-day motivation, but looking into the past, where the patterns for many of our behaviors and fears and needs are established. Let's see what the dictionary has to say about the word *trauma*: 1. *Medicine*. A serious injury or shock to the body, as from violence or accident. 2. *Psychiatry*. An emotional wound or shock that creates substantial, lasting damage to the psychological development of a person, often leading to neurosis. The word comes from the Indo-European root *ter*, to rub, turn, with some derivatives referring to *twisting*, *boring*, *drilling*, and *piercing*. Think about the related words, the definition, and synonyms while you are doing this exercise. What happened to

> "The first thing that makes a reader read a book is the characters."
> —JOHN GARDNER

your character as a child that shaped him, wounded him, left substantial emotional damage? Write about the event and the results. Consider your own life, of course, as a source of material, and the lives of others. Consider doing this with all of your significant characters.

TIME TO GO DEEP. Describe one of your central character's obsessions, or something that haunts her, something you know about, or you have an inkling of, but which does not appear in the story, at least not in black and white. Write about the obsession in as much detail as you can. (Maybe it's an obsession of your own—one you don't understand.) Now trace that obsession back to its source. Something happened in your character's childhood. You get an image, a person, an event. Write about that. (Your character is obsessed with security, with saving money, with playing it safe, because every payday Dad and Mom would have a fight about the family finances, frightening arguments for a five-year-old.)

> "I was reading E. M. Forster who was writing about plot, and he said the awful thing is you create those wonderful characters and then they won't do anything; they won't be bothered to get involved in a plot!"
> —JOHN MORTIMER

A DAY IN THE LIFE. We want to know what your character does every day. The little things, the rituals, the habits, and so on. Describe her waking up. What does she do on a typical morning? What does she have for breakfast? Describe her workday in detail. Her friends there. What she does for lunch. Does she call anyone during the day? Whom? Why? When work's over, what does she do? With whom? Back home she does what? Give us a typical day, in other words. What's on her mind while she's doing everything else? Probably she does a few things that are unusual or odd.

ON THE SEVENTH DAY. On an NPR Summer Reading segment a while back, the editor leading the chat said that reading was a leisure activity, intimating that reading ought to be an amusing diversion in the manner of movies or television. (You know: "beach books" and "summer movies.") I thought she was demeaning books, and perhaps she was, but she was also demeaning leisure, in the same way that the seventies male fashion industry did. (You know: "leisure suits.") Leisure is, in fact, when everything creative and interesting in our lives ought to happen, when we live our real lives and they aren't on loan to the marketplace. Anyway, you've written about your character on a typical day. But now it's Sunday. A day of relative freedom. Leisure. Sundays and free time can bring out the worst in people. Things happen on Sundays that don't happen on other days. Family obligations, perhaps. For the religiously affiliated, there may be worship services. Write about your central character on Sunday.

PLEASE ALLOW ME TO INTRODUCE MYSELF . . . Let your central character speak in his or her own voice. Let him introduce himself to the world, to you. He can be formal, informal, funny, sober, or whatever. What does he think is important for us to know? Will he keep anything from us? From himself? How does he feel about talking this way to strangers?

———

NOW LET'S SEND your central character on a vacation. Wherever he wants to go, for as long as he wants to go there. Life as a journey is one of our oldest metaphors, so with that in mind, we'll consider his own brief journey from oblivion to oblivion as well. (Rilke: "The only journey is the one within.") Am I being too pessimistic? (Oliver Goldsmith: "Life is a journey that must be traveled no matter how bad the roads and accommodations.") Every novel is a journey, for that matter. Writing it and reading it.

DESTINATION. A. Where is she going and why? What are her plans when she gets there? What kind of planning has she done? Does she believe that planning is half the fun, or does she leave it to the travel agent? Let her dream about what might happen when she gets there. **B.** She has a destination planned for her life—where is she going and why? What is her five-year plan? Ten-year plan? What might stop her from getting there? What does she have to do to achieve her goals?

BAGGAGE. A. What does he pack to take on the trip? Fill every inch of that suitcase, briefcase, overnight bag. What does he forget to pack? What does he take that he won't use? **B.** We all carry around psychological baggage, wounds from our childhood, betrayals by ex-lovers and supposed friends. Make a list of some of the baggage your character carries with him.

DINING OUT. A. Your central character has at least one divine meal on her holiday. Describe it in loving and precise detail. The meal, the place, and the company, if any. Use your five senses and cookbooks and wine books and whatever else you need. You also notice that she has some peculiar eating habits or rituals. Look closely. What are they? **B.** Despite the meal, your character is disturbed. It's the memories of other, less pleasant, even painful dinners. What were those? Put us there at the tables.

SLIDE SHOW. A. Your central character has brought along a camera. What kind? He takes photos of people and places on the trip. Why does he photograph what he does? Show us the pictures. Give us a real sense of the place and the culture. Let him look at the pictures when he gets home. What does he feel, looking at them? **B.** The slide show gets your character interested in visual images of himself. He takes out the old photo albums. Write about the photos he sees. Let us see them. What do they tell you about the character's life and growth? Who is in the photos? Who is missing? What are the expressions on the faces? Look at some of your own photos to stir your imagination.

THE ENCOUNTER. Your central character meets someone on the trip. An intriguing stranger, unlike anyone she's ever encountered. What is it about this person that first catches her attention? They spend time talking. For some reason your character opens up to this stranger. She tells this person things she hasn't told anyone. Let's hear the conversation.

THE TRAVELER. A. When we travel, visit new places, we tend to be alert, to notice things that we might ordinarily not. We notice the unusual flora and fauna, the peculiar architectural details, the illuminating local customs, and the strange food. Travel trains us to notice. We are open to new experiences; we welcome new interaction with people. We allow ourselves to become susceptible to the stimuli around us. We are, in fact, a lot like fiction writers when we are travelers. What did your central character notice on his holiday? What did he see, taste, touch, smell, say, hear for the first time? What did these stimulants do for him? How did they make him feel about his own life back home? **B.** Let him come home and apply this elevated sense of awareness to his house, his city, and his surroundings. What does he find that he has failed to notice before?

> "The characters you create in a novel become as real in your mind as movie stars."
> —NORMAN MAILER

EVERY JOURNEY MUST end. And that journey we call life, when we're waxing poetic, ends in the same place for all of us. We're all on a one-way trip to nowhere. Well, that's one way of looking at it.

DAY OF THE DEAD. Let your central character write his own obituary. As if he were dying now. As if he were to die when he accomplished everything he wanted to. Now let him make the plans for his funeral and memorial service.

DEAR DIARY. Your central character is going through her closet/ attic/cellar and finds her diary from elementary school. She reads it with interest and trepidation. She remembers old friends she hasn't thought about for years. She remembers smells and tastes and places, some fondly, others with embarrassment. She learns something about herself that startles her. She was not the child she thought (until now) she was. She had always thought of herself as free-spirited, let's say, but realizes after reading this diary that fear and anxiety directed her days. Or she thought she was happy, but senses the sadness under the breezy entries. How does she feel now about this revelation?

THE BIRTHDAY PARTY. It's your central character's birthday. What's his sign? (And what are those astrologers doing about their Pluto problem?) How old is he and how does he feel about his age? All the appropriate characters in the novel are there. And some folks who aren't in the novel. Let him open his gifts. Who gave him what? Did he get what he wanted? What was that? Spend some time at the party. Watch him, eavesdrop on his conversations. After the party, he's alone, and he remembers a birthday party from his childhood. Why this particular one? What does he remember? Be specific, concrete. Render the honest emotions then and now.

THANKSGIVING. Your central character has plans for the holiday. He's spending at least part of the day with family—however he defines the term. They'll eat. Write a scene about the meal. Describe the food in detail, the talk, the place. Use all of your senses. Let your character talk or think about his mood on this day. What does he have to be thankful for?

ANSWERING MACHINE. Your character is troubled as usual. What is today's specific problem? Write about it. Now he comes home and sees the red light flashing on his answering machine. A message. He plays the message and is surprised to learn that the message solves his problem, alleviates his trouble. Play the message.

YOU CAN'T ALWAYS GET WHAT YOU WANT. For each of the important characters you have so far, make a list of ten things he or she wants. Some items will be obvious. Some will be complete surprises to you. You may have to do some brainstorming to come up with ten. Some will have no seeming connection to your novel. That's fine.

DAYS OF FUTURE PAST. Examine the central character's past (or any character's past). Make a list of important dates. A timeline. Dates are doorways into a person's life. Birth, move to new city, graduation, first date, college, trip to Europe, death of father, arrest. Be as specific as you can. (Creating a character who is about your age, who comes from the same region as you do, who has a similar educational and cultural background, can be very helpful later on—the research is easier. The downside is maybe you don't get to imagine the world as clearly or as energetically.) Who were her early friends, best friends? What were her hobbies? Where does she go on vacations? Did she have a secret place? What did she dream of becoming when she grew up? Write about her school days and play days and the difficulty of adolescence. If your character has had any marriages or significant

> "By the end, you should be inside your character, actually operating from within somebody else, and knowing him pretty well, as that person knows himself or herself. You're sort of a predator, an invader of people."
> —WILLIAM TREVOR

relationships that are no longer viable, write about them. Has she had children? Write about the births and the early days of parenthood. What does she remember as the significant relationships in her life? The crucial decisions that she made? When does she consider herself to have become an adult? And so on.

'TWAS THE NIGHT BEFORE CHRISTMAS. It's Christmas Eve. Your central character is awake, alone, sitting in the living room or the kitchen or the bedroom, remembering ghosts of Christmases Past. Let her remember. Write about the memories and the feelings they engender. Many Christmases with many people, many trees, many drinks, and many friends, some of whom she's never seen again. If Christmas is inappropriate for your character, substitute a similar holiday. New Year's Eve will work for most of us.

CAST IN BRONZE. Leonardo da Vinci: "An emotion, a state of mind, always finds expression in a person's face and body. When a man is angry, he shows his teeth and frowns; his eyes seem to shoot darts; he tightens his facial muscles and his whole posture, stiffening his neck and balling his fists. Such emotion might be temporary or habitual. An habitual emotion imprints itself on a person's face like an inscription in bronze; it becomes character." Let's read the face of your central character. If you can see the face clearly, begin to describe it in terms of its inscription—the lines around the eyes, the wrinkles between the brows, the dimples or absence of them, the cast of the eyes, the set of the jaw, the brow furrowed or smooth. Is the face symmetrical? What does the inscription tell us? If you can draw, draw the face in as much detail as possible. If you can't quite see the face, look through books of photographs and find it there. Now describe it and write about what the face tells you.

Weeks 19 & 20:
The Plot Thickens

We want incident, interest, action:
to the devil with your philosophy.
—*Robert Louis Stevenson*

THIS MORNING—a few minutes ago, actually, during my first cup of coffee—I came across a drawing by Swedish caricaturist Albert Engström on a Web site called *Applied Abstractions*. In the drawing, a fully clothed and mightily disheveled man sprawls on a rumpled bed, his boots still on, and an open decanter on its side, spilling wine onto the tangled sheets. The caption reads, in English: "During a convivial gathering there is talk of the unhygienic aspect of using galoshes. One of those present chips in: 'Yes, I've also noticed this. Every time I've woken up with my galoshes on, I've had a headache.'" The lesson here, according to the Web site, is that *covariation* does not mean *causality*. "Just because something moves at the same time or later than something else, the first does not necessarily cause the other." If that were the case, we could say that global warming was caused by Baby Boomers going through menopause.

In philosophical circles, the term *post hoc ergo propter hoc* addresses this issue. This is a logical fallacy meaning "after this, therefore, because of this." In other words, because A precedes B, A must be the cause of B. However, because your character cut himself shaving in the first scene of the story does not necessarily mean that the nick caused the death of his father in the second act. The danger for the fiction writer is that she misunderstands causality and chronology. Just because one incident in the story precedes another does not make it a cause. Because the rooster crows before the sun rises does not mean the rooster causes the sun to rise. Unless you're into magical thinking. All of which brings us back to plot, a causal, not covariant, sequence of events.

Yes, we've talked an awful lot throughout the book about plot, and we're not finished yet. If you don't have a plot in your novel, if you're not going to tell the reader a story, what do you have to offer her? Your spectacular display of language? If we want language, remember, we have Shakespeare, Nabokov, and Joyce, and each of them gave us plot as well as sublime language. Your incandescent characters will not fire our imaginations unless they are involved in a struggle. A character is what he does. Plot is action, not simply activity. Action is motivated behavior. Movement, not simply motion.

We read novels because we need stories; we crave them; we can't live without

> "The problem of narration is not . . . the problem of finding the words, but that of choosing and placing events, of allowing or instigating their wordless dialogue."
> —JOHN BERGER

telling them and hearing them. Stories are how we make sense of our lives and of the world. When we're distressed and go to therapy, our therapist's job is to help us tell our story. Life doesn't come with plots; it's messy and chaotic; life is one damn, inexplicable thing after another. And we can't have that. We insist on meaning. And so we tell stories so that our lives make sense. Here's A. S. Byatt on stories: "Narration is as much a part of human nature as breath and the circulation of the blood. Modernist literature tried to do away with storytelling, which it thought vulgar, replacing it with flashbacks, epiphanies, streams of consciousness. But storytelling is intrinsic to biological time, which we cannot escape. Life, Pascal said, is like living in a prison from which every day fellow prisoners are taken away to be executed . . . and we all think of our lives as narratives, with beginnings, middles, and ends. . . .

"Stories keep part of us alive after the end of our story."

Now, once you have a plot, once you've given us a reason to read your novel, then you can also dazzle us with your display of graphotechnics, make us fall in love with your irresistible characters, and provoke us with your trenchant ideas. But first things first.

PLOT SOUNDS EASY enough. Here it is one more time (thanks to John Gardner):

- A central character
- Wants something (intensely)
- And goes after it
- Despite opposition (conflict)
- And as a result of a struggle (protracted action)
- Comes to a win or a loss

But it's hard to do! Plot is where we separate those who want to write novels from those who actually do it. Plot is not imposed on the novel, remember. Plot emanates from the thoughts, feelings, and behaviors of the characters. You can't really separate plot from character. Plot, then, gives your characters something to do, and it engages the reader in the story. To reiterate: No matter how interesting a character is, no matter how luminous your writing, no matter how fascinating your themes, if we don't have a plot to follow, we're not going on the journey. Period. Plot makes the reader want to know what happens next and reassures the reader that what will eventually happen won't simply be a random series of events, but events that will add up to meaning. Every event in a plot is predicated on an earlier event and gives rise to succeeding events. And they are all related. Plot is your context. Plot is the unifying principle of your novel. It's what holds this world of characters, settings, language, and themes together. "Plots are what the story writer sees with," Eudora Welty said. You don't want to walk into this world blind. You spent all this time writing a novel, and you want others to read it. Give them a suspenseful plot, and they will.

STOPPING TIME. In a previous exercise we worked from a visual image to a narrative. This time we're going to imagine an event and then capture it at a telling moment, the way a photograph might. What we are trying to do is to fix an event in time and space, to make the resulting image work symbolically. (Ritual events, like weddings, funerals, baptisms, graduations, and so on, work well in this context. They represent moments

> "Essentially and most simply put, plot is what the characters do to deal with the situation they are in. It is a logical sequence of events that grow from an initial incident that alters the status quo of the characters."
> —ELIZABETH GEORGE

that we'd like to save and treasure.) The moment becomes an emblem of the larger story. The formal wedding photo, for example, represents our culture's faith in family and in romantic love. It suggests much more than it states. Like the haiku, it starts us thinking. The suit, the tie, the white wedding gown, the crucifix, the flowers, the rings, and the candles, all are symbolic. And as a writer/photographer you know that what is left out casts its shadow onto the story.

Imagine you are a photographer who wants to snap the picture that will suggest what is going on in that room, in that church, in that backyard. The mood, the tension, the atmosphere. You want your picture to reveal the character of these people, not just their personalities. Will your picture be black and white? Color? Interior? Exterior? Candid? Posed? Who is it that has caught your attention?

Watch your characters, see what they're doing. You need to assess what it is you think is at the heart of this business. And what's behind it. Take your photograph just when they're doing something that expresses the essence of the ritual or the conflict.

> "A story to me means a plot where there is some surprise. Because that is how life is—full of surprises."
> —ISAAC BASHEVIS SINGER

Now that you've taken the photo, describe it in elaborate and precise detail. You'll notice things now that you perhaps did not see through the viewfinder. And now you can crop the photo, darken or lighten. Look at all of the details. The position of the hands, the keys on the table, the light from the lamp, that ring, the scar. And now your task is to describe the photograph in such a way as to reveal the narrative that lies beyond the borders of the picture.

SEEMING TO DIGRESS. Now let's try this. Take your central character and place her in a situation that you just know does not belong in this novel. Let's say she's a wife struggling to save her troubled marriage and keep her family together. Her husband has a girl-friend; her friends are telling her to leave the creep; the kids miss their daddy. She's at her wits' end. She's desperate. Have her train to run a marathon. What is that about? Her friends are asking her how she has time for that. This isn't getting her struggle under way, is it? Do we have time for this? While she's out on the road, hubby is romancing his sweet young thing. You don't think it's a good idea, but let her do it. Go with her on one of her runs. Talk to her. Write down what she thinks about, what she's feeling as she runs. What about that metaphor of the long-distance run? Can you use it? What about running through "the wall"? What does she learn about herself? What do you learn about her? Maybe this isn't a tangent at all. Maybe running serves as an important insight into her character. When in her life has she run from something? Toward something? And maybe this is a subplot. Isn't it great when these opportunities drop into your lap? She wants her husband back. She also wants to complete a marathon. She's putting everything she has into both endeavors.

> "The novel requires a certain slowness of progress that allows the reader to live with the characters and become accustomed to them."
> —ANDRÉ GIDE

STRANGERDOM. One of the oldest plot devices in literature is the stranger who rides into town. So now let's think about your central character and consider every way that he may be a stranger. To his family and friends, to himself, and to the world. There are obvious ways, perhaps (he just moved to town), and other, more subtle ways. Does he see himself as a stranger? Does he feel out of place in some circumstances? Does she ever feel like she belongs somewhere else? In what areas of her life is she a newcomer? Does she ever feel exotic? Has she ever been a guest? Has she ever been a visitor, someone just passing through? Has she ever acted the stranger—affected a distant manner? What is she a stranger to? And now you might want to consider the strangers in her life. Who are they? Did they stay in her life or pass on?

THE SEARCHER. Another venerable plot device is the person who sets off on a quest. What has your central character searched for or pursued in his life? Did he get what he was after? Was his quest a solo one or done with others? If so, with whom? Has he sought wisdom, wealth, comfort, security, love, friendship?

STORY LINE. You know that a plot is not a chronological sequence of events. It's a causal sequence of events. The rhythm of a story line suggests inevitability: this happened, which causes this to happen, which causes this to happen, and so on. Build on all the work you've done so far, including the scenarios, plot points, scene outlines, and so on. Now map out a story line from your opening scene on till the last scene in terms of cause and effect. Like this one I did from *Louisiana Power & Light*:

> *Situation:* Billy Wayne wants to be a priest.
> *Complication:* He meets Earlene.
> *Result:* He marries Earlene.

Which causes this new situation:

> *Situation:* Billy Wayne regrets his decision.
> *Complication:* Billy Wayne meets Tami Lynne.
> *Result:* He has an affair with Tami Lynne.

Which causes:

> *Situation*: Billy Wayne regrets another decision, this dalliance.
> *Complication*: He realizes his marriage is in jeopardy.
> *Result:* He confesses to Earlene.

Which causes Earlene to leave him. And so on.

Or think of the rhythm as *problem-solution-problem-solution,* etc.

Problem: Parents are poor.
Solution: Get rid of the children.
Problem: Children don't want to leave.
Solution: Take them for a long walk in the woods.
Problem: Children are stranded, lost.
Solution: Are found by a little old lady.
Problem: The lady is a child-eating witch.

And so on. Plot out the novel in this way. Remember this is all just imagining what might happen, and nothing is struck in stone, and you remain completely flexible. You're just blazing a trail that might lead to the destination. But you also know it might not. We're trying to approach our characters, our worlds, from all different angles, not knowing where or when some intriguing information will turn up. We're trying to be illogical and unanalytical. We're storytellers, not scholars!

MINING THE ORE. Read through all of your notebook entries—all these exercises you've been doing and all the other writing you've been doing—with story in mind. I highlight or otherwise note those items, names, images, ideas, plots, characters, et al., that you think you will use or might use or could use in the coming novel. Don't worry that those items don't seem to connect yet. They will later. Write them down and elaborate on them. Do you have any ideas yet on how they might appear?

THE FAMILY PLOT. The family plot is that little piece of land where the living bury their kin. Some families, of course, bury their kin before they're dead by disowning them, by keeping them or their deeds a secret from the world. What is your central character's family tree? Make one up, put it on a chart. (I just Googled "family tree" under *images* and found many sample trees you could use. Apparently genealogy is big business on the Internet.) Trace her family back a few generations. Give everyone a name. Aunts, uncles, cousins, grandparents and great-grandparents. Both sides of the family. Did either the paternal or maternal families have a certain reputation in the area as, say, cantankerous ("the querulous Quinns"), intellectual, comely, miserly, or cursed? Any illnesses run in the family? Any unsavory conditions or predilections? Remember that we are all ruled to some degree by our DNA, our selfish genes. Some fates we can run from, but never elude. Make up the family tree, visit the family plot, look through the family Bible, and write about the people who interest you there. Who was your central character named for? Why that person? What relative does the family always say she reminds them of? Who does she *really* take after? Who was your central character close to? Whom did she avoid?

> *"As regards plots I find real life no help at all. Real life seems to have no plots."*
> —IVY COMPTON-BURNETT

Weeks 21-24:

Draftsmanship

A careful first draft is a failed first draft.
—*Patricia Hampl*

Y OU'RE WRITING A *first* draft. Don't expect to get it right; just try to get it written. Keep in mind the epigraph above. No need to be meticulous and conscientious yet. If at first you succeed, try, try again. Here's John Steinbeck's advice on what we might think of as the discovery draft: "Write freely and as rapidly as possible and throw the whole thing on paper. Never correct or rewrite until the whole thing is down. Rewrite in process is usually found to be an excuse for not going on. It also interferes with flow and rhythm which can only come from a kind of unconscious association with the material." You should write as serenely as you can. Chekhov said he tried to write as calmly as if he were eating blinis. You have nothing to worry about and nothing to fear. No one sees this draft but you. The fact is, as I've said, that much of the important writing comes during revision, but you have to have something to revise. You need to get black on white. Your task these four weeks, then, is to finish, to write a beginning, middle, and end of your novel— as bad as it is, and it *will* be worse than you had hoped. So don't worry. It's that way for all of us and for each novel we write. You will also have accomplished the hardest part—the first draft, where you have had to allow yourself the opportunity to fail. Failure's a more humbling experience than most of us want to suffer. Call the draft a *rehearsal* if you want. That may take the pressure off. Write fast and don't cross out or toss out anything just yet—you might find whatever disappoints you now useful later on; it may not, in fact, be so loathsome as you think it is. To err is human, to revise, divine. The first draft is where you are most human, most fallible. David Mamet wrote, "I used to say that a good writer throws out the stuff that everybody else keeps. But an even better test occurs to me: perhaps a good writer keeps the stuff everybody else throws out."

> "First drafts are for learning what your novel or story is about."
> —BERNARD MALAMUD

Maybe the worst thing you could do at this point is to expect too much from this first draft. Shoot the works. Don't hold anything back. I should just let you write and be quiet. But here are a few suggestions.

THE DEVIL'S WORKSHOP. I had a habit of daydreaming in grammar school (and high school and college), of staring out the window at the three-deckers on Grafton Street and imagining myself elsewhere: in the Amazon basin of Brazil or on a ranch in Wyoming roping mavericks, or climbing the Matterhorn, or turning a 5-4-3 double play at Fenway Park. Sister would interrupt my reverie with a slap at my empty head or a whack on the hand with a ruler. And she would reiterate that an idle mind was the devil's workshop. I wanted to be anywhere but in the classroom reciting answers to the questions in the *Baltimore Catechism* or calculating the rate of interest on a bank loan that I would never get. I was making up a more exhilarant world for myself, a flagrantly idle pastime at St. Stephen's School.

You have to get over the notion that you are wasting your time by sitting and writing, by thinking and feeling frustrated at what you've written, and staring out the window and doodling and closing your eyes and seeing these made-up people and imagining their lives. You are doing your job even if those who peek into your writing room and see you gazing off into space think you're squandering your life—they can't see what you see. Put up a sign on your writing room door that says THE DEVIL'S WORKSHOP or AUTHORIZED PERSONNEL ONLY. Creativity is all about the idle mind, the mind freed of the bonds of commerce.

> "Novel, beginning one: *any subterfuge seems preferable.*"
> —E. M. FORSTER

We've all internalized the capitalist notion of time in which success equals production; time is money and all that nonsense. In the writing business, time is far more important than money, and time does not serve money. Thank God for the devil who says, No, thanks, I'm busy right now, who doesn't go along with the crowd. Until you can relax, you won't be able to write effectively. *Effectively*, alas, does not often equal *efficiently*. Idle your mind! Envision your resplendent future! Write!

ALL'S WELL THAT STARTS WELL. Yes, read your opening scene again, the one you wrote in Week 13, this time looking for moments that are begging for embellishment, exploration, resonance, for opportunities that you wrote into the scene but have yet to exploit, capitalize on. One of the joys of revision is that you get to open the scene up, not close it down. Often these moments are when you were surprised (*then* in the writing or *now* in the reading) when a character did or said something or learned something unexpected. If you find these moments, you might look through your notes and see if you've got something that might fit there. Or you might make a note to return to this in revision.

WRITING AT GUNPOINT. At the end of Flannery O'Connor's extraordinary story "A Good Man Is Hard to Find," the Misfit, having shot the grandmother, turns to his cohort Bobby Lee and says, "She would have been a good woman . . . if it had been somebody there to shoot her every minute of her life." We might say the same about the erstwhile writer—he'd have been a good novelist if someone had held a gun to his head every day and said, "You best move that pen, mister." I've never been to journalism school, but I would guess that the first lesson on the first day of class is called "Have It on My Desk in the Morning." Journalists understand that they don't have time for writer's block.* They cover the news. We need to know the news right now. Getting it done is more important than getting it perfect. The novel, you recall, means *new*—you're writing news that will stay news, to paraphrase Ezra Pound. The best way to succeed as a novelist is to write the novel today and every day. Don't put it off. All right, then. Do what I tell you, and no one gets hurt. Pick up the pen . . . nice and easy . . . don't try anything foolish. Now write. There you go!

> "And this is the way a novel gets written, in ignorance, fear, sorrow, madness, and a kind of psychotic happiness as an incubator for the wonders of being born."
> —JACK KEROUAC

THE BIG PICTURE. Take a look at the diagram of Aristotle's Incline back in Week 8. Note the structure: opening, plot point 1, mid-

*No one can stop you from writing. There is nothing at all difficult about it. What's difficult is writing splendidly, but you don't have to do that yet. In fact, you can't. Writing is your job now. And you have to go to work every day, like every other worker in every other trade. Carpenters don't call in to the foreman and say they can't come to work because they have carpenter's block. "Just don't feel up to driving nails today, Bob." No, they show up, and they hammer away, and so they bend a few nails, so what?

point, plot point 2, climax, and wrapup. With those key moments in mind, let's schedule the work we need to do in the next twenty-eight days.

- Days 1–3: write the opening scene; rewrite it; write any summary that precedes it; build the momentum of the novel.

- Days 4–8: write to plot point 1, that critical moment, the key scene, when something happens that spins your novel off in a new direction, intensifies the suspense, and makes the goal seem more difficult to achieve, perhaps; we get to know the central character; we understand his problem, his goal, his struggle, and his

> *"The first draft of anything is shit."*
> —ERNEST HEMINGWAY

motivation; make it to this plot point in any way that you can, even if you have to scribble in notes of a scene not finished—get there, this is only a draft; we're setting a rapid pace to ensure that you don't expect to get more out of a first draft than it is intended to do; no excuses for not going on; you're mining the ore, not polishing the gem.

- Days 9–15: write to the midpoint of the novel during these seven days; perhaps this scene represents your central character's lowest point, when all seems hopeless; again, something happens that intensifies the struggle and makes the goal seem unattainable and perhaps reverses your central character's fortunes; you're halfway home.

- Days 16–22: write to plot point 2; your hero might fail in this scene; danger abounds; obstacles everywhere; again, be sure to get there; keep moving forward; don't worry that what you've written is not as good as it could be, as good as it will be; make notes about what you intend to fix and go on; everything will change.

- Days 23–28: write the climactic scene and then wrap up all your loose ends and write the final scene; you did it.

You did it! It's a mess, but you got to the end, and now you have something to revise. And you're coming to understand that plot is a process, that the story emerges on the page and did not really exist until the writing.

WHEN ALL IS SAID AND DONE. Think about that ending. I like to start a story or a novel quickly and to end it lyrically. Endings can't be loose, can't drift. Endings in contemporary fiction are often muted. The novel, in other words, has made its point or it has failed. The ending should be inherent in the opening line and should not go on beyond the story—not try to portend or moralize. It should look within the novel. Leave us with a compelling image of the central character, one that is so resonant and mesmerizing that it stays with us after we close the book. A novel doesn't do our thinking for us, but it should start us

> *"The picture is not thought out and determined beforehand, rather while it is being made it follows the mobility of thoughts. Finished, it changes further according to the condition of him who looks at it."*
> —PABLO PICASSO

thinking. So when does a novel end? When the conflict you set out to explore has been resolved. We don't need the resolution of the character's life, just the resolution of this particular struggle.

Take one of your beginning paragraphs and think about writing the last paragraph. What is there in the opening of your novel that suggests the ending? Look ahead to possible resolutions now. Imagine your central character doing something at the finish of the novel. See her clearly. Look closely. How does she feel? What is she thinking? She has gotten what she wants or has not. You are surprised she is doing what she's doing but you realize that it perfectly depicts her emotional state. Leave us with a picture of the character. A freeze frame.

———

THIS IS THE first draft, and you do not have to get it right. "First drafts are for learning what your novel or story is about," Bernard Malamud said. And you do not have to write the scenes in order. You do whatever you need to do to get it done. Remember that any reversal that happens in the novel, anything crucial in the development of character, needs to be shown and not told. Otherwise the reader can't share the experience, can't be moved along with the characters, and may not understand or necessarily believe in the character's change. If you find yourself bogged down in a scene, follow Raymond Chandler's advice and bring in a man with a gun. Actually, any weapon will do, of course. Your man with a gun might, in fact, be a teenage girl armed with sarcasm. As you write, you're looking for moments that are beyond what you thought was going on. You'll more likely find them in revision than now. Writing a novel is a labor of love, but it also has to be a love of labor.

Weeks 25 & 26:
Craftsmanship

All of us failed to match our dream of perfection. So I rate us on the basis of our splendid failure to do the impossible. In my opinion, if I could write all my work again, I am convinced that I would do it better, which is the healthiest condition for an artist. That's why he keeps on working, trying again; he believes each time he will do it, bring it off. Of course, he won't, which is why this condition is healthy. Once he did it, once he matched the work to the image, the dream, nothing would remain but to cut his throat, jump off the other side of that pinnacle of perfection into suicide.

—*William Faulkner*

L ET THE REVISIONS BEGIN! Elie Wiesel said, "Writing is . . . like sculpture, where you eliminate to make the work visible. Even those pages you remove somehow remain. There is a difference between a book of two hundred pages from the very beginning and a book of two hundred pages which is the result of an original eight hundred pages. The six hundred pages are there. Only you don't see them." If you followed my advice in writing the novel, there may be much extraneous material because you followed the accidents in the hope of discovering revelation and significance—and not all of those digressive paths led to enlightenment.

Revision is not a matter of choice. Now that you've got black on white, you've got something to work with. Now the real creative writing begins. You're job—your duty—is to work the novel over and over until you get it right. Get the words right, the sentences right, the music right, the scenes right, and the plot right. If you are hesitant to

> "I cut adjectives, adverbs, and every word which is there just to make an effect. Every sentence which is there just for the sentence. You know, you have a beautiful sentence—cut it."
> —GEORGES SIMENON

proceed, consider why that is. You don't care enough about the characters to spend the time? Well, why have you written about characters you don't care about? You can, if you want to, settle that matter in revision. You can get to know them well enough to care about them. Why else wouldn't you revise? You wanted to write a beautiful novel, a heartbreaking one, but you failed. Now you do it again and do as Samuel Beckett said: Fail better.

No doubt you've done some revision already. You've revised words in a problematic sentence, changed a character's name several times, made chapter five chapter seven, and so on. In a sense we're always revising as we write. Writing is a messy, erratic, repetitive, and slow process. Nothing is linear or logical about it. Planning, drafting, and revising are always going on simultaneously and are probably not even distinct tasks. Your job as a writer amid all this chaos is to remain calm and confident—later, by degrees, you'll sort all this out, make sense of disorder. But not right now. This is the state that Keats called *negative capability,* and if you don't have it, you'd better cultivate it, or you're doomed to writing easy, formulaic, superficial, and inoffensive entertainments. Here's how Keats defined negative capability in a discussion about Shake-speare: "when a man is capable of being in uncertainties, mysteries and doubts, without any irritable reaching after fact & reason." Maybe he means that the writer possessing negative capability is comfortable with seeming contradiction and chaos, and is without a personal agenda, and is able to fill herself with an understanding of, or sympathy for, or empathy with, the subject of her creation, her characters, and her themes. Keats spoke of poets as being "the most unpoetical of anything in existence." We may substitute *writer* for *poet* and continue with Keats's comment: "Because he [the writer] has no Identity—he is continually in for—and filling some other Body."

Revision, as you know, means "seeing again." Now you can read your novel, see what you've said, and sense what still needs to be said. Revising means casting a *critical* eye on your work. *Critical* meaning, *Characterized by* careful, exact evaluation and judg-ment. Also meaning: *Having the nature of a* turning point; *crucial or decisive*. And: Indispensable; *essential*. And: *Fraught with danger or risk*. All of the above definitions apply to the revising process. You reorganize material; examine words, phrases, and paragraphs; consider character and plot; look at beginnings and middles and transitions and ends. You add, delete, rethink, reshape. In this stage your imagination should become deeply engaged with your mate-rial. This is when and where you come to know your characters— who they are, not who you think they are—and begin to perceive their motivations and values. In other words, revision is not the end of the process of writing, but a new beginning. It's a chance to open up the novel and discover what's there, what could be there.

> *"Fall seven times, stand up eight."*
> —JAPANESE PROVERB

Read the novel out loud, if you can, and note where the language is not working, the music is jarring. Take notes. Listen to what the story is trying to tell you. Try to visualize the characters. In the second part of the novel you might find things that were not prepared for in the first. Make a note. There might be something you started in the opening that fades away, fails to resonate. Places where you forget you're reading and enter the world of your book these are the parts that work. Examining these good parts might help you strengthen the weak.

> "It took me six years to finish [Legs]. I wrote it eight times and seven times it was no good."
> —WILLIAM KENNEDY

You are a writer, so in reading you see what's really there, not what's supposed to be there, not what you told yourself is there. That's your job, after all. You see what you wrote, not what you thought you wrote. You look at the current draft and you ask the right questions: Have I shown and not told? Has my central character changed? Does each character have a distinctive voice? Are the details vivid, precise, and revealing? You ask the questions, answer them honestly, make the necessary changes that the answers necessitate and the changes elsewhere that those changes suggest and so on. Then you read it again, ask more questions. What is my novel about? Was that my intention? What emotional experience do I want the reader to have? Have I caused that to happen? Is the story as clear as it can be? And so on.

All of this can't be done at once. Take your time, concentrate on one task at a time. Relax. The first draft was an act of discovery where you indulged yourself and your characters. These next drafts will be less indulgent, will be at times ruthless. The novel will improve with each revision. Revision is not about editing. Editing is a small, but important, part of rewriting. This is a time to invent and to surprise, to add texture and nuance. In writing fiction, you must be honest and rigorous. You cannot judge your characters or want to say something so much that you manipulate them, twist the plot, or ignore what their reactions and responses would be. Your job is to do justice to their lives. Revision continues until you feel that you have done all you can to make the novel as compelling and truthful as possible. Ask yourself if you care enough about these characters to put in the time, energy, and thought it takes to work a story into shape. If you quit, if you won't revise, then you don't care enough.

I've been talking about revisions, but in our six-month project you have only two weeks left (went by fast, didn't it?), so we're concentrating on only the first revision, the one that will result in a more polished, more textured, more lucid, and more compelling first draft than you hold in your hands right now. That means you'll be rereading to rewrite. Rereading with a pen in your hand. So before you do anything else, print out a hard copy of the draft. You may have to do some of these readings and responding after the two weeks, no doubt. That's fine. You might also feel comfortable combining the readings and doing two or three or more tasks at once. But remember we're not after efficiency alone. So you've got the hard copy and all of your notes on the desk. You've got your coffee and you've put up your DO NOT DISTURB sign. The phone is off the hook.

> "Since revising is the discovery of the heart of the story, it's a progressive process; each revision brings you closer to success."
> —JEROME STERN

Reading and Responding to Your Novel

1. *Below the Surface.* As with cemetery plots, novel plots are important for what's below the surface. Read your draft with plot in mind. As you do, ask yourself if you know why the

central character does what she does at every moment. Note those places where the motivation is unclear. You'll want to get it clarified in revision. Pay attention to the struggle. Have you dramatized that struggle? Are all the important moments in scene? How can you intensify the struggle? What's the worst that could happen? Has it? Will it? Where is the plot weak? Is there enough at risk for the character? You'll want this information handy as you write on, and certainly as you revise.

2. *A Field Guide to Your Novel.* Now read the draft again. (As John Gardner says, you have to read your novel a hundred times. As you do, you'll be making the small changes that become large changes down the road, changes that deepen the vision of the story.) This time note all of the natural and man-made objects in your story. The tables, houses, flowers, fish, and trees. Highlight them. Now go back and see if you can be more precise and accurate about all of them. Not a grove of trees but of cottonwoods (and once you know they're cottonwoods, you know that those cottony seeds might be floating by a window in another scene, but is it an eastern cottonwood or a black cottonwood, a plains, a Southern, or a swamp cottonwod?), not a chair, but a maple Morris chair, not a glass of wine, but a crystal goblet of Merlot. You get the idea.

3. *It Don't Mean a Thing if It Ain't Got That Swing.* Read the new and improved draft again and listen to the music of the prose. Just the sound, that's all you're interested in today. Whenever you find yourself stumbling, whenever the text is difficult to read, make a note. You'll want to smooth that out later, if not immediately. Are some parts of the novel more lyrical than others? Do you know why? Is that what you want? You might consider audiotaping yourself, although that can be

an unnerving experience for other than literary reasons. Prose can often look gorgeous on the page, but rattle in the ear.

4. *Words.* Spend the day rereading what you've written and highlighting all of the significant nouns and verbs. Then look them all up in your dictionary and your thesaurus. Consider all of the possible denotative and connotative meanings of the word in question. Is it precisely the word you want? Does it have metaphorical potential that you have yet to exploit? If it's not the accurate word, of course, replace it.

5. *Hunting for Qualifiers.* Mark Twain said, "If you find an adjective, kill it." He also said, "The adverb is the enemy of the verb." Read through what you've written for the fifth time (and always read out loud, if possible), and this time mark all your adverbs and adjectives. Then get rid of every single one that you can. Read the sentence without the offending word, and only if the qualifier is absolutely essential should you keep it. What you may need is one strong verb rather than a weak verb and a qualifying adverb. Not "He walked unsteadily," but "He staggered." Like adverbs, many adjectives are unnecessary. Often the adjectival concept is in the noun modified. A night *is* dark, an ache painful, a needle sharp, a skyscraper tall. Color is often redundant, as in *blue* sky, *green* grass, and so on. Other adjectives are too conventional, like a *tender* heart or a *sly* fox. If you've described something with adjectives, like that sly fox, you might write another sentence that illustrates the adjective and fleshes out your intention. The fox runs into a hollow log and out the other side, leaving the hounds howling at the arboreal cavity.

6. *Furniture.* In a letter to Aleksandr Semenovich Lazarev, Chekhov wrote, "One must not put a loaded rifle on the stage if no one is thinking of firing it." We have to use our furniture ("equipment that is necessary, useful, or desirable"). There is

no room for extraneous furniture in a novel, just as there is no room for the extraneous character or the extraneous word. List every inanimate object in your novel. The sofa and easy chairs in the living room, the loose change in the pocket, the automobile, the whatever. Think about what other use you can put the objects to. Can a character pick up the rattle that the baby dropped and stuff it in his pocket? Might it rattle later on at some significant moment? Attend to each object. If you can't put it to further use, do you need it in the novel? (You might.)

7. *Instant Revision.* This is not meant to be a thorough revision of a draft. More complete revisions have preceded this "instant" phase, and others will follow. But let's say you have a draft in decent shape now. It's coming along. Get yourself a cup of tea, sit down at your desk, and read the novel again. Now take the following steps:

1. Delete the first chapter. (Ouch!) The beginning of our novel is often an introduction. Introductions are intrusive and unnecessary. They may have been essential parts of the creative process, leading us to our material, perhaps even generating that material, but unnecessary in the final version. So start reading the novel at the second chapter. Often that is where the novel begins. (Or in the third or the fourth chapter.)

2. Delete the final chapter. The end is often a summary, a pulling of the punch. Sometimes we lose faith that we have made our point, and here we attempt to restate it. If we haven't shown it by now, unfortunately, it's too late. Don't tell us what the novel we've just read was about. Don't telegraph a message. Read your novel and stop at the penultimate chapter. Is it better?

3. Make sure that each sentence justifies its existence. If the paragraph makes sense without it, if it's not revealing character, expressing theme, advancing plot, what is it doing there? Conrad said: "A work that aspires, however humbly, to the condition of art should carry its justification in every line."

4. Strengthen each verb. Circle them all. Ask yourself if you have used the exact verb that you wanted. Is this guy really walking or do I see him strolling, swaggering, or limping? Is he trimming the hedge or lopping at it? Especially take a look at verbs that are modified by adverbs. How often have you used the verb "to be"? If you are like most of us, the answer is *too often*. Strengthen all of those that you can.

8. *The Line Edit.* This will be one of the last things you do when you think you've got the story told and the writing sparkles. Look at the first paragraph of your novel. Read it and justify your use of punctuation for each sentence. Why you put in a mark of punctuation or why you did not. Now do it with the entire book. Use conventional punctuation. Check for clichés, for repetitions, for redundancies and superfluous expressions like: blinked *his eyes,* stood *up;* nodded *yes,* thought *to himself.* You don't need the italicized words. And while you're at it, check your spelling, and don't rely on spell-check or you might end up with "She gripped my arm tighter and steered me father down the sidewalk," or "When Jimmy awoke from his comma he had no idea where he was."

9. *One More Time.* Read the novel one more time and ask yourself what you can cut without damaging the novel. Whatever it is, cut it. Are there any sentences, clever lines, jokes, phrases, scenes that you aren't quite sure about? Cut them. If you are wondering whether a sentence, an image, a word belongs, it does not.

OTHER READERS. It's not a good idea to give your draft to anyone in the family. This will only cause problems. Mom's going to love it, but still wonder when you're going to stop this nonsense and get a real job. Your husband's going to lie if he has to. You can't blame anyone for not wanting to jeopardize a relationship. Don't put that weight on them. But you might want certain friends whose aesthetic values you trust to read it. If you're brave enough to hand out copies, you need to understand that not everyone will be a generous and sympathetic reader of your material. Listen to what people have to say—if they can be specific about it—and when a response makes sense, then pay attention to it. Disregard all the rest.

> *"Read and revise, reread and revise, keep reading and revising until your text seems adequate to your thought."*
> —JACQUES BARZUN

If you give your story to a friend or a colleague to read, try to be specific about what you're looking for. Have them read with a question or two in mind—this way they can be specific and helpful and won't feel they are endangering a friendship: Can you tell me if the central character has earned your sympathy? Do you think the boy tried hard enough to win the heart of the girl? Does the setting add meaning and significance to the plot? Asking someone to simply read and respond is asking for vague generalities. Set your agenda for the response. When you find someone who is a careful and honest reader of your material, give her more of your work. But that means you owe her a dinner or two.

THE RACONTEUR. You know your novel pretty well by now. So tell your novel to someone. Pour him a drink, maybe. Have him settle back in an easy chair. After you tell the story, you'll know which parts are working. Your friend sat up, smiled, flattered your strategy. When you see his eyes glaze over or his eyelids droop, you know you lost him and that's where you may have let the tension slip, and it's just one thing after another. You'll learn that when you have to keep a listener's attention, you'll want to avoid long digressions. You'll find you'll need to keep on the plot track. If at the end of your story your auditor says, "And then what?" you can be sure you haven't resolved the plot he thought he was following. You'll be deflated, but you'll be wiser. When you're finished, wait for his response or encourage it if you have to.

Think about the differences between writing a story and telling one. How can the differences be translated across genres? Why do you tell a story to someone? To a specific someone? You pick your listener and tell him a story you think he'll enjoy and find entertaining and illuminating. (Do you also *write* your story for a particular someone? Should you?) I think the element of entertainment is an important one. We don't want to be preached at. Stories told by fathers to sons, by teachers to students, by preachers to the congregation, to impart a lesson are seldom listened to because they are boring, predictable, condescending, and self-serving. Don't preach; don't send a message; don't talk down to the listener or to your reader. When you're telling a story, you can see if the listener is paying attention, and if he's not, you can respond with a remedy for the boredom immediately. But how do you anticipate the bored reader of your novel? I'm not sure, but you'd do well to find out, and remedy that situation as well. I will say that you have to anticipate the questions a reader will have. You must become the reader as you revise. You tell a story with confidence. You know the story is fabulous, and you understand every nuance. You just know it's going to pay off. Revise your novel with that same confidence—it inspires the reader to pay attention, to trust the narrator. You can't change your tone of voice when you're writing, but you can modulate the tone of the story to help the reader understand what's going on below the surface. You don't have the benefit of a spellbinding voice if you're writing, but you can enchant the reader with the music of your prose.

Checklist and Prompts

A. Ask yourself the following questions. If you can answer them, you have a grasp of your novel.

- In fifty words, what is the basic idea of your novel?

- What is the central aim of the novel? State your answer as a question. For example, "Will Hamlet finally seek revenge for the murder of his father?"

- What is the novel's main conflict? Is it internal or external? Another way to think of this question may be: Is your plot character-driven or action-driven? What is at stake for your central character?

- How does your central character change during the course of the novel as you understand it now?

- How do you maintain tension throughout the novel?

- How does your central character bring about the climax of the novel?

B. Underline as you read the first interesting sentence in your novel. If it isn't the very first sentence, why isn't it? What is the best sentence in your opening chapter? Why is it the best? Could you make that the first sentence?

C. Describe one of your characters' obsessions or something that haunts her, something you know about but which may not appear in the novel, not yet anyway, at least in black and white. Now trace back that obsession to its source. Something in that character's childhood. An image, an event, a person, something. Write about it. Work it into the novel.

D. Insert the following lines in your draft and continue with them. *This time last year, I was . . . ; Five years from now I'll be . . . ; She heard a knock at the door.*

E. Insert the following: a menu; a portion of a radio show; an original song.

RX FOR YOUR AILING NOVEL. You're not satisfied with the novel yet. You shouldn't be. You aren't quite sure what's wrong with it, so you can't make it better. Here are some simple, quick remedies that might get you started. Answer the questions in your notebook.

1. Have you made things hard enough for your central character? We want struggle. It can't be easy for the central character to get what she wants. The storyteller's job is to obstruct. The harder a character has to try to get what she wants, the deeper she digs into herself, and the deeper she digs, the more we'll know about her, and the more we know, the better we'll like and understand her, and the better we like her, obviously, the more we'll care about her. And now there is more at stake. So throw some more obstacles in the character's way. Make it impossible for her to get what she wants. (And then watch her get it—maybe.)

2. Have you chosen the correct point of view? Have you arranged for the reader to get the most efficient access to the mind of the central character? Try changing the opening paragraph by altering the point of view. Write it in first person as the story is happening. Now write it in first person told by a reminiscent narrator. (I remember when . . .) Write it in third-person limited, third-person omniscient, third-person objective. If any of these new vantage points seems intriguing, press on and see what happens to your novel.

> "Begin again."
> —ALBERT CAMUS

3. If your novel is based on autobiographical material, there may be a tendency to be slavish to the facts and not to the emotional truth of the story. Your allegiance should belong to the story and not

to your life. You may need distance to achieve this allegiance. So do this: Change the gender of all the characters. The character you thought was Emily is now Emile. The character you thought was you is not. You might also arbitrarily make the young people old and the older people young. Or change the locale of the novel. It's not winter in St. Paul; it's summer in Houston.

4. Have you shown and not told? Have you written the obligatory scenes and only the obligatory scenes? Have you made the quick expository cut from scene to scene? Go through your story and look at the exposition. Did anything important happen there (offstage, as it were)? If so, make a note to put it in scene. Is there anything you can cut from exposition? Now look at your scenes.

> "In the writing process, the more a thing cooks, the better."
> —DORIS LESSING

Any small talk? Cut it. Any attempts at getting expository material in the scene? Any furnishing of rooms in dialogue? ("My, that's a lovely velvet painting of a panther over your plaid couch, Marge.") Cut it. If the room needs to be furnished, let the narrator decorate.

THE STORY'S HISTORY

> The last act of writing must be to become one's own reader. . . . To begin passionately and to end critically, to begin hot and to end cold; and, more important, to try to be passion-hot and critic-cold at the same time.
>
> —John Ciardi

Write a history of your novel when you've finished it, not now but after the second or third or fourth draft. When did the idea for the novel first occur to you? The inspiration. Write about how it incubated, how you knew you were ready to write. What were your original intentions and how did they change? Why did they change? What worked for you in the writing process and what did not? Remember those times that you felt stuck. How did you come unstuck? How did the second draft differ from the first, the second from the tenth, and so on? Was there a breakthrough moment on this story? What was it? The Eureka Moment. When did you know you were finished and how did you know? What do you think you did well?

The idea here is, of course, to learn from your own work and to reassure yourself, if you need it, that you've done this before—you've imposed order on the chaos that was the nascent novel—and you can do it again. You've got the proof and a blueprint for your successful process. As you experience success in solving problems, you no longer think of problems as obstacles, but as opportunities. Writing a story's history allows you to make more efficient use of your talents and will alert you to technical and procedural pitfalls. Writing the history will help demystify the writing process. It's not luck and it's not miraculous. Writing, you'll see, is work and persistence, and it is solving problems. You solved a technical problem this way last time, and you can do so again.

———

Yes, there will be more drafts, and you'll look forward to them. You'll be afraid to stop because you might have missed something that would have improved the book. Reread, rethink, rewrite. Again and again. As you gain experience in revising, you'll build up a stockpile of solutions that you can use when you confront a familiar problem or when a new problem occurs.

Now What?

———

Finishing a book is just like you took a child
out in the yard and shot it.
—*Truman Capote*

YOU'RE DONE! Well, not quite. You did the hard part, and now
comes the fun part. You began this journey with nothing other
than your desire and your talent. You developed patience and tenacity. You came to understand that writing a novel is itself very much a
plot. You wanted something—to understand the lives of your characters, which meant resolving the trouble in your central character's life, which meant completing the novel—and you wanted it
intensely. If you didn't finish, your life, you believed, would have
been significantly diminished. And so you pursued your goal and
battled every obstacle, not the least of which was yourself and your
lack of confidence, your obstructionist tendencies, the world calling for your attention, the chaos of the characters' lives, those elu-
sive words, and so on. You sat day after day. You worked diligently
and relentlessly in joy and in frustration. You trusted in the writing
process and in yourself. You began by writing about your personal
experience and came to realize your life was far more interesting
than you had thought because you thought deeply about it and got
past the obvious clichés. And then you engaged your imagination
in the same way you'd used your memory. You created a brave new

world and peopled it with characters who *in time* came to breathe. You constructed a plot, managed your tone, animated the characters in scene, experimented with point of view, questioned your decisions. You struggled, and at last you finished your draft.

You learned that writing a novel was not as hard as you thought it was that first day when you recapped your pen, put the pristine tablet back in the drawer, slouched away from the desk, poured yourself another drink, avoided your mother's phone calls, chastised yourself for your ridiculous dreams, decided that the whole project was impossible, childish, and arrogant. The dream might have ended there, but you went back to the desk and wrote and came to understand that writing a novel is, among other things, an act of love, and you remembered what Diana Ross told you. "You can't hurry love." So you listened to your heart.

> *"The profession of book-writing makes horse-racing seem like a solid, stable business."*
> —JOHN STEINBECK

THE FIRST THING you want to do today is put the manuscript away in a drawer. Keep it there for as long as you can, so that when you go back at it, the novel will be somewhat fresh to you. Put it away and begin writing your next novel. (Or a short story if you'd prefer a speedier sense of accomplishment.) Take notes, sketch scenes, do some of the exercises in this book, maybe some of those that worked especially well for you the last time. Read a novel or two. Reacquaint yourself with your family. And then after the manuscript has had a chance to cool, and when you can't wait any longer to get back at it, take it out and begin to read with a pen in your hand. Read and take notes. See where you can open up the story. Be ruthless with your cuts. The delete key is your best friend. Trim the rejectamenta. You reread and you revise. Your novel improves with each pass. You look for solutions to the problems in the novel itself. You realize you are writing better than you ever thought you could. You see that these made-up characters of yours have become vivid and intriguing people who live interesting and often terrifying lives. You begin to resent the time spent away from them.

You work on the novel until it's as good as you can make it. Apply your critical skills as well as your creative talents. *That's not working. How can I fix it?* By the way, while you're revising, you'll be getting ideas for characters and places and plots that you can't use in this novel. Write it all down in your notebook. You're alert to lines and images in the

> "The moment a man sets his thoughts down on paper, however secretly, he is in a sense writing for publication."
> —RAYMOND CHANDLER

world around you, and you collect them, and you save them for your next book. Begin to make files on the new characters and on the other narrative elements you discover—you're getting a jump start on the next project or the next several. But don't abandon this novel for those —this one you must finish. The others will wait. The best advice you will ever get on writing the novel is: Finish! You *will* feel discouraged; you *will* lose confidence in your abilities, you *will* be bored with the characters—and the only way to overcome these obstacles is to write your way through them. And writing always works. Always. You can't solve problems if you're not working on the manuscript.

> "I would advise any beginning writer to write the first drafts as if no one else will ever read them—without a thought about publication—and only in the last draft to consider how the work will look from the outside."
> —ANNE TYLER

You work at the draft every day and eventually you're done. And now you've proven to yourself and to the world that you can do it. You're a writer, a novelist, dammit! You've taught yourself how to write a novel. And how to write the next one and the next.

What I Was Reading
While I Was Writing

H ERE ARE THE books on writing and related matters that I was reading while I was putting all of this together. You might find some of them useful. I'll provide the publication information for the editions that I have here in my room. You can find newer versions for most, I'm sure.

20 Master Plots (And How to Build Them) by Ronald Tobias, Writer's Digest, 1993.

101 Plots Used and Abused by James N. Young, The Writer, Inc., 1945.

Advice to Writers, edited by Jon Winokur, Vintage, 1999.

The Artful Edit by Susan Bell, W. W. Norton, 2007.

The Art of Fiction by John Gardner, Vintage paperback, 1985.

The Art of Subtext by Charles Baxter, Graywolf Press paperback, 2007.

Aspects of the Novel by E. M. Forster, Edward Arnold, 1961.

Becoming a Writer by Dorothea Brande, Tarcher paperback, 1981.

Camera Lucida by Roland Barthes, Hill and Wang paperback, 1983.

Characters and Viewpoint by Orson Scott Card, Writer's Digest Books, 1988.

Conversations with Eudora Welty, edited by Peggy Whitman, Washington Square Press paperback, 1985.

The Copyeditor's Handbook, edited by Amy Einsohn, University of California Press paperback, 2000.

A Dash of Style by Noah Lukeman, W. W. Norton paperback, 2006.

A Dictionary of Literary Terms by J. A. Cuddon, Penguin paperback, 1979.

The Elements of Style by William Strunk, Jr., and E. B. White, Macmillan paperback, 1979.

Essentials of the Theory of Fiction, edited by Michael Hoffman and Patrick Murphy, Duke University Press paperback, 1988.

The Faith of a Writer by Joyce Carol Oates, Ecco Press paperback, 2004.

Get That Novel Started (And Keep It Going 'Til You're Finished) by Donna Levin, Writer's Digest, 1992.

How to Write Killer Fiction by Carolyn Wheat, Perseverance Press paperback, 2003.

How to Write Your Novel by Margaret Chittendon, The Writer, Inc., paperback, 1995.

I Could Tell You Stories by Patricia Hampl, W. W. Norton paperback, 1999.

If You Want to Write by Brenda Ueland, Graywolf Press paperback, 1987.

Making Shapely Fiction by Jerome Stern, W. W. Norton, 1991.

Naming the World, edited by Bret Anthony Johnston, Random House paperback, 2008.

Narrative Design by Madison Smartt Bell, W. W. Norton paperback, 1997.

A Natural History of the Senses by Diane Ackerman, Random House paperback, 1990.

Nonconformity by Nelson Algren, Seven Stories Press paperback, 1998.

Novel Ideas by Barbara Shoup and Margaret Love Denman, Alpha Books paperback, 2004.

Novelists on the Novel, edited by Miriam Allott, Columbia University Press paperback, 1966.

On Becoming a Novelist by John Gardner, Harper & Row paperback, 1983. (The dried binding glue dropped out of this copy as I reread it. Time for a new copy.)

On Becoming a Writer by Eudora Welty, Modern Library, 2002.

The Ongoing Moment by Geoff Dyer, Pantheon, 2005.

A Passion for Narrative by Jack Hodgins, St. Martin's Press, 1993.

The Passionate Accurate Story by Carol Bly, Milkweed Editions paperback, 1990.

Plotto by William Wallace Clark, Writer's Digest, 1941.

Poetics by Aristotle, University of Michigan Press paperback, 1994.

A Primer of the Novel for Readers & Writers by David Madden, Scarecrow Press, 1980.

Reading Chekhov by Janet Malcolm, Random House, 2001.

Reading Like a Writer by Francine Prose, Harper Perennial paperback, 2006.

Ron Carlson Writes a Story by Ron Carlson, Graywolf Press paperback, 2007

The Scene Book: A Primer for the Fiction Writer by Sandra Scofield, Penguin paperback, 2007.

Screenplay by Syd Field, Dell paperback, 1994.

Shoptalk, edited by Donald Murray, Boynton/Cook Heinemann paperback, 1990.

So You Want to Write a Novel by Lou Willett Stanek, Avon paperback, 1994.

Steering the Craft by Ursula Le Guin, Eighth Mountain Press paperback, 1998.

Story Plotting Simplified by Eric Heath, The Writer, Inc., 1941.

The Stuff of Fiction by Gerald Warner Brace, W. W. Norton paperback, 1969.

Sudden Fiction International, edited by Robert Shapard and James Thomas, W. W. Norton paperback, 1989.

Technique in Fiction by Robie Macauley and George Lanning, St. Martin's Press, 1987.

Techniques of Fiction Writing: Measure and Madness by Leon Surmelian, Anchor Books paperback, 1969.

Tell It Slant by Brenda Miller and Suzanne Paola, McGraw Hill paperback, 2003.

The Thirty-six Dramatic Situations by Georges Polti, The Writer, Inc., 1977.

This Year You Write Your Novel by Walter Mosely, Little, Brown, 2007.

The Weekend Novelist by Robert J. Ray, Dell Trade paperback, 1994.

What If? by Anne Bernays and Pamela Painter, second edition, Pearson Longman paperback, 2004.

The Writer's Chapbook, edited by George Plimpton, Viking, 1989.

The Writer's Idea Book by Jack Heffron, Writer's Digest paperback, 2000.

The Writer's Life, edited by Carol Edgarian and Tom Jenks, Vintage paperback, 1997.

The Writer's Mentor, edited by Ian Jackman, Random House Reference, 2004.

Writing Mysteries, edited by Sue Grafton, Writer's Digest paperback, 2002.

Writers on Writing, edited by Jon Winokur, Running Press, 1987.